This War without an Enemy

Richard Ollard

This War without an Enemy
A History of
The English Civil Wars

FontanaPress
An Imprint of HarperCollinsPublishers

For Juliet O'Hea

Reprinted 1992

First published by
Hodder & Stoughton Ltd.
This Fontana Press edition
first published by
Fontana Paperbacks is a
division of the Collins
Publishing Group
ISBN 0 00 686189–X
Printed and bound in Great Britain
by Butler & Tanner Ltd, Frome and London

Contents

Colour Plates

Preface

Terrorism, kidnapping, violence of one sort and another are now so familiar an element of political life in the once sedate centres of Western civilization that we are perhaps better equipped to enter imaginatively into the experience of civil war than the great scholars of the Victorian and Edwardian age – one thinks particularly of S. R. Gardiner and Sir Charles Firth – whose mastery of the sources has put all subsequent writers in their debt. Like it or not, we have at times been driven to wonder what we would do if civil order were to break down. The affinities between the seventeenth century and our own, so often remarked, seem to increase rather than diminish.

Since this book is addressed to the general reader and prints no new manuscript material I have cited no authorities and supplied no bibliography, though I have, I hope, made clear how much I owe to the scholars who have extended and enriched our understanding of this period during the past twenty or thirty years. For the same reason when quoting a contemporary source I have sometimes followed the orthography and spelling of the seventeenth century and sometimes not, depending partly on whether a modernized printed text is available, partly on whether unnecessary difficulties were presented to a twentieth-century reader. I have tried to be accurate without being pedantic but I am aware that both terms are relative.

In dating I have followed the usual practice of combining the Old Style with a year that begins on 1 January. On the spelling of names I have not thought it necessary to affect a punctilio agreeably absent from the age itself. I have further taken the liberty of adopting the style by which a man is best known to history. For instance, throughout the book I refer to Clarendon as Clarendon, not as Edward, or Sir Edward, Hyde, although of course the title was not conferred on him till after the Restoration.

Whatever merits may be found in this book arise either directly or at one remove from the illustrations. The stimulus to write it came partly from the two Van Dyck exhibitions in the Queen's Gallery and at Messrs Agnew, partly from the Samuel Cooper exhibition at the National Portrait Gallery and above all from the great 'Age of Charles I' exhibition at the Tate Gallery. Other exhibitions and the riches of various permanent collections, national and private, have nourished the excitement and fascination I have found and have tried to communicate in the authentic, speaking likenesses of this intensely individual age.

My debts to the kindness of owners who have allowed their pictures to be reproduced and to curators and custodians who have afforded every facility are separately, if inadequately, acknowledged. But there are some that I would also wish to record here. The generosity of Sir Oliver Millar, the Surveyor of the Queen's Pictures and the moving spirit of the exhibitions I have mentioned, has met every call on his limited time and inexhaustible knowledge without ever seeming to confer an obligation. The staff of the Print Room at the Ashmolean Museum, Oxford, have been helpfulness itself; and as a publisher's editor myself I am well qualified to know how fortunate I have been in my editor at Messrs George Rainbird, Mrs Penny Miller.

Richard Ollard
March 1976

ILLUSTRATIONS ON PRECEDING PAGES *Oliver Cromwell by Samuel Cooper* (half-title); *Charles I at His Trial by Edward Bower* (frontispiece); *Three Children of Charles I (Princess Elizabeth, James, Duke of York, and Henry, Duke of Gloucester), attributed to John Hoskins* (p. 4); *John Pym by Samuel Cooper* (p. 5); *Henry Ireton by Samuel Cooper* (p. 7)

LEFT *Queen Henrietta Maria by John Hoskins*

Chapter 1
Why and Why Not

Three centuries have passed since the civil wars, yet historians still disagree profoundly as to the nature and cause of the conflict. It is even possible to find the result in dispute. We all know that the first civil war was won outright by the Parliament and that as a result of the second the army leaders decided that it was impossible to do business with Charles I and cut off his head. But in 1660 Charles II was restored to the throne and a number of those who had signed his father's death-warrant were themselves executed. And why should we strike the balance at that point rather than another? Twenty years later, in the collision between the King and the dominant party in the House of Commons over the bill to exclude James, Duke of York, from the succession, England again trembled on the brink. 'Forty-one is come again' was the common judgment of those who had seen it all before. People who have lived through civil war are notably reluctant to repeat the experience. This, combined with the immeasurable superiority in political sense that Charles II had over his father and brother, averted catastrophe. But within a further ten years his brother had been turned off the throne in one of the most efficient and painless revolutions in history. All this suggests that the civil wars were never fought to a finish.

This was certainly the objective of the wisest and best of the leaders on both sides when with sinking hearts they saw that violence had become inevitable. To stop the war without either side winning was the aim of Royalists like Clarendon and Parliament men like Manchester or Hampden. It was not, it was emphatically not, the aim of Charles I or of his queen, Henrietta Maria. And historically if not genealogically Charles I and Henrietta Maria begat Oliver Cromwell. Peaceful development such as England has generally been fortunate enough to enjoy depends upon a known readiness to give ground. Intransigence generates its own equivalent reaction. No explanation of the civil war that does not put Charles I at the centre will stand for long.

This is not, of course, to deny that the issues for which men consciously contended, the social resentments, the economic interests, the religious beliefs, the legal and political principles, were not infinitely more complex and more interesting, lay much deeper and extended far wider than the limited mentality, the hesitant, devious inflexibility of the King, so aptly expressed in his slight but wiry figure, his wide, appraising eyes, his weak mouth and his indecisive chin. If the civil war were indeed coterminous with the mind and personality of Charles I it would not touch the imagination and the sympathy as powerfully as it does. Still less would it provide so happy an illustration of the late Pieter Geyl's definition of history as a debate without an end. But if Charles I is removed from the scene it is difficult to believe that it would have been fought.

Paradoxically the generation that suffered this calamity were more conscious than any before or since of their good fortune in not being involved in civil war. Everywhere they looked their neighbours were. In Germany and central Europe the indescribable horrors of the Thirty Years War, begun in 1618, were still in full swing. France with brief intervals of a decade or so had been racked by civil war since the middle of the sixteenth century. Spain was faced in 1640 by the revolt of the Catalans and had been fighting for three-quarters of a century a war in the Netherlands that the luckless inhabitants might classify as such. Italy, less plagued by this disease than in earlier periods, had by no means a clean bill of health. Europe in the age of James I and Charles I might well cause peace-loving Englishmen to shudder.

Modern historians surveying this scene of carnage and ruin have naturally inferred a common cause for so hideous and widespread a distemper. Apart from the obvious and perpetual sources of tension in any society, such as the struggle for power and wealth, the seventeenth century, like its predecessor, was an age of fierce religious conflict. Of this every thinking man was well aware. What contemporaries perhaps did not realize, since they lacked the language to describe and the techniques to measure it, was that they lived in an age of inflation. By our standards it was nothing much. Prices rose by one hundred per cent in the hundred years that divide Henry VIII from the civil war. But wages and rents did not rise in sympathy so that both the property owners and the poor found themselves the victims, in very different degrees and at different times, of economic adversity. The effects were felt through the whole of society. The discontent so produced, sometimes acute to the point of violence or revolution, sometimes a moody truculence towards a government obscurely felt to be responsible, has led historians to talk of a general crisis of the seventeenth century and to look for social and economic causes proportionate to so vast a concept. In this great tidal movement of history Charles I and Cromwell, the Royalists and the Levellers, the Presbyterians and the Independents, are swept along, sometimes afloat, sometimes awash, but never in fact controlling the direction or the speed with which they are borne forward.

Perhaps. And perhaps not. The view of history most powerfully stated in Braudel's *The Mediterranean and the Mediterranean World* is the vision of a genius, unsearchable in its riches and imperfectly communicable to those who do not combine the grasp of his mind and the reach of his learning. To the ordinary plodding historian as to the general reader the inestimable value of the great system builders is that they make him a little less crass and unimaginative than he would otherwise have been. One does not have to be a Marxist to be conscious of the immense debt everyone who writes or thinks about history owes him.

To come to particulars, it may be that the events with which this book is concerned took their origin beyond the horizon of the Stuart age or the British Isles. What people said and did and wrote and thought may be

significant only if it can be related to some historical cause or social tendency stretching far out of their sight. I do not much believe this: but those who do are well served by some of the most brilliant historical writing that England and America have produced since the war. Unlike Dr Johnson's old schoolfellow I have not tried very hard to be a philosopher. Curiosity about people would keep breaking in. And how rich a variety, how sharply defined, how imperishably described by pen and brush, the individual characters appear. Dull would he be of soul who could pass by. Caroline England is the first great age of English portraiture and of English biography. In painting, which owed so much to the direct patronage and inspired connoisseurship of the King, Mytens and Van Dyck precede the two native Englishmen Dobson and Samuel Cooper who are themselves succeeded by a further pair of Continentals, Lely and Kneller. In literature Clarendon's *History of the Great Rebellion* owes its place among the acknowledged masterpieces of English historical writing chiefly to the characterization, mostly drawn from life, on which the author took such pains. On a very different scale John Aubrey's *Brief Lives* achieves a seemingly effortless intensity that has not been surpassed by any subsequent biographical writer. This is but to mention a few of the most famous names. They were surrounded by a host of others and by a wealth of memoirs, letters and diaries in which the close observation of character for its own sake is a dominant note. People were interested in people as individuals, not simply as souls to be saved or as examples of sociological phenomena to be explained. It is one of the marks that distinguish the particular sensibility of the age.

This thread of individual identity, whether of persons, families, regions or status, runs through and through the great general and national issues over which men fought. It colours not only the religion and the politics, the economics and the sociology, the conduct of war and the writing of history but the very apprehension of ideas on these subjects. Behind every abstraction lie unspoken connections of persons, families, local interests and so on. The true ideologue who holds his opinions and arrives at his conclusions by faith or reason uncontaminated by personal circumstance is a type hard to recognize in the first civil war that ended with the total defeat of the Royalists in 1646. He is perhaps discernible in the debates and controversies that followed when Parliament and its army found themselves unable to agree on where they were to go next. But the more the traditional labels are studied, Royalist and Parliamentarian, Presbyterian and Independent, Cavalier and Puritan, the less they seem to mean. What emerge are knots of men, connected by friendship or family or local patriotism, sharing this belief about religion or that principle in politics, detesting such and such a minister or distrusting such and such another, despising the Scots or loathing the Irish and generally ready to be convinced that the Pope and his shock-troops the Jesuits are at the bottom of all the trouble. As the kaleidoscope is jarred by the succession of events, the groupings change their pattern. The man who came to the Long Parliament in 1640 determined to destroy the constitutional instruments of Charles I's power and to have the blood of his principal minister might find himself two years later rallying to the Royal Standard. Indeed Clarendon himself did exactly that. The man who had fought for the Parliament in the dark days of 1643 when the Royalists were winning victory after victory might find himself later so far out of sympathy with the way things were going as to think a restoration of the monarchy the best, or at any rate least disastrous, consummation. Such was the position reached at different times by the most successful Parliamentary commanders in the field, Waller and Fairfax, and by some of the original political leaders such as Holles and Manchester.

Matters are not made easier by applying the political and social conceptions of our own time. In particular the idea of class has only a limited usefulness. While it is certainly true that some men of working-class or at least non-gentle origin rose high in the army and the navy of the Parliament and that none did on the Royalist side, the civil war could not have taken place at all if the owning and governing classes had not been deeply divided. As the war went on a number of Parliamentarians grew more and more apprehensive of a stampede into social revolution led by religious fanatics, themselves the product of the

The frontispiece to Clarendon's History of the Great Rebellion

tolerance so notably championed by Cromwell and Manchester in the army of the Eastern Association. Royalist propaganda made the most of these fears. In his history Clarendon is emphatic on the social inferiority of the Parliamentarians. Lamenting the casualties among the Royalist officers at the second battle of Newbury he remarks: 'the officers of the enemy's side were never talked of, being for the most part of no better families than their common soldiers'. To him, as to most of his contemporaries, educated or uneducated, Royalist or Parliamentarian, society was like a chess set. A major piece, an earl or even the head of a large landed family, was hardly to be valued on the same scale as a pawn. This was not mere vulgar snobbery. It was the principle on which a clearly stratified, largely static, society worked. Authority was a function of social position. Put that in question and it would be like leaving each motorist to decide for himself which side of the road to drive on.

In disparaging the promotion of persons of humble birth Clarendon was stating a principle that the vast majority of his opponents would have asserted with equal fervour. What they would not so easily have accepted is the substance of Clarendon's criticism. His partiality, they would have argued, betrays itself in citing regrettable exceptions as instances of the normal rule. Lucy

*Staunch Parliamentarians,
John (ABOVE) and
Lucy Hutchinson*

Hutchinson, a vigorous partisan of the Parliament, and her husband John, who commanded the important Parliamentary garrison of Nottingham throughout the war, were exactly of Clarendon's opinion. Mrs Hutchinson tells us that her husband as a young man was admired by 'a young maid, beautifull and esteemed to be very rich, but of base parentage . . .' She was, it appears, the grandchild and heir of the Hutchinson's old family doctor. But 'his greate heart could never stoupe to think of marrying into so meane a stock', scruples that were evidently not shared by the earl's son who subsequently married her. Colonel Hutchinson abated no whit of his principles under the stress of war. As his wife remarked: '. . . allmost all the Parliament Garrisons were infested and disturb'd with like factious little people, insomuch that many worthy gentlemen were wearied out of their command, some opprest by a certeine meane sort of people in the House whom, to distinguish from the most Honorable Gentlemen, they called *worsted stocking men*'.

Again and again in the civil war one is struck by the unanimity of those who were on opposite sides. And yet is this so strange? England was one nation. The articulate, the educated, the ambitious and the powerful might, as in every age since the world began, disagree, might argue, might compete fiercely for power, for wealth and for position. But that they should share the vast proportion of the presuppositions on which the civilized life of any age must rest is hardly surprising. The civil war divided families, divided the communities of town and county that composed the nation: it divided merchants, landowners, lawyers, clergymen, scientists and poets. It did not divide the rich from the poor, the gentle from the simple, for the good reason that the poor and the simple had no ticket of admission to the great theatre at which the drama was to be performed. But it is in the nature of such performances that events take charge. Within a few years of the outbreak of war social and political doctrines of a radical, even a revolutionary, character were being preached or printed. Ideas of democracy and of social and economic equality were thus the product, not the cause, of the convulsion.

The cause of the civil war was the total collapse of Charles I's government. Even that would not have been sufficient had it not been for the unique combination of ineptitude and slyness, of obstinacy and vacillation, with which the King frustrated friend, foe and neutral alike from constructive action. Governments and ministers had fallen often enough, policies had changed or had been reversed without the country having to pay so terrible a price. But Charles I was no ordinary man and no ordinary King. It is to his character and mentality that we must now turn.

Charles's elder brother, Henry, who died of typhoid at the age of eighteen

Chapter 2
The King

Perhaps no monarch in English history has so touched the hearts of those who knew him, or the imaginative sympathies of those who have looked at his portraits or read of his misfortunes. What might not Shakespeare have made of the man and of the tragedy when, in his hands, Richard II moves us so powerfully? In pathos and dignity the closing scenes of the play rival, but do not surpass, the historical reality of Charles's last days. And the Richard of the play is the creation of genius not the portraiture of history. Medieval biography and the materials for it are like dried milk. The warmth and humanity is Shakespeare's own.

Unlike most of his predecessors Charles I was brought up in an atmosphere of domestic happiness. James I was a most affectionate father and Anne of Denmark a gay, good-tempered, empty-headed mother. Her entire devotion had been lavished on Charles's elder brother, Henry, Prince of Wales, whose sudden death in 1612 robbed the nation of a most popular and attractive heir-apparent. Prince Henry was everything that his father was not: good-looking, graceful, dignified without stiffness, a Prince Charming of the early seventeenth century. He appears to have inherited his father's undoubted intellectual ability and to have combined all these qualities with a conspicuous enthusiasm for the good old freebooting policy of overseas expansion that his father was most anxious to play down. Sir Walter Ralegh, the last, half-legendary personification of the age of Drake and Hawkins, whom the King kept a prisoner in the Tower of London was the friend and mentor of the Prince. It was to the Prince that he dedicated his *History of the World*, that best-seller that Milton and Cromwell himself read and admired. Along with Foxe's *Book of Martyrs* it formed the sacred literature of those who believed in Puritanism at home and a vigorous, aggressive foreign policy based on sea-power. To both of these ideas James I was by temperament, conviction and experience deeply opposed.

Charles never succeeded to his brother's place in his mother's affections. It is therefore natural that he should have been more his father's son, conscious as he must have been of lacking both the splendid presence and the intellectual adventurousness of his more dashing brother. Not that he did not derive some tastes from his mother and study some qualities that had characterized her adored elder son. Notably Anne's passion for masques, that combination of entertainment and propaganda, of theatre and allegory, acquired with monarchs such as Louis XIV and Charles himself a deeper and more serious symbolism. And physically Charles, lacking all his brother's natural advantages, modelled himself on his grace, not on his father's grossness. James I's habits of personal hygiene revolted a society that was anything but exacting in such matters. Charles was fastidious in every detail and, in marked contrast to his father, a man of rigid self-discipline.

> He was a person, tho' born sickly, yet who came thro' temperance and exercise, to have as firm and strong a body as most persons I ever knew, and throughout all the fatigues of the warr, or during his imprisonment never sick. His appetite was to plain meats, and tho' he took a good quantity thereof yet it was suitable to an easy digestion. He seldom eat of above three dishes at most, nor drank above thrice: a glass of small beer, another of claret wine, and the last of water; he eat suppers as well as dinners heartily; but betwixt meales he never medled with anything. Fruit he would eat plentifully; and with this regularity he moved as steddily as a star follows its course.

This account given by one of his most intelligent and perceptive servants, Sir Philip Warwick, whom Pepys in the next reign was to admire for his mastery of Treasury business, establishes his essential features. There was nothing loose, convivial or ill-bred about the King. The coarseness and buffoonery of his father were alien to him. The stillness, the withdrawn majesty of the great Van Dyck portraits are true to the character of the sitter as well as to the conception of kingship they were intended to convey. In his speech from the scaffold Charles told his people: 'A subject and a sovereign are clear different things.' The famous phrase enshrines his personal and political creed, interchangeable terms since, on Charles's principles, there was no distinguishing between the King as head of state and the King as an individual. In all he did and was and said and thought, he was directly and solely accountable to God.

Such a theory makes no sense unless its religious foundation is first admitted. Here indeed Charles, a man of serene and profound piety, found no shadow of difficulty. The divine right of kings which his father, a much wider-ranging and more acute thinker, had intellectualized in his book *The Trew Law of Free Monarchies* required no such mental exertion from the son. It was as clear as daylight, as palpable as the force of gravity. God, the creator of the world, had instituted the Church which threw the mantle of its divine authority over the Crown. In all kingship there was an element of priestly authority and in England since the Reformation this mysterious capacity had been explicitly stated in the statutes of the Realm. Charles was supreme governor of the Church that had anointed him King. Unlike all his predecessors since Henry VII he could not look back in any period of his life (he had left Scotland at the age of three) at which there had been any question of his belonging to any other communion but the Church of England. To that Church his love and loyalty were unqualified. To the order and beauty of its public worship, to Cranmer's Prayer Book and his father's Bible, how could so fine a perception not respond? No English king, no European monarch, has displayed a purer taste in the arts than Charles I. It is hard to think of any collection of paintings ever formed by one man that could stand comparison with his. Although he was no intellectual he was an aesthete of the first order. With so intense an artistic sensibility, no wonder if the day-to-day affairs of life, money, business, management of men and analysis of policy, were to seem less real than the

non est potestas nisi a deo.
Rom. 13. 1

THE
Diuine Right
and
ORIGINALL
of the ciuill
MAGISTRATE
from God.
Illustrated
and
Uindicated

By Edward Gee

Sould by Geo: Euersden
at ye Maidenhead in St
Paules Church yard

ΑΥΤΟΧΕΙΡΑΡΧΙΑ

ΘΕΟΧΡΑΤΙΑ

2. Sam: 18.   2. Sam: 20.

A title page presents the choice between Divine Right and Anarchy great design, framed by the divine artist, to which, as mere details, such matters were subordinate. Seen in this light the King might appear more truly, more fully King when showering peace and plenty on his people in a masque than when sitting at his council table considering expedients for raising revenue or filling vacant offices.

Even in the seventeenth century such a view of kingship would have been extreme. But it would not have been so bizarre as our modern hindsight makes it. The distinction that Bagehot drew so brilliantly between the dignified and the efficient parts of the constitution owes most of its point to the fact that Victorian England was changing rapidly into an industrial and democratic society while retaining in unbroken continuity the outward forms of the middle ages. The comic opportunities of such a situation were not lost on Gilbert and Sullivan. But the seventeenth century was nearer both in time and temper to the medieval world. All authority depends upon obedience, voluntarily given, tacitly conceded or enforced by violence and terror. In the middle ages panoply and display were a conventional assertion of authority. Dignity, that is to say, was part and parcel of efficiency. Hence the fierce sumptuary laws minutely regulating expenditure on dress, length of stay in the capital and other such details, the enforcement of which already infuriated so many of the rich and powerful. The magnificence of Charles I's court was therefore not simply the indulgence of the sovereign's personal tastes but the discharging of what he felt to be an important part of his function. In this as in so much else the King was insensitive to changing opinion and shifts in the spirit of the age. The order that he admired in the arts and practised in the regulation of his own life was disconcerted by what was new or strange. His mind was slow, his character diffident. Confronted by the unfamiliar his instinct was to obstruct or at best to play for time.

Of the charm and attraction that arose from his nature the evidence is abundant. Sir Philip Warwick, already quoted, wrote a quarter of a century after the King's execution that when he thought of dying it was one of his comforts that when he parted from the dunghill of this world he should meet King Charles. James Harrington, whom Parliament appointed to attend the King when he was their prisoner, according to Aubrey 'passionately loved his Majestie . . . I have oftentimes heard him speake of King Charles I with the greatest zeale and passion imaginable, and that his death gave him so great a griefe that he contracted a Disease by it; that never anything did goe so neer to him'. Clarendon, who began his Parliamentary career by opposing the policy of the Court and was always far from an idolatrous or even uncritical Royalist, wrote of himself that: 'He had a very particular devotion and passion for the person of the King; and did believe him the most and the best Christian in the world.' All these are intimate, not public, tributes and it would be easy to multiply them. Formal to the point of haughtiness in acting his great role – even on campaign he insisted on being served on the knee – the King's true nature was gentle and easy.

Yet the very qualities that endeared him to his private circle unfitted him for the real business of government. The harsh and the overbearing make more effective rulers than the courteous and the friendly. Charles's readiness to defer to others was, as he himself at last recognized, a dangerous weakness. What made it fatal was his inconsistency and his bad judgment of men. Matters had been made much worse by his father's example. James was notoriously open to the influence of favourites. The last and most magnificent of them, George Villiers, Duke of Buckingham, had won such an ascendancy over the young Prince of Wales that he retained or rather increased his power in the new reign. Only his assassination by a crazy ex-officer with a grievance left Charles suddenly on his own resources. The effect was to turn the King's love and loyalty towards his wife, Henrietta Maria, with whom his relations had not up to that point been happy. But the transformation was complete. The couple became and remained devoted to each other and to their children. Unfortunately the Queen herself was only too ready to accept the vacant position of political favourite, a fact in itself sufficiently indicative of her unfitness for it. Ignorant and contemptuous of the politics and religion of her husband's kingdom, a patriotic Frenchwoman and a bigoted Roman Catholic, she united in her person everything that was most hated and feared. The relations between the King and his subjects were endangered from the start.

It is ironical that so staunch a Church of England man as King Charles should have been so bedevilled by the anti-papal frenzy that smouldered through the seventeenth century, always ready to burst into flame at the lightest breeze. A wife so indiscreet and partisan in her Catholicism as Henrietta Maria would have been enough in herself. But there were many less obvious causes. James I was, after all, the son of that scarlet Papist Mary, Queen of Scots. And though his mother had had no hand in his religious education, though he had shown no sign of overt Catholicism, an international movement with a highly developed secret organization spread then, as it spreads now, a wide penumbra of suspicion. James had in any case reversed the policy of freebooting and privateering. He had enjoyed the most cordial relations with the Spanish ambassador and, under Buckingham's influence, had hurried his son from one Catholic marriage project to another. His wife, Anne of Denmark, was generally believed to be a secret convert to Catholicism. When his Calvinist son-in-law, the Elector Palatine, had challenged the Catholic powers of central Europe thus precipitating the Thirty Years War James had resisted the popular clamour to lead a Protestant crusade to his rescue. It might, on the other hand, be argued that the only authentic Catholic plot of the century involved blowing James sky-high and that the only foreign war of his reign was that declared on Spain against his better judgment in the last months of his life.

Similarly with his son. Although before the Scottish affair that brought matters to a head in 1640 Charles's only operations of war had been undertaken against Catholic powers, even in support of Protestants – the disastrous expeditions against Cadiz and the Ile de Rhé – the tone of his foreign policy was by no means that of Queen Elizabeth of glorious memory. And worse, far worse, was the King's ecclesiastical policy and its execrated architect, Archbishop Laud. This, it was argued, was the real thin end of the popish wedge. The Church of England was to be Catholicized from within so that her walls would collapse at the first blast of the Romish trumpet.

FROM TOP TO BOTTOM:
Charles's father and mother, James VI and I and Anne of Denmark; Frederick, Elector Palatine and King (for a few months) of Bohemia, and his wife, Charles's sister, Elizabeth (they were Prince Rupert's parents); and Charles before he became Prince of Wales

Laud, like his royal master, was wholly innocent of any such design. But again like Charles his words and his actions, his style and his manner, lent plausibility to the accusations of his opponents. There are striking affinities and contrasts between the King and his most trusted minister – for Laud besides being Archbishop of Canterbury was a prominent member of the Council and presided over such important Commissions as the Plantations, Foreign Affairs and even, for a time, the Treasury. Sharp, tetchy, red-faced, with nothing of the aristocrat in bearing or manner, the Archbishop was in externals the direct opposite of the King. But they shared a rigidity of mind and a resentfulness of opposition that goes far to explain their tactlessness and political ineptitude, since it never seems to have occurred to either of them to imagine what it might be like to be somebody else. Most important of all, their view of the Church, its place, its nature, its relation to society and to government, was essentially one and the same.

The King and Queen in Inigo Jones's designs for a masque

In so many respects behind their time, in one Charles and Laud were ahead of it. They were Tories before Toryism had been invented. The toast of Church and King epitomizes their creed. The King whose nature was artistic understood this in images of divinely sustained regality, painted by Rubens or Van Dyck or staged in a masque designed by Inigo Jones. To Laud whose nature was essentially didactic and disciplinarian it meant licking the Church into shape, seeing that it taught what it was there to teach, redrafting the rules, turning out the idlers and those who answered back, restoring or rebuilding churches, in a word doing on a national scale what he had already done as President of St John's College, Oxford, where the quadrangle that bears his name is his most beautiful memorial, and as Chancellor of the University, where his reform of the statutes opened a golden age.

And what was the Church to teach that, in Laud's view, it was not already teaching? First and foremost it was to stem the tide of Calvinism – or Puritanism as it was loosely called – and bring its teaching and practice back to the example of the early undivided Church, before England's breach with Rome, or Rome's breach with Byzantium. The altar and the sacrament, not the preacher and the pulpit were to be the focus of public worship. A rigid high-churchmanship was to be imposed on a nation that had largely lost the tradition of ceremonial and whose intellectual and social leaders were by education and sympathy generally opposed to any such programme. So powerfully entrenched were these forces that there was never the slightest chance that Laud and the King could coerce the whole country, although they might frighten or irritate by local persecution. In the diocese of Norwich, for instance, where Christopher Wren's uncle, Matthew, was Bishop from 1635 to 1638 the Puritans were severely handled. To escape this a number of them emigrated to New England. It was easy to argue that bullying of this sort was a foretaste of the Inquisition and all the horrors of Popery.

From Laudianism flowed a logical, coherent philosophy which was Tory and paternalist. Authority whether of priest or king was God-given, mysterious, not to be questioned. On the other hand Puritanism though often in practice fully as dictatorial and intolerant in its manifestations opened the door if not to democracy at least to oligarchy. Whether one accepted some form of predestinarianism, of vessels elect unto salvation and vessels elect unto wrath, or tempered it with a belief in an Inner Light by which the Holy Spirit guided the individual soul, the distinction between the minister ('priest' could only be understood in a Laudian or Catholic sense) and his flock was not absolute. The polarization of religious opinion which Charles and Laud were bringing about thus bore a dangerous resemblance to those between King and Parliament and King and Common Law.

Chapter 3

The Approach of War

It has often been asserted that England enjoys an inestimable advantage in not having a written constitution. This might not have appeared a self-evident proposition to the men of 1640. What was the relation between the King and the Law? Was he, the fountain of justice, above it or was it above him? In the preceding reign Titans such as Coke and Bacon had championed opposing views. Questions of this kind are much better not asked since the answering, even the framing, of them divides people who would have been content to jog on together. If the King were under the law, who was to tell him when he broke it or punish him if he persisted in his criminality? The judges? But they were appointed by the King and might be dismissed at pleasure. The High Court of Parliament? But the King was under no obligation to summon Parliament if he could manage without it. And it was not yet law that a Parliament could not be dissolved without its own consent.

We think of Parliaments as a part of the permanent machinery of government whose main function is to support an administration and to pass such new laws as may be necessary. Apart from that it is the great national debating society where issues of policy are argued and questions aired. Such a body bears little relation to any Parliament that met before 1640. Even Queen Elizabeth whose virtues the critics of the Stuarts never tired of extolling called Parliaments only infrequently and dismissed them soon. During the whole of her reign of nearly forty-five years Parliament was in session for a grand total of just under two and a half years. James I and Charles were even less ready to face them. The vitality of the House of Commons, its skill in taking the initiative, is all the more remarkable when it is remembered how rare were its opportunities of practising the arts of politics. Like the dragonfly it had to make the most of a short span.

Since Parliaments were, as a rule, only called when the Crown needed an extraordinary supply of money to pay for a war or to fit out a fleet, the technique was to refuse to grant supplies until grievances had been redressed. It was this that had led Charles to govern for eleven years without calling a Parliament. His last Parliament had been dissolved with a proclamation forbidding any one to speak of calling another. Naturally this lent substance to those who argued that the King was really determined to subvert the laws and customs of England. The King at this stage of his life had not in all probability thought enough about the matter to have any such objective. He was sure in his conscience that he had no motive other than to fulfil the duty laid on him. He would answer to God on the Day of Judgment and was accountable to no one else. If the Parliament obstructed his purposes by refusing him the

TRUTH.

JUSTICE.

THE CHURCH

THE STATE

THE
HOLY
STATE

By
Thomas Fuller
Bachelour of Divinitie, &
Prebendary of Sarum.
late of Sidney Colledge in Cambridge.

CAMBRIDGE,
Printed by R: D:
for John Williams
at the Signe of the
Crowne in S.t Paules
Church-yard
1642
W: Marshall sculpt.

A visual summary of
Charles I's political philosophy

supplies he needed, why, he would find ways of raising taxes without them. It was they, not he, who were violating the spirit of the law.

Such an interpretation of the central constitutional question was by no means perverse. None of our ancestors, Cavalier or Roundhead, would have approached it with the two assumptions that have coloured our view: the idea of progress and a knowledge of English history in the eighteenth and nineteenth centuries, when the development of our constitution was admired and imitated both in the old world and the new. The idea of progress seems almost self-evident to a technological society; the car, the gramophone, the dishwasher of 1970 has only to be compared with its counterpart of 1950, to say nothing of 1930, for the case to be established. Later means better. Therefore progress, like growing older, is an ineluctable process. The same holds true of the experimental sciences. But England in the first half of the seventeenth century was a pre-industrial society and, outside a tiny circle in London and Oxford and Cambridge, a pre-scientific one. There was thus no general prejudice in favour of the idea of progress. Some might think the world was getting better, some worse. But the overwhelming assumption was that it had its ups and downs and would go on, as it always had, in much the same way.

Similarly the view that our constitution developed in a regular, symmetrical, easily discernible pattern from the first laws of the Kings of Wessex down to the Reform Bill of 1832 had not dawned on the eye of the seventeenth century. The great common lawyers, such as Coke in James's time and Selden in Charles's, certainly ransacked the legal records for precedents that would support the advancement of Parliamentary power and the checking of prerogative. But that sprang from the very nature of the Common Law, a law that followed previous decisions and was not therefore subject to the whims and caprices of a sovereign, which the prerogative was. This fossicking in the archives, to borrow Professor Trevor-Roper's phrase, gave the movement for representative government and liberty of the subject its strongly antiquarian and historical character. It probably contributed to the popular mythology of history that represented the Saxons as a free and freedom-loving people who were brought under the yoke of arbitrary and aristocratic government by the Normans in 1066. But its great paladins never dreamed of calling themselves democrats and did not assert large abstract claims based on the patterns and rhythms of history. To them as to the King history was not a process that followed some ascertainable and therefore predictable pattern but the gradual unfolding of God's inscrutable purposes. A belief in Providence, the all-seeing eye whose range is not restricted by merely human perspectives, is almost the antithesis of a belief in progress. Progress is something that anyone can see for himself. The workings of Providence are proverbially mysterious.

Thus the King and his opponents shared some preconceptions about the nature of politics and law that would be widely questioned today and knew nothing of many ideas and attitudes that we are ready to read into their acts and utterances. In particular the rights that the King claimed for himself would, until the war was on the point of breaking out, have been generally admitted. Indeed all through the first civil war the Parliament claimed, however insincerely, to be fighting for the King, to be his rescuers from the wicked men under whose influence he had fallen. It was not so much what the King might legally do but what he actually did that was the rock of offence. Had Puritans with a forward foreign policy taken the places of Laudians and peace-party men as his advisers and servants, many constitutional issues would never have been raised, at least in the form they were. The hated prerogative courts, Star Chamber and High Commission, were loathed for the unpopular policies pursued by court favourites often against their social superiors, much more than for offending against the genius of the English Constitution. Both had been constantly employed by the Tudors, not least by the glorious Queen Elizabeth. No one doubted that the King must rule and must have adequate instruments. It was the poisonous and perverted notions that had been put into his head that were bringing ruin on the kingdom.

For his part the King was quick enough to learn the tricks of his opponents though he would never condescend to understand their aspirations. He too had lawyers who could search the records for precedents and could find there perfectly legal means of raising the revenue that Parliament had denied him. He revived the Court of Wards and Liveries, an obsolete but lucrative mechanism of a defunct feudal order. Furious tenants-in-chief found themselves paying huge sums for the right to give their children in marriage, to compound for the dues incident on death and other resented exactions. Anyone owning land worth £40 a year could be compelled to become a knight, an expensive proceeding, or else to compound for the privilege of avoiding it. The Forest Law, a long disused codification of the Crown's hunting rights drawn up when great tracts of country that now supported a fair population had been reserved for deer and boar, was pressed into service. And, most famous of all these expedients, Ship Money was levied first on coastal and then on inland counties to finance the King's naval programme. In all these methods of taxation the King was either technically within his rights or at the least had a very good case. But Hampden, Pym, Holles and the rest had the sympathy of many who were to shed their blood for the King in the civil war when they challenged the by-passing of Parliament. Charles's reaction, to resort to force where he could, to bring pressure to bear on the judges, even to dismiss those who delivered opinions unfavourable to himself, confirmed men's fears. Finally besides antagonizing the Puritans and Common Lawyers who were the backbone of the future Parliamentary party the King alienated a great part of the trading interest by his grants of monopoly. These touched the acme of Stuart ineptitude. Granted to favourites and courtiers they yielded little to the Crown at a cost in resentment, jealousy and a sense of social and economic injustice that can hardly be exaggerated.

The King's chief ministers during the eleven years when no Parliament sat were with two exceptions men of no great mark. When the storm burst they either fled abroad or sank into obscurity. One of the exceptions was of course Archbishop Laud and the other was Thomas Wentworth, Earl of Strafford. Strafford, to give him the title he enjoyed for so short a time before he was to bequeath it to history, was a much more formidable politician than Laud or the King. In the Parliament of 1628 he had detached himself from the leadership of Pym and Holles (whose sister he had married) to head a middle party,

Mr. Alexr. Henderson.

Alexander Henderson, a leading Presbyterian minister who opposed Charles I's ecclesiastical policies in Scotland and helped draw up the National Covenant

whose strength centred in the House of Lords. But middle parties were irrelevant to a man such as Charles I. After the dissolution and the imprisonment of several of the leaders of the Commons Wentworth entered the King's service, becoming, whether at Whitehall or at York as President of the Council of the North or at Dublin as Lord Deputy of Ireland, the most vigorous and effective administrator of the whole reign. He, if anyone, was the King's best hope. But characteristically Charles neither liked nor altogether trusted him. Wentworth had been outspoken in his criticism of Buckingham, the greatest favourite of all, and that was not easily to be forgiven. There was too a fierceness, an arrogance, a provocativeness about him that made him as much hated as Buckingham had been, and, for his far superior abilities, much more feared. In Laud's rigorism he recognized a fellow spirit, a man who had thought his position through and did not shrink from alarming or unpleasant consequences. Both had much more in common with each other than with the King they served. Together they created and carried through the famous policy of 'Thorough' with which Strafford's name is forever linked. 'Thorough' meant the assertion of the Crown's authority to whatever limit might be found necessary or expedient.

Laud and Strafford, the mainstays of the Court party, were not courtiers. Charles I's natural companions had more time for the splendours of civilization and less for its necessities. Connoisseurs like Endymion Porter and Sir Thomas Hanmer, collectors and patrons like the Earl of Arundel and the Earl of Pembroke, great riders to hounds like his brother the Earl of Montgomery, or magnificoes like the Earl of Holland, a favourite of the Queen, set the tone of taste and expense. Their essence is distilled in the Marquis of Hamilton who, in Clarendon's words 'had the greatest power over the affections of the King of any man of that time'. In wealth, in territory and in lineage Hamilton towered over the other Scottish grandees. Like the King, whose cousin he was, he loved hunting and the arts. Again like the King his profound sense of his position urged him to military and political eminence far beyond his natural capacities. He had raised and led a contingent of his own to the wars in Germany but had fortunately been prevented from commanding them in battle. Less fortunately he was the King's most trusted adviser on Scottish affairs. His instinct for magnificence as at once the end and the means of political authority, his instant retreat into deviousness when faced by any difficulty, exactly complemented the King's.

The amateurism of the courtiers exemplified by Hamilton, the ideological rigidity of Laud and the teachings of 'Thorough' were a sufficiently explosive mixture. Scotland detonated them. In 1633 Charles returned to the kingdom he had left as a boy of three to be crowned at Holyrood. The religious form on which the King insisted offended the prevailing Calvinism of the noblemen who attended. Annoyed, the King resolved to bring his northern subjects to that better order Archbishop Laud was establishing in England. Misinformed by Hamilton of the real state and strength of opinion, he introduced the Prayer Book of 1637. The reaction was a riot in Edinburgh, followed by petitions from every part of Scotland. The King's anger was matched by Scotch resentment, as much patriotic as theological, at the attempted imposition of an English religious system. A year later the signing of the Scottish National Covenant paved the way for an Assembly at Glasgow that met without the King's permission and abolished episcopacy. Charles had the choice of capitulation or resort to force. There could be little doubt which he would take.

The tension was heightened by the course of affairs in England. In the most famous of all his many unpopular and oppressive acts Laud had obtained in Star Chamber a sentence of mutilation against three hostile pamphleteers, William Prynne, the lawyer, and two less learned authors, Burton and Bastwick. Cutting off the ears of educated men for an expression of opinion offended the

Prynne, Burton and Bastwick at the pillory

sensibilities of an age that felt nothing but satisfaction in watching felons or traitors undergo the same or worse. The ship-money issue, too, was recoiling on the crown. The expedient of postponing judgment in Hampden's case, of referring it from one court to another, had not proved a success. It gave the opposition the chance of reviving it when it might have died down: it fortified some counties into petitioning against it: it even raised doubts in the minds of some of the judges. Clarendon in his history talks darkly of the great contrivers, Hampden, Pym, Warwick, Mandeville (soon to succeed to the earldom of Manchester) and Saye. But no contriver could have orchestrated so menacing a concert as the King himself.

In the spring of 1639 the Covenanters gathered an army and appointed Sandy Leslie, an officer of considerable recent experience in the Thirty Years War, as commander-in-chief. Charles at once retaliated by charging them with rebellion. The so-called First Bishops' War had begun.

To most Englishmen only one result would have seemed possible. Scotland was very much poorer and smaller than England. The hereditary feuds between the clans, the bitter jealousies between the lowland nobles, the absence of any tradition of strong central government deepened the inequality. Certainly the King counted on a quick and decisive victory. He had been planning for war, insofar as he could be said to plan for anything, for at least a year. That is to say he had come to hope for it and to see in it the readiest way for God to chastise his disaffected subjects and to vindicate the divine institution of kingship. The idea that God might allow rebels to win wars against anointed kings was one that Charles resisted in the teeth of over-whelming evidence until the civil war itself was all but over. Some practical steps were taken: arms were ordered, inventories made, fortifications surveyed. Attempts were made abroad to raise loans and hire mercenaries. There were even plans of campaign. But to a dreaming visionary nature like the King's image and reality easily merged. When the war actually broke out the Coven-anters possessed themselves at once of all the King's strongholds, seized his projected bases and, finding themselves masters of Scotland, were soon in a position to threaten the stronger country.

Charles succeeded in raising an army that was much smaller than the force on which his original projections were based: 6000 horse 'and about that number in foot, all very well disciplined men, under as good and experienced officers as were to be found in any army in Christendom', according to Clarendon. That this did not apply to the generals chosen to command the expedition the same writer makes clear. The commander-in-chief was to be a great nobleman of advanced age whose connoisseurship in the arts came close to the King's and who in lack of executive experience or talent surpassed him:

> He chose to make the earl of Arundel his general, a man who had nothing martial about him but his presence and his looks, and therefore was thought to be made choice of only for his negative qualities: he did not love the Scots; he did not love the puritans; which good qualifications were allayed by another negative, he did love nobody else.

The lieutenant-general was a much more rational appointment. Robert

A corner of Berwick fortifications

Devereux, Earl of Essex, was a great noble whose immense popularity, like his reputation in military circles, can only be explained by his honesty and his lack of malice. As a boy he had been favoured by James I and there is a charming picture of him hunting with Prince Henry. He had seen some, but not much, service in Germany. He had served as vice-admiral in the Cadiz fiasco of 1625. His religious and political connections were moderately puritan, so that in reclaiming him for the court Charles was, apparently, acting with unusual foresight and magnanimity. Gloomy, conscientious, kindly and unintellectual Essex belonged to a type which Englishmen of every generation prefer in positions of responsibility to those with more glittering but perhaps more alarming endowments. Essex was sound.

Nothing of the kind could be said about the Earl of Holland, whom the King appointed to command the cavalry. As a young man he had served a campaign or two with the Dutch army but he had soon found that good looks and charm of manner could open much more profitable and agreeable prospects at court. He married a rich wife, obtained places and embassies and lived in great splendour. Holland House, the Mecca of Whig Society in the days of Macaulay and Sydney Smith, and Holland Park, the glass of educational fashion in the 1970s, owe their name to him. Clarendon who never tires of describing him sums him up at last: 'He was a very well-bred man, and a fine gentleman in good times: but too much desired to enjoy ease and plenty . . . and did think poverty the most insupportable evil that could befall any man in this world.' The contrast between him and his brother, the Earl of Warwick, a vigorous puritan, an ardent imperialist, a practical seaman with a dashing record of privateering and a thorough grasp of politics and war, could hardly be more extreme.

Even less happy was the choice of Hamilton to command the fleet. His

A Parliamentary view of the Pacification of Berwick

single qualification for command, that as a great territorial magnate he might easily rally support amongst his tenantry, was thrown away at sea. His defects, amateurishness, indecision and pride, were made more absurdly evident. Under him the navy accomplished nothing. Far worse, the appointment was a gratuitous insult to a young and able nobleman who was actually Charles's Lord High Admiral, the Earl of Northumberland. His territorial importance, if not quite so vast, was still great and more obviously relevant to the operations of a fleet supporting an army up the northeast coast. Northumberland had shown talent and energy in command of the ship-money fleets of 1636 and 1637. No doubt he had been exasperated by the feebleness of direction that had prevented him from achieving any result proportionate to his exertions. His supersession by Hamilton was a public slight that was noticed by others besides its recipient. It was to cost the King much.

While Sandy Leslie, whose literacy, the unkind said, only extended down the alphabet as far as the letter 'g', was recruiting his officers from his fellow professionals in the Swedish service, Charles was admiring his cavalry perform their evolutions. The most magnificently accoutred troop was that raised by Sir John Suckling, the poet, but its subsequent performance in the face of the enemy prompted verse more ribald than his own. At the end of March the King had joined the army at York. By that time the Covenanters were in undisputed control of Scotland. News came in that loyal noblemen, on whose support Charles's policy rested, had signed the Covenant. Outraged, the King summoned the lords attending their sovereign to take a new oath of fealty in the coming war. Two of them, Lord Saye and Lord Brooke, refused. It was not a happy start.

Essex, on the other hand, whose political and religious sympathies the Scots attempted to work on, behaved impeccably, showing the King the secret letter they sent to him. In his military capacity he acted with promptness. Berwick, the key to the east coast route, still today retains the formidable system of fortifications that Queen Elizabeth had erected on the best continental model. The Scots were reported to be close and then to be in possession of it. Undeterred by these alarming reports Essex did not rest until he had secured it for the King. It was the only display of military competence on the English side. When the remainder of the army came up, disenchanted by foul weather and totally inadequate provision of food and shelter, an advance into Scotland was ordered. Holland pushed on with the cavalry, characteristically losing touch with the foot who naturally marched at a slower rate. It was early June. The weather had now changed to heat and heaviness. Late in the afternoon Holland suddenly observed a large and well-found force of foot occupying the hills in front of him and extending its wings to cut him off. After an exchange of summons to retreat Holland ignominiously returned to Berwick without engaging the enemy. A few days later the two armies faced each other across the Tweed. The order and efficiency of the Scots camp discouraged the more realistic from any light-hearted adventure.

This first encounter of Charles I's army gave ample scope for what was to prove the most enduring talent of its senior officers, that for fighting amongst themselves. Holland, attacked for his gross incompetence, blamed the guides

A View of Greenwich, by Adriaen van Stalbemt and Jan van Belcamp, shows Charles I and Henrietta Maria with their eldest son, Charles, and attendants, including Endymion Porter (on the left, with stick), next to him possibly Philip Herbert, Earl of Pembroke, and, climbing the hill in a blue dress, Lucy Percy, Countess of Carlisle. In the background is the palace at Greenwich and the ground floor of the Queen's house which was begun by Inigo Jones for Anne of Denmark and completed in about 1635 for Henrietta Maria

provided by Arundel, the commander-in-chief. The Earl of Newcastle, governor to Charles, Prince of Wales, and in that capacity commander of the Prince's troop, was furious with Holland for having posted him at the rear instead of in the van of the cavalry. As the most expert equestrian of his age and one of the richest peers he would have been a much more appropriate choice for the command of the cavalry. Usually the commander-in-chief commanded the horse in person. Arundel already resented Holland's pretensions and took his criticisms of the guides as insulting to himself. Nothing of this kind, we may be sure, went on when Leslie called a council of officers.

In spite of everything the King was still disposed towards an active prosecution of the war. How far did he see himself as concerned with the brute realities of power, money, force, men, bases, munitions, supplies and the rest, how far as the central character in some great masque of monarchy?

He did more intend the pomp of his preparations than the strength of them and did still believe that the one would save the labour of the other.

Clarendon's judgment, applied to an earlier stage of the war, suggests how difficult it was for the King to draw this distinction. But his council were in no doubt that the campaign must be called off and a truce, if not a peace, at once concluded. Strafford who had been watching events with increasing alarm pressed this view from Dublin. The King's defeat in battle by the Covenanters would mean the end of 'Thorough' and of a great deal else besides. In fact the situation was already so threatening that nothing but his own presence at the King's side as his Chief Minister could restore it. To this conclusion the King himself at last had come. An unsatisfactory peace treaty was cobbled together at Berwick and the Lord Deputy received the invitation for which he had been waiting.

The City of London, as it was before the burning

A The Tower.
B Algate.
C Bellinsgate.
D London Bridge.
E The three Cranes.
F Queene heuse.
G Pauls Wharfe.
H Baynards Castle.
I Common stayres.
K Blackfriers.
L Bridewell.
M The Temple.
N Sommerset house.

O The Savoy.
P Durham house.
Q Whitehall.
R Bow church.
S Saint Som Pichers.
T Saint Giles in the fields.
V Westminster bridge.
X Charing Crosse.
Y Pauls steeple.
Z Saint Iames.
1 Lambath marsh.
a Paris garden.
3 Winchester house.
4 Saint Saviours.
5 Saint Olives.

CIVITAS LONDINVM

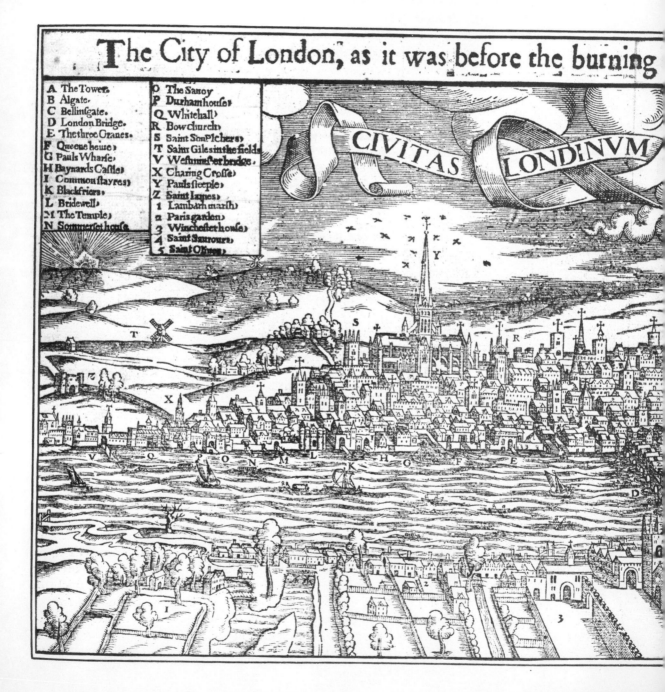

Chapter 4
Charles I's England

The great difference between reading about the past and experiencing the present is that time presents an illusion of pattern and order and perspective that we cannot make out in the events that slip and slide around us, smothering our sense of direction. Yet nothing is more fundamental to an understanding of history than the simple recognition that it wasn't history to the people who lived through it. The point may seem an insult to the meanest intelligence, a truism of truisms: but even the best historian has to fight to hold on to it as his artistic instinct and his habits of scholarship marshal in his subconscious mind the rabble of disorderly reality into the formations that are shortly to march across his page.

The course of events sketched in the preceding chapter and soon to be resumed seem to us like the current of a river as it approaches a waterfall. It gathers speed, the roar of catastrophe grows louder and closer. Within three years neighbours who had been the best of friends all their lives, whose children had intermarried, whose interests and tastes were sympathetic, whose common loyalties it had never occurred to anyone to doubt, were, often in agony of spirit, trying to kill each other. These people did not know, in 1639 or 1640, that they were going to be called Roundheads and Cavaliers, Parliamentarians and Royalists. The mere act of so classifying them seems to give a spurious rationality to what would have seemed, two or three years before the event, revolting and unthinkable. English society in the age of the early Stuarts was not bitterly divided; on the contrary, it was, by comparison with the two preceding centuries, harmonious and tranquil.

> O thou, that dear and happy Isle,
> The garden of the world erewhile,
> Thou Paradise of the four seas
> Which Heaven planted us to please,
> What luckless apple did we taste
> To make us mortal and thee waste?

So wrote Andrew Marvell, who took no part in the war but, like Milton, served Cromwell's government and was wholly opposed to everything the Stuarts stood for. Exactly the same point is made at greater length and even more emphatically by Clarendon who served the Stuarts through thick and thin. During the 1630s, 'this kingdom, and all his majesty's dominions . . . enjoyed the greatest calm, and the fullest measure of felicity, that any people in any age, for so long time together, have been blessed with; to the wonder and envy of all the parts of Christendom'.

Aula Domus Arrundeliana. Londini, Meridiem versus,

The south side of Arundel House in the Strand during the civil war

Sir Theodore Mayerne. His obstetrical advice was especially valued: Sir Henry Slingsby consulted him about his wife, and during the war he was given a safe-conduct to attend Henrietta Maria's last pregnancy

What was England like as the storm clouds gathered? Who were these people who were soon to be pinned down in the showcase of history as Royalists and Parliamentarians? Apart from London, Bristol, Norwich and a few other ports wealth and status rested largely on the ownership of land. The clothing industry was important in some towns of the north and west: the iron and steel furnaces of the Weald of Kent and Sussex were still more numerous than those of Derbyshire or the West Riding, an indication of the tiny scale of production. The coalfields of the northeast were important for domestic, not industrial, consumption. Water-wheels and windmills harnessed the only sources of inanimate power. Roads were few and bad. Bulk transport was only possible by inland or coastwise navigation. Overseas trade and colonization thus offered markets and opportunities for investment the more welcome because so little was available at home.

Apart from trade, the openings for the ambitious and talented were few and narrow. Most of the professions that we know did not exist. The Church and the Law offered most to an educated and intelligent man. Medicine and music though nominally represented in the two universities were fringe professions. Musicians learned their art in a society where singing and playing were among the chief recreations by apprenticeship rather than formal instruction. Amateurs and professionals were not distinguished by the existence of a career structure. Such posts as there were were in the gift of Church and Court; otherwise the uncertainties of private patronage were all that was to be hoped for. Medicine was neither lucrative nor respected except in the case of a few extremely successful practitioners such as Sir Theodore Mayerne, Charles I's doctor and later Cromwell's. Such men who had studied either in Holland or in Italy really belonged not to the medical profession but to the small circle of scientists of which Gresham College in London was the nucleus and which was beginning to establish a cell or two in Oxford and Cambridge.

There was no regular army and the navy employed no permanent commissioned officers. It did retain a few boatswains, carpenters and suchlike technical experts, but these were men of very different expectations. The man who wanted a military career would have to find it in the Dutch service, where many of the civil war commanders learned their trade, or even further afield.

The Law had supplanted the Church as the most likely route to administrative office. The Inns of Court were much more what the university is now in the education of a man who wanted to play some part in public affairs, and the universities were more like present-day grammar or public schools. The age of entry was much lower in the seventeenth century. Clarendon went up to Oxford when he was only thirteen and Milton had just passed his sixteenth birthday when he was admitted to Cambridge. The universities were not only wholly clerical – a Fellow of a college who did not take orders would have to resign – but almost entirely celibate. Only the heads of houses were allowed to marry. The affinity with the monasteries that had been suppressed only a century earlier was not close but it was perceptible. It was therefore natural that the intellectual life of the universities should concern itself principally with the Church and with theology. And it was still axiomatic that religion was the bond that held society together, even that it was the basis of all political organization. The collision between the Laudians and the Puritans was thus not a remote and specialized controversy but a conflict on a matter of central importance. No doubt many people wished that Laud and his opponents would not be so violent but probably very few thought their disputes trivial or irrelevant or futile. Both universities included powerful and learned champions of the two schools of thought but Cambridge was predominantly Puritan while Oxford largely supported the archbishop.

Such men were by no means necessarily bigots or even on bad terms with their opponents. Not all High Churchmen were persecuting authoritarians and by no means all Puritans were the snivelling sanctimonious killjoys so brilliantly caricatured in the plays of Ben Jonson. Among the High Church party were to be found such people as the Ferrars of Little Gidding who turned their house into a religious community and ran a school where children were not only freed from the beatings that formed such an important part of contemporary education but were even provided with story books specially written for them. George Herbert's too brief ministry as a country parson at Bemerton expressed a beauty of holiness that his hymns have kept bright for succeeding generations. The shrill, bitter notes of party warfare that untune even Milton's religious poetry are worlds away. So, too, one would have thought, were the rigidities of Charles I. Yet he admired and favoured both Herbert and the Ferrars.

Again, the rising school of Puritan intellectuals, the so-called Cambridge Platonists, under whose influence Milton came as an undergraduate, were notably tolerant and large-minded. Men like More, Whichcote and Worthington, who were to hold high office in the university after the Royalists had been displaced, were very much on speaking terms with such men as Hales and Chillingworth who enjoyed Laud's favour and were to suffer for their Royalism in the civil war. The circles, in religion, in politics, in family and kinship, intersect. The hard lines that party managers and partisan historians love were forced on an England much more flexible than that of a century, or even half a century, earlier.

Hales and Chillingworth were members of a circle that more than any other distilled the learned, civilized, open flavour that characterizes the finest spirits of the age. This was the circle for ever associated with Lord Falkland and his house, now long vanished, at Great Tew. No description of it can rival that written long after the war had scattered or killed its intimates by the most famous of them, Clarendon himself:

> He [Lord Falkland] was wont to say, that he never found reluctancy in anything he resolved to do, but in his quitting London, and departing from the conversation of those he enjoyed there; which was in some degree preserved and continued by frequent letters, and often visits, which were made by his friends from thence, whilst he continued wedded to the country; and which were so grateful to him, that during their stay with him, he looked upon no book, except their very conversation made an appeal to some book; and truly his whole conversation was one continued *convivium philosophicum* or *convivium theologicum* [a feast of philosophy or theology], enlivened and refreshed with all the facetiousness of wit, and good humour, and pleasantness of discourse, which made the gravity of the argument itself (whatever it was) very delectable. His house where he usually resided (Tew, or Burford, in Oxfordshire) being within ten or twelve miles of the university, looked like the university itself, by the company that was always found there. These were Dr Sheldon, Dr Morley, Dr Hammond, Dr Earles, Mr Chillingworth, and indeed all men of eminent parts and faculties in Oxford, besides those who resorted thither from London; who all found their lodgings there, as ready as in the colleges; nor did the lord of the house know of their coming or going, nor who were in his house, till he came to dinner, or supper, where all still met; otherwise, there was no troublesome ceremony or constraint, to forbid men to come to the house, or to make them weary of staying there; so that many came thither to study in a better air, finding all the books that they could desire in his library, and all the persons together, whose company they could wish, and not find in any other society.

Falkland, too, like Clarendon, was a friend of John Selden and on easy terms with most of those who were to be prominent in the two Parliaments of 1640.

This note of gentleness, affection, domesticity, good nature (to use Clarendon's own favourite expression) sounds no less insistently in the lives of the future Parliamentary leaders. Hampden was not only, on the evidence of Royalist members, one of the best liked men in the House of Commons, but also among his neighbours in the country. When the war broke out and the canons of Windsor, the clerical equivalent of the King's bodyguard, were turned out of doors, it was to Hampden as an old and valued friend that one of them applied for redress on the violation of the safe conduct for the wagons bringing his goods through Buckinghamshire. Bulstrode Whitelocke, a prominent Parliamentarian who was to hold high office under the Commonwealth and Protectorate, had been a favourite pupil of Laud at St John's and an intimate of Clarendon's when they were both young barristers of a gay and social disposition. Again like Clarendon, Whitelocke was happy and affectionate as son, husband and father. The degree of social harmony, the balance and

Clarendon's closest friend and political associate, Lucius Cary, Viscount Falkland, killed at the first battle of Newbury

good temper of the tone in which men wrote and talked is much more remarkable than the signs of division. The frenzied rivalries of Italian Renaissance towns, the feuds and vendettas of poor and backward societies strike no echo in the prosperous placidity of England before the civil war.

This inviting picture takes no account of the poverty and hunger that so many people were condemned to, not because these sufferings are beneath the historian's notice but because they were not felt by the people who were being propelled towards the terrible choices of civil war. The men who were to call each other Cavalier and Roundhead were not starving or in rags. In town and country, at the bar or in the universities, they were living much the same sort of life, cherishing often the same ambitions, thinking, so far as one can see, much the same thoughts.

Take, on the Puritan side, the future Colonel Hutchinson whose biography written by his widow is one of the most compelling documents of the civil war. His father was a rich and cultivated country gentleman, several times

Bulstrode Whitelocke, another friend of Clarendon's, who chose the opposite side

chosen to represent his native county of Nottingham and was to die '. . . in the yeare 1643, a sitting Member of that glorious Parliament that so generously attempted, and had almost effected, England's perfect liberty'. It comes as something of a shock to find that the son, the future Parliamentary governor of Nottingham, was in 1639, after two agreeable years idling in the country, trying to meet the increased expense of a growing family by buying an office of profit in the court of Star Chamber, that hated instrument of Stuart oppression. In physique, in piety, in fastidiousness he closely resembled the King he was to fight against, some of whose pictures he was even to buy when the royal collection was sold off by the Commonwealth. Or take another Parliamentary officer whose widow has left a description of him, Sir William Springet, of Ringmer in Sussex:

Thy grandfather declined bishops and common prayer very early . . . In his zeal against dark formality and the superstitions of the times, he having taken the Scotch Covenant against all popery and popish innovations, as also the English Engagement, when his child was about a month old, he had a commission sent him to be colonel of a regiment of foot, when the fight was at Edge-Hill, and he raised without beat of drum, eight hundred men, most of them professors and professors' sons [i.e. Puritans], near six score volunteers of his own company, himself going a volunteer and took no pay . . .

He rarely ever was idle, but when he could not be employed abroad in shooting at a mark with guns, pistols, cross-bows or long-bows, managing his horses (which he brought up and managed himself, teaching them boldness in charging) . . . then he would fence within doors, make cross-bow strings [etc.]. He was also an artist in shooting and fishing, and making of lines and ordering of baits for that purpose. He was a great lover of coursing, but he managed his dogs himself . . .

Such men are not readily distinguishable from those who were so soon to meet them on the battlefield. And if the Puritans did not disdain the pleasures and pursuits of the Royalist gentry, the Royalists were not necessarily less spiritually minded than they. Sir Henry Slingsby of Scriven, a few miles west of York, occupied much the same position in his county as Sir Thomas Hutchinson did in Nottinghamshire. Like Sir Thomas he was returned to serve in the Long Parliament but his subsequent history was very different. He fought on the Royalist side throughout the first civil war. He was among the garrison of Newark that surrendered only on the King's direct order after one of the longest and hardest sieges of the war. Thereafter he refused to take any of the oaths required or to make any terms with the victors for the preservation of his estate which was duly confiscated. He lived mostly in hiding, corresponded with the exiled court and in 1655 was arrested for his part in a Royalist conspiracy. In 1658 he was beheaded on Tower Hill, one of the very few Royalists who could claim the full status of political martyrdom. Here if anywhere we should find the true type of last-ditch Cavalier. Fortunately for us he kept a diary so that we do not need to rely on guesswork.

And what did a man of this unusual strength of character and clarity of decision think and feel as the sands were running out for peace? Much the same as his devout, serious-minded future opponents. The tone is what we should call puritanical. On a visit to York he meets one of the canons in the Minster library and argues against Laudian practices. 'I thought it came too near idolatry to adore a place with rich cloaths and other furniture.' His anti-clericalism would have won Milton's approval:

When we come into a Church we come with our hatts off, and endeavour to lay aside all worldly cares, and compose ourselves to more serious matters, considering where we are; but if in a place Clergiemen are, and enter into their acquaintance, for ye most part we shall receive no benefit, but rather harm; whose example shall teach us rather to embrace ye world than forsake ye world.

These reflections are no hot-house exotics, interlarded as they are with down-to-earth details of estate management and the cares of a good employer for the men and women who serve him. Sir Henry Slingsby was sensitive, intelligent and well-read but the duties and pleasures of his life are those of a conscientious, happily married Yorkshire landowner. The prospect of civil war, in which category he includes war with the Scots, appals him.

> The 3rd of January (out of curiosity to see ye spectacle of our publick death) I went to Bramton [Bramham] moor to see ye training of our light horse, for which service I myself had sent 2 horses, by commandment from the Deputy Lieutenants and Sir Jacob As[t]ley who is lately come down with speciall commission from ye King to train and exercise them. These are strange, strange spectacles to this nation in this age, that have lived thus long peaceably, without noise of shot or drum and after we have stood neutrals and in peace when all ye world besides hath been in arms, and wasted with it; it is I say a thing most horrible that we should engage ourself in a war one with another, and with our own venom gnaw and consume ourself.

When, finally, the Long Parliament met he went up to take his seat in a state of mind much more to be expected of a supporter of Pym than of the Court whose extravagance and frivolity he deplored.

> The 2nd of November I took my journey to London to be at ye Parliament, and came thither 2 days after it had begun. Great expectance there is of a happy Parliament where ye subject may have a total redress of all his grievances: and here they apply them to Question all delinquents, all Projectors, and Monopolizers, such as levi'd ship mony, and such Judges as gave it for law.

Clarendon and Falkland were to come up to Westminster with the same cheerful hopes of reform.

Enough has been said to emphasize the homogeneity and the health of the society that was to be soon and so cruelly divided. It knew itself to be fortunate, its confidence in its powers and in its values was absolute. If the points made in this chapter seem to render the fact of the civil war more puzzling, perhaps they help to explain why it was fought with so little vindictiveness and barbarity, to an extent that foreigners considered desultory and lackadaisical (if not downright cowardly), and why the political scars it left healed so quickly.

Chapter 5

Strafford

Strafford's recall to the centre of power had been left too late for safety. But safety and King Charles I are politically irreconcilable concepts. In the event everything combined to bring on the collision that the great minister had been brought back to avoid.

In the first place Strafford's unpopularity had recently been heightened by well-publicized accounts of his tyrannical behaviour in Ireland. With characteristic arrogance he at once added to it by taking as one of his titles when the King raised him to an earldom the barony of Raby. This was a mortal insult to the owner of Raby Castle, Sir Henry Vane the elder, who was himself a member of the Privy Council and a great favourite of the Queen. The reader, in Gibbon's famous phrase, may smile, but Clarendon believed that this, more than anything else, was to cost Strafford his head. He had enemies enough at court, notably the Earl of Holland. And Essex, the only major figure to emerge from the Scots war without discredit, bore an old and bitter grudge against him. It was characteristic of Charles to yield to the Queen's pressure and promote the elder Vane to be Secretary of State in February 1640. His radical Puritan son, Sir Henry Vane the younger, had returned the year before from Massachusetts, of which he had been governor, to become Joint Treasurer of the navy. The Vanes, rich and well connected with both Court and Opposition, were a dangerous pair to have antagonized.

This was soon demonstrated when in April 1640 the Parliament that Strafford had urged the King to call actually met. Clarendon who was a member of it draws a strong contrast between the Short Parliament of 1640 and its far more famous twin that was to meet in the autumn. It is his argument that it was precisely because of its moderation that men like Pym and Cromwell were ready enough to provoke the King into a premature dissolution, counting on his having to call another whose mood would be much less conciliatory. By his account the part that the elder Vane played in misrepresenting the King to the Commons and the Commons to the King, was all part of a plot to ruin Strafford. Certainly Vane did, intentionally or not, mishandle the Commons; and his son's transmission to Pym of his alleged notes of the Privy Council that met early in the morning when dissolution was decided on was a piece of dirty work that could hardly have been effected without the father's active or passive collusion. This was to prove one of the most effective of the many effective propaganda *coups* of the Long Parliament. The most damaging allegation was that the troops Strafford had provided for raising in Ireland before his departure were intended to cow English Puritans not to drive back the Scots.

The dissolution of the Parliament without the voting of any supply to defend the kingdom against the threat of a Scots invasion would seem to imply, if not to impose, some modification on the Government's policy towards the Covenanters. Even one of Strafford's few wellwishers in the Council, the Earl of Northumberland, argued for bringing policy into alignment with resources. But Strafford, though he had prevailed on the King to make Northumberland commander-in-chief in Arundel's place, was still, like his master, ready to double his stake as the run of the game went against him. Preparations for war went ahead through the spring and summer. The attempts made by the Scots to turn the Pacification of Berwick into a permanent settlement had been sharply rebuffed by the King and the Archbishop. Far from retreat, the call was for advance. Laud drew up a new set of canons, as the rules of Church administration and doctrine are called, which included the imposition of an oath highly provocative to Puritan consciences. There were

Warachtige afbeeldinge en verhael vanden vreeffelijcken en bloedigen, doch victori
mando des Admiraels d'Oquendo, en de Scheeps Armade der H.Mog.Heeren Staten der vereenighd

riots in London. Lambeth Palace was attacked. The Lord Mayor called out the trained bands but the storm had blown itself out before they came to action. The young seaman who had led the mob against the archbishop's palace was hung, drawn and quartered, a savage act of revenge on the part of the Government that Laud's enemies were not slow to exploit.

The King provided further evidence of the great popish conspiracy against the people of God. When the Queen gave birth to a son he released all the Roman Catholic priests then awaiting trial as an act of thanksgiving. Together with the fact that some of the officers now obtaining posts in the army were undoubtedly Roman Catholics, this helped to raise the temperature. And Charles's endless schemes for obtaining subsidies from either France or Spain that would enable him to finance his Government without reference to Parliament were widely suspected. The troubles of the Spanish Empire

England's maritime impotence under Charles I: Tromp destroys the Spanish convoy sheltering in the Downs while the tiny English squadron watches helplessly in the background

committed to an interminable war in the Low Countries which, since the taking of Breisach late in 1638, could no longer be reached overland from the Spanish possessions in North Italy, presented a natural opportunity. If England's naval power could protect Spanish troops and money passing up the Channel, could not the gold and silver of the Indies solve the King's problems? Negotiations on these lines were certainly conducted between Strafford and the Spanish minister Olivares in the summer of 1640 but came to grief probably because neither party was in a position to deliver the goods. The Royal Navy had been publicly humiliated in the autumn of 1639 when a Spanish squadron and the convoy it was protecting took refuge in the Downs. The Dutch fleet under the great Tromp followed them in, watched by an English force far too weak to uphold the sovereignty so loudly asserted by the Stuarts, and after four weeks riding within range of each other fought an action in England's principal anchorage. To fit out a fleet strong enough to prevent this sort of thing would take much more money than Charles could command and more resources than his dockyards and magazines could supply. Even supposing this problem could be overcome, manning and officering a fleet to be used in support of a Catholic power trying to subjugate a Protestant one would be difficult and dangerous.

Strafford, if anyone, could perhaps have engineered such a policy. But now there was no time. The situation must be met out of the means immediately available. How perilous it was only became clear when it had passed all hope of remedy. Lulled by complacent reports from the English commander in the north Strafford and the King were still preparing to teach the Scots a lesson when they heard that Berwick had been outflanked and that the Scots army had crossed the Tyne at Newburn, routing the English force that opposed it. The surrender of Newcastle followed. The Earl of Northumberland who should have been on his way north to assume the command fell ill. Whether his illness was purely tactical or, as C. V. Wedgwood more charitably suggests, psychosomatic, there is no doubt that this shrewd and capable aristocrat steered a remarkably smooth course through waters that others found tempestuous enough. The civil war, the Protectorate and the Restoration all saw him enjoying the delights of Petworth and the respectful goodwill of whoever happened to be in power.

Whatever Strafford's faults he was not the man to pull the bedclothes over his head when things looked frightening. He set off at once for the north to take personal command, but his health failed him. He had long suffered from both gout and the stone, two agonizing conditions that seventeenth-century medicine could identify but not palliate. Although he was able to struggle after the King, who had himself at once headed north and established his court at York at the news of the Scotch victory, he found when he arrived that the situation was past remedy. 'Never came man to so lost a business', in his own eloquent phrase. The King was troubled by no such doubts. He summoned a Great Council of the Realm to York, a piece of medieval window-dressing aimed to suggest to the Parliamentary leaders that he might govern simply by relying on the great landed magnates. He signed a treaty with the Scots at Ripon, committing England to pay for the maintenance of the Scotch

York about the time of the civil war

army until a satisfactory settlement of Kirk affairs had been reached. Most important of all, he issued writs for another Parliament to meet.

The King's optimism united the profound and the superficial. Beneath and behind all was the serene, as yet unshaken certainty that God would sustain his anointed against all comers. On the superficial level, the level of day-to-day developments, what Braudel has called *l'histoire événementielle*, Charles's disinclination or inability to think any problem through was a great source of consolation. Something was bound to turn up. And when it did, his over-riding responsibility to God relieved him of any lesser obligation he might have incurred by promising this or swearing that and left him free to exploit every opportunity to the full. So viewed, the situation offered many possibilities. The Scots might, and probably would, fall out among themselves. This had indeed, unknown to Charles, already happened. Montrose who had led the Covenanting army across the Tweed at Coldstream was soon to hear of the plundering of a Highland neighbour to whom he had given his protection by the followers of his great rival, Archibald Campbell, Earl of Argyll. The King himself was a Scot; his cousin Hamilton, the chief man of the kingdom, was his trusted counsellor. As for the men of ill-will he would keep them in play and bamboozle them. So, too, with England. He would offer places in his council to the leaders of the Opposition in Lords and Commons, easily dividing and beguiling them. Meanwhile the balance of force could soon be redressed by the troops Strafford had set about raising in Ireland. And then there was France and his wife's relations. And Spain with whom something could no doubt be arranged. And Holland, where he was considering marrying one of his daughters to the son of the Prince of Orange.

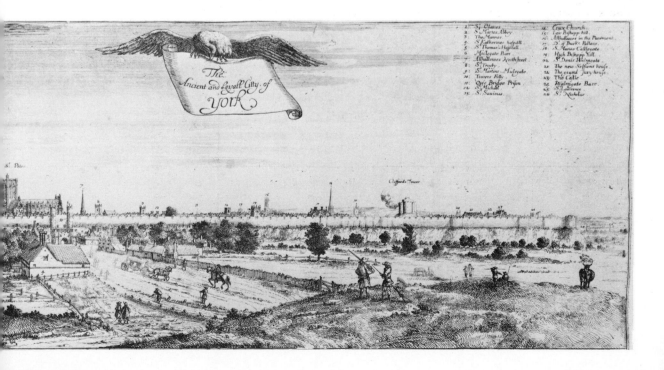

Each of these options could well have yielded some advantage if the King had chosen which to take up. But he was, it seems, temperamentally incapable of recognizing that some were mutually exclusive. France, for instance, was at war with Spain, as was Holland. If an approach were to be made to Pym and Hampden, then Strafford's scheme for an Irish army and Laud's Church policy would both have to take a reef in their sails. It is generally admitted that one cannot have everything. Charles I, on the evidence of his policies, disputed this. The meeting of the Long Parliament, however, transferred the initiative to other and more purposeful hands. By the terms of the Treaty of Ripon Charles had committed himself to finding what was then a huge sum – between £800 and £900 a day – to pay and feed the Scottish army over and above the normal expenses of government. The Puritan leaders could be relied on to make the most of their stranglehold on Parliamentary supply.

When the two Houses of Parliament met, Pym and his friends rapidly asserted their ascendancy. They obtained control of the committee that decided all disputed election results, a key position in the Parliamentary battles of the seventeenth and eighteenth centuries. The Court had in any case played into their hand by mismanaging the election of the Speaker so that the Houses ended up with a hitherto unknown lawyer, William Lenthall, who was far from being the wise and experienced servant Charles had been counting on. Lastly the Scotch Commissioners appointed by the Treaty of Ripon were established in London, making it easy to co-ordinate tactics with the Puritans and difficult to forget that the King and his ministers had twice been defeated, expensively and humiliatingly. It was thus clear that the game must begin with the overthrow of the two men who would egg the King on to try a third time if they got the chance, Laud and Strafford.

Strafford was far and away the more formidable. Nothing shows Pym's generalship more sharply than the fact that he did not at once lead an all-out attack on the hated and now disastrously unsuccessful minister but held his forces in check until the mistakes of his opponents gave him a favourable opening. He had not long to wait. George Digby, son and heir of the Earl of Bristol, an ambitious but temporarily estranged courtier, moved the drawing up of a Remonstrance against the ministers who had so misled their royal master. A committee was appointed and the hunt was up. Within twenty-four hours the Commons voted Strafford's impeachment, his trial before his fellow peers with the House of Commons acting as prosecutor, on a charge of high treason. He was arrested as he arrived to take his seat in the Lords.

The trial of Strafford that opened after more than three months' preparation was a battle of the Titans. Ill as he was, close prisoner in the Tower and with none of the resources commanded by his attackers, Strafford fought them to a standstill by the brilliance and force of his mind and by his mastery of the legal issue. Men might be entitled to the opinion that he had been a curse to his country but that was not the same as producing evidence that he had committed acts of treason. In the end all pretence of fair play was abandoned. His enemies dropped the impeachment and proceeded by Act of Attainder, a form of judicial murder whose heyday had been the Wars of the Roses. Strafford was thus voted a traitor by statute, not convicted by process of law.

TOP *The Family of Arthur, Lord Capel, by Cornelius Johnson. Capel, one of the most effective Royalist leaders of the second civil war, was executed shortly after Charles I*

BOTTOM *Algernon Percy, 10th Earl of Northumberland, by Van Dyck. Charles's negligent treatment of him as Lord High Admiral made him an ally of Parliament*

The statute required the assent of the King who had pledged his word to his minister that he should not suffer in life or estate. This breach of faith weighed heavily on the King's conscience. It was not at all the same thing as deceiving opponents by promises he never meant to keep. It was breaking his word, and breaking it against what he believed to be just and right. In the end he came to see his defeat in the civil war, even his own execution, as divine retribution for signing Strafford's death-warrant. It was conscience, not as so often with the Stuarts, partiality. Strafford's imperious isolation is demonstrated by the fact that of the three hundred or so MPS who ultimately sided with the King only fifty-six voted against the Attainder. Sir Philip Warwick, one of those who did, does not conceal how much Strafford's 'soure and haughty temper' and a roughness in his nature amounting almost to injustice made him disliked.

During the interval between the impeachment and the trial much went forward besides the building up of the case against Strafford. The two issues on which the King had all but united articulate opinion against him were Religion and Ship Money. But even here he held good cards. Pym himself, Puritan though he was, was no extremist. Clarendon explicitly states that he was not in favour of abolishing episcopacy and would have been contented to leave the government of the Church as it was, providing of course that Laud and his policies were disowned. To have conceded in good faith and with good grace what would otherwise be extorted with humiliation and ill-feeling was so obviously the path of wisdom that there was little fear that Charles would take it. The King swerved with the swift unpredictability of a snipe towards the man who had given Pym his opening against Strafford, George Digby, soon to be Earl of Bristol.

Bristol's nature combined the King's irresponsible optimism, political shallowness and personal daring with a most unfortunate brilliance in public speaking and private debate. He had attracted the King's favour by the courage and ability with which he had opposed Strafford's attainder (having been, it will be remembered, a prime mover in his impeachment). Did Charles's subconscious emotions thrill at the recognition of a kindred spirit? He was to remain disastrously in the ascendant at each of the few moments when there was a plausible chance of preventing or stopping the war and, after the King's execution, to lend valuable support to the mischievous political influence of Henrietta Maria on the young Charles II. It is impossible to understand the protracted success of so eminent a failure unless allowance is made for the charm of his personality. Half of Clarendon's active political life was frustrated by the frivolous and futile activities of this figure, yet after it is all over, he describes him with amusement and affection, even with a certain admiration for his sparkle and his spirit. And for all that he did to negate their policies it was he who convinced Charles I that Clarendon and Falkland must be brought into his service. His first act, however, was to embroil his master with both Houses over the position of the bishops, themselves highly unpopular, and to give the religious radicalism that had so far hardly identified itself its first taste of political success. The Parliamentary agitation for the total abolition of episcopacy culminating in the Root and Branch Bill became so powerful that those like Pym who would have been happy to settle for much less could

Miniatures of Cromwell
(TOP and BOTTOM)
and of his son-in-law Henry Ireton
(MIDDLE)
by Samuel Cooper

THOMAS *Graaf van Straffort, Onder Koning van Ierland, Binnen Londen Onthalst, Den 22 van May 1641.*

I.L

A Dutch print of Strafford's execution

not stand against it without prejudicing their success on wider issues.

It was in November 1640, Sir Philip Warwick tells us, that he, a rather exquisite young courtier MP, first noticed his fellow member, Oliver Cromwell:

... I vainly thought myselfe a courtly young Gentleman: (for we Courtiers valued ourselves much upon our good cloaths.) I came one morning into the House well clad, and perceived a Gentleman speaking (whom I knew not) very ordinarily apparelled; for it was a plain cloth-sute, which seemed to have been made by an ill country-taylor; his linen was plain, and not very clean; and I remember a speck or two of blood upon his little band, which was not much larger than his collar; his hatt was without a hatt-band: his stature was of a good size, his sword stuck close to his side, his countenance swoln and reddish, his voice sharp and untunable, and his eloquence full of fervor; for the subject matter would not bear much of reason; it being in behalfe of a servant of Mr Prynn's, who had disperst libells against the Queen for her dancing and such like innocent and courtly sports; and he aggravated the imprisonment of this man by the Council-Table unto that height, that one would have believed the very Government itselfe had been in great danger by it . . . he was very much hearkened unto.

So the name that, linked with Charles I, springs into every mind at the mention of the civil war makes its first impression on a young, well-informed and exceptionally intelligent contemporary. The picture has all the distinct undoctored truthfulness of first-hand recollection. Its author, half ashamed of his immature preoccupation with dress, half amused by it, lets it shape our vision, and in doing so lets us see and hear the disturbing passion and force of this somewhat unbalanced country gentleman. Simply by virtue of them he was already known and valued in that circle of cousins and connections by marriage – Hampden, St John, Warwick, Manchester, Saye – who formed the real nucleus of the Puritan party. As colleagues in the Providence Island and Massachusetts Bay companies they were both the heirs to the age of Drake and in touch with important city merchants. Many of them were prominent in the great Puritan movement to engross the patronage of the Church of England by buying up the presentations to livings, that body known as the Feoffees for Impropriations. But outside these small, interlocking circles Cromwell was not yet much known.

With Strafford executed in the teeth of the King's reluctance, with the bishops imprisoned and deprived of their rights to sit and vote in the Lords, the way was clear. Before the Houses were prorogued in August 1641 the Courts of Star Chamber and High Commission had been abolished, as had the Council of the North. Ship money had been declared an illegal tax and the Triennial Act had ensured that there would be no going back (short of a *coup d'état*) to the Eleven Years' Tyranny. Above all the King now had in Sir John Culpepper and Lord Falkland two ministers who had come from and sympathized with the House of Commons, not the Court. That Clarendon had, as yet, not taken office was simply because he believed he could serve the King better if he maintained his private character. He, like Falkland, his dearest friend, was admitted to the King's private audience and tendered his advice. The trouble was that the King could never stick to one adviser or to a consistent policy. The itch to put something on every horse in the race contradicts the first and harshest maxims of politics and war. The Queen, the Earl of Bristol, military adventurers in the Scottish and English armies, Irish and Scottish noblemen with scores to settle: there were plenty of people ready to give advice and to promise exciting results.

Chapter 6
The Command of Resources

No doubt it was in the confidence that Scotland might be reclaimed as a support that Charles spent the last summer of peace revisiting his native realm and presiding over the Estates as the Scotch Parliament was called. But the air of Edinburgh was as thick with plots, rumours and accusations as that of London. Indeed the two capitals acted on each other by a constant stream of messages and reports to intensify the atmosphere of anxiety. Edinburgh received Charles on his arrival in August with the same outward signs of loyalty and enthusiasm as London showed on his return in November. But the real political reception in both cases was cooler. For all the ceremonies and feasting Charles did not get any change out of the Estates. And when he returned to London it was the morrow of the passing of the Grand Remonstrance, in one of the most fateful divisions in Parliamentary history, by a mere eleven votes. As the members, dog-tired and used to earlier hours than our present legislators, trooped out of the House of Commons at two o'clock in the morning, Cromwell told Falkland 'that if the remonstrance had been rejected, he would have sold all he had the next morning, and never have seen England more; and he knew there were many other honest men of the same resolution'. 'So near,' comments Clarendon in relating the story, 'so near was the poor kingdom at that time to its deliverance.'

So near, it might more truly be said, had Clarendon and his friends come to winning back control of the Commons from Pym, a political feat of no ordinary quality when to having Pym as an adversary is added the consideration of Charles I as an ally. But Pym and the others knew now that they must exploit the antagonism the Remonstrance was designed to inflame before the moderate men outflanked them. As its name suggests the Remonstrance was a long recital, at times unctuous, at times offensive, of every grievance and complaint to which the conduct of affairs in Church and State had given rise in the past fifteen years. Some of them, Star Chamber, Ship Money and so on, had already been remedied, so that their inclusion was certain to exacerbate those who were already urging the King to treat his Parliament rough and teach them manners. Others brought most happily and opportunely into view the terrible spectre of the Pope and all his devilish minions. Only a few weeks earlier the Irish Catholics had risen in revolt and repaid with hideous atrocities the injustice and oppression of Protestant colonization. Now that the popish bogey had put on such timely flesh Englishmen must be made to realize that the massacres in Ireland might very easily happen in their own country if the King continued to flirt with Catholicism.

The Irish Rebellion gave a new twist to the struggle with the King. To restore order an army would have to be sent over. Parliament would have to vote the necessary supplies but the King would appoint its officers and thus effectively control its operations. This was undoubted law and custom. But could the Puritan leaders, now that they had driven the King into a corner and had forced his conscience over Strafford's execution, calmly vote him an unlimited military power that might so easily be turned against themselves? From the moment the question presented itself it became the central issue. Control of the militia was the point on which all attempts at compromise broke down. 'By God, not for an houre. You have askt that of me in this, was never askt of a King.' Charles's outburst to the Earl of Pembroke's suggestion in March 1642 that he should accept the Parliament's militia ordinance for a trial period shows that such a proposal violated his whole conception of his office. It was not just that he recognized control of the armed forces as a prime source of political strength, though no doubt he did. But at his deepest level Charles did not think politically. Kingship was a sacramental concept. Trading bits of it away in a general market-place of power was sacrilegious. Such a view may seem strange today but it was perfectly comprehensible in the seventeenth century, to Charles's opponents as well as to his friends. Pym and Cromwell and the younger Vane were just as theological in their fundamental approach to political questions, though infinitely more flexible and intelligent

Whitehall from the river in Charles I's time

Sould by Iohn Overton at the white horse neere the fountaine tavern without Newgate

in their political apprehensions. They were politically minded. The King, unhappily for his subjects, was not.

It was on some such reading of the King's mind that Pym and his friends based their strategy. The malice and wickedness that Clarendon in his history attributes to men whom with all his genius as a portraitist he yet fails to make into convincing villains becomes an unnecessary hypothesis if it is once allowed that Charles would never freely and fairly concede the minimum on which they were prepared to settle. If negotiation is impossible there is nothing left but an appeal to force. And to Charles there was nothing unthinkable in this. Part of a sovereign's duty was to assert his authority by force whether against foreign enemies or rebellious subjects. This, after all, was what he had been blamed for trying to do in Scotland and was now being urged to do in Ireland. To the Puritan leaders it was a far more searching question. Except in the case of a national revolt against a foreign oppressor such as had taken place in the Netherlands, rebellion and revolution had none of the romance that they have acquired in the last two centuries. Lawlessness and anarchy held no picturesque charm for people who knew what was going on in Germany. The inequality of risk was well understood. 'He that draws the sword against his Prince must throw away the scabbard' as Clarendon's old friend Bulstrode Whitelocke reminded the House only a few weeks before the war broke out. For this reason once the risk had been accepted it was crucial to secure a quick and irreversible decision. A long-drawn-out war was bound to offer advantages to the Crown. As the Earl of Manchester, himself one of the original Parliamentary leaders, was to put it after two years of war, 'If we fight a hundred times and beat him ninety-nine times, he will be King still. But if he beat us but once, or the last time, we shall be hanged, we shall lose our estates, and our posterities be undone.'

If Pym were to bring off his *coup*, two conditions had to be satisfied. He and his party must be in effective control of such military and naval forces, bases and munitions as were available at the time of the breach, which would further enable them to deny the King access to supplies from abroad. And, since the whole aim was to win a war without fighting one, the battle for public opinion must be won in the comparatively bloodless arena of propaganda and tactical manoeuvre that was to precede the trial of strength. Unexpectedly it was in the second field that this past master of political warfare met his match.

The reason was that in this battle of propositions and counter-propositions, of propaganda broadsides delivered in the form of an exposition of constitutional law, Charles was content to be guided by Clarendon, even to the extent of the drafting and timing of his answers. Clarendon at once seized and held the middle ground from which moderate opinion was most sure to be influenced, preaching a reason and a conciliation that, had he occupied the throne, he no doubt would have practised. Charles was content to appear in such a *persona*, and was probably conscious of no hypocrisy. The father of his people, the wise and watchful guardian of their law and custom, was one of the aspects of kingship that he approved and no doubt sincerely tried to fulfil. That he understood Clarendon's arguments in gross and in detail is clear from his masterly use of them at his own trial seven years later. For all his diffident, unimpressive powers as a speaker, his lack of political sense or intellectual rigour, Charles had a mind that compelled respect from men of high abilities. Sir Philip Warwick says of him that like Francis I of France he learned more by ear than by study.

But Clarendon's constitutionalism was only one among the many mutually conflicting policies that the King was pursuing. This fact was brought home to his new advisers with flabbergasting effect when early in January 1642 the King appeared in the House of Commons at the head of a troop of cavalry with the object of arresting five members, Pym, Hampden, Hesilrige, Holles and Strode together with Manchester, one of the active party in the Lords. What price would the King's care for constitutional rights fetch now? Clarendon's work had been rudely knocked aside to make way for yet another of Lord Bristol's miraculous cures for the nation's troubles. Pym, as he hid in the City, knew that he had been handed a major victory. In less than a week the King left London, never to return as its acknowledged sovereign.

One of the reasons why the King abandoned his capital was, most probably, one that had contributed to his insane attempt on the Five Members: anxiety for his Queen. This the Parliamentary leaders had played on for all they were worth, making sure that rumours of a move to impeach her should come to her and her husband's ears from sources that would carry conviction. Even with the anti-Catholic fever raging over the atrocities in Ireland it hardly seems likely that the impeachment and execution of Henrietta Maria would have been a profitable venture for the Puritan leadership, supposing that men like Manchester could be brought to contemplate it. But the Queen's excitable incomprehension of English politics produced acceptance in the quarter intended. Of all the many sources of bad advice open to the King she was the most unerringly disastrous. Her departure for the Continent towards the end of February was no doubt a relief to the moderates who still hoped for a composing of matters in dispute. But it is characteristic of the relation between Charles and Henrietta Maria that she had made him promise not to re-admit any of the Parliamentary leaders to his favour without first securing her approval. Their parting touched those who witnessed it by the depth of mutual affection. After the Queen's ship had set sail for Holland Charles rode along the cliffs to keep her in sight as long as possible.

Apart from making sure of her safety the object of the Queen's voyage was to obtain money and arms. Until they arrived the most important single source of munitions was the magazine within the walls of Hull, a well-fortified port convenient for the supply of the army with which the King and Strafford had intended to discipline the Scots. It was to the securing of this that the King's thoughts turned. Coming up the Dover Road as far as his great palace at Greenwich, where Inigo Jones's splendid pleasure house begun for Anne of Denmark and finished for Henrietta Maria remains to connect his vanished court with Wren's no less magnificent Naval Hospital, he set eyes on London but did not set foot in it. He crossed the Thames and headed northwards in a leisurely progress through what was to be the heartland of the Parliamentary cause, stopping at Newmarket to exchange sharp messages with the Parliament and at Cambridge to be entertained by the University. Before the end of

March he had established himself in York, where he was joined by his second son James, and his tutor the Marquess of Hertford. The young Prince of Wales, whose seizure as a hostage the King feared, had already joined him at Greenwich and travelled north in his company.

The nucleus of what was to be the Cavalier party was already forming in the northern capital. Noblemen and gentlemen came in with horses and servants. The last of the King's servants in London such as Clarendon and the Lord Keeper of the Great Seal slipped quietly away and travelled north by cross-country routes. Now that there seemed so little chance of King and Parliament avoiding an open conflict men tried in despair to patch up local non-aggression pacts that would at least keep the war out of their own part of the country. Even the Yorkshire gentry with the King on their doorstep made strenuous efforts to this end, as did some of the leading families in East Anglia where Parliament was strongest. But the Parliamentary leaders were alive to the danger. The simple force of inertia and the desire not to upset the continuity of existing authority were the greatest threats to the cohesion and strength of their movement. People must be made to choose.

In Ireland such islands of constituted authority as survived in Dublin and a few strong points looked more to the Parliament at Westminster than to the King at York. The rumours of a Royalist-Catholic conspiracy were easy to believe. Parliament had seized the excuse to put the penal laws against the priests of the English mission into force in all their barbarity and even the King at York thought it prudent to prove his Protestantism by executing two of them. But the time for propaganda and psychological warfare was running out. Parliament levied troops to defend itself against the King and appointed Essex Lord General. Charles prepared to occupy Hull where he would not only find the magazine for last year's army but would control a port ideally suited to receive the arms the Queen was buying in Holland.

Hull was commanded by Sir John Hotham, a local landowner whose sympathies inclined, though not very decidedly, to Parliament. Towards the end of April the King sent over the young Duke of York to convey a letter giving private notice of his intention of entering the city next day. Hotham was delighted and honoured to entertain the Prince but manned the walls and raised the drawbridge as a sign that he would not betray his trust. When Charles appeared in person he respectfully declined to admit him. The King furiously declared him a traitor and returned to York. It was not an auspicious beginning. However, the Earl of Bristol was at hand with his usual fertility of resource. A few weeks later he was captured and brought into Hull where he adopted the identity of a Frenchman who had secret knowledge to reveal. Hotham saw him in private and was soon persuaded by that glib master of fore-doomed intrigue to promise the surrender of the town if the King would appear before the walls with at least a token force and fire a shot or two for the look of the thing. Early in July Charles marched over at the head of two thousand troops, a respectable force by the standards of the civil war. Hotham, however, had had second thoughts. Whether it was fear and jealousy of his son whom the active party at Westminster were using to spy on his father, whether a recalculation of local interest and prestige had convinced him that

Sir John Hotham, who refused to admit the King to Hull in the summer of 1642

The Right Worshipfull S.r Iohn Hotham K.t: Gouernour of Kingston vpon HVLL

The King's humiliation before Hull

it would not do to sell out too soon, he again manned the walls and flooded the surrounding country. Hardly a year later Hotham was arrested by his brother-in-law and sent prisoner to Parliament for being in correspondence with the Earl of Newcastle, the commander of a large and well-found Royalist army then threatening the town. Both he and his son were ultimately executed after trying to save their skins at each other's expense. But in July 1642 the King was humiliated a second time before Hull and retired again to York.

Parliament's retention of Hull both during the war and in the twilight period that preceded it can be seen in retrospect as invaluable. The North and the West were the regions most strongly Royalist in sympathy. Hull and the Humber offered the natural route for arms and supplies from the Continent. From the rivers that fed its estuary, the Trent, the Aire, the Ouse, the Don, a great part of the northeastern Midlands drew their health and strength. York, the King's temporary capital on the eve of the war, was a bare thirty miles away. Yet even here, at the very heart of Royalism, the Parliament could defy him.

The real significance of this was Parliament's virtually complete control of the navy. Hull was protected and could be reinforced, supplied, animated and encouraged from the sea. The war was to show many examples of heroic sieges endured when all hope of relief had long gone. The courage that inspires people to such extraordinary acts is essential to any military enterprise beyond a walk-over. But courage that is grounded on rational hope and demonstrable ability wears better. The Parliament was to need all of this when, against all expectation, the first year of the war produced a series of Royalist successes. Had the King then had control of the sea things might have gone very differently. It was the battles that were not fought, the battles at sea, that more than anything else dictated the shape and determined the outcome of the war.

How was it that the Navy Royal, to give its name in the form more familiar to Charles I and his generation, came to adhere to the Parliament? Had not the King incurred great unpopularity and run some dangers on its behalf by his imposition of Ship Money? Was not the *Sovereign of the Seas* by far the most beautiful and by far the most powerful warship ever built? Did not the fleets fitted out to protect the shipping lanes of the Channel and the villages of Devon from the pirates of Algiers and Sallee mean more jobs at sea and prospects of promotion and prize money? All of these questions presume, as no doubt the King did, a strong predisposition within the service to support a Government that had expanded the navy.

The explanation of the King's failure to retain a loyalty he had more right to expect than most on which he counted lies, as so often, in his own ineptitude. He had built ships, some of them like the *Sovereign* of a standard never previously reached, and some, like the *Whelps*, of a type intelligently designed to satisfy a real need for the policing and patrolling of home waters. But the arming, storing, equipping and manning of these vessels had marked little improvement on the lamentable standards of his father's navy. The men were not properly paid or fed; the officers were disgusted at the shoddiness and corruption of the administration; the uses to which the fleet was put were trivial and tiresome. Above all Northumberland who had won excellent opinions as Lord High Admiral had neither been encouraged nor dismissed. His temporary supersession by Hamilton at the time of the First Bishops' War had been a public slight. Yet in spite of his obvious coolness towards the King he had still been left in office. As the war daily drew nearer the responsibilities of the Lord High Admiral became acute. Northumberland could be relied on to take refuge in pleas of ill-health, real or evasive. Much too late the King decided to appoint Sir John Pennington, a popular and experienced sea officer, who had had the unenviable command in the Downs while the Dutch and the Spaniards cannonaded at each other. Northumberland, however, had already invited the Earl of Warwick to act as his deputy, an appointment at once confirmed by Parliament. When Charles sent letters to the individual captains annulling Northumberland's commission and the authority that Warwick derived from it as his deputy only four felt strongly enough to attempt obedience. The feeling in the fleet was so overwhelming that they were easily dealt with. Without a shot fired in anger the Parliament had possessed itself of the whole navy.

Part of the reason, a large part perhaps, may be found in the character of Warwick. Unlike Cromwell he started with the advantage of a proved reputation as a fighting leader: as a noble and as a territorial magnate he had the social and economic standing expected of a commander-in-chief; as a Parliamentarian he had been distinguished by imprisonment in the Tower; and as a Puritan he controlled a great deal of Church patronage in Essex which he had used with characteristic thoroughness. For all that, as the splendid Van Dyck portrait of him shows, here was no mild milk-and-water pulpiteer but a vivid man of action with a touch of the freebooter, earthy, vigorous, decisive. A born military leader is what the painter brings before us and how amply that reading of him is confirmed in the civil war. Keynes said of Lord Jellicoe in 1914–18 that he was the only man who could have lost the war in an after-noon and the judgment, though it does not fit exactly, comes close to describ-ing Warwick's part in the first civil war. He was in full operational control of the fleet from the beginning of the war till its end was plain, a position such as was held by no land commander on either side, and the quality of his achievement as strategist, as tactician and as leader is attested by the fact that hardly anyone, then or since, has noticed it. In an age of furious and expert pamphleteering and political in-fighting Warwick's inadequacies would have been seized on avidly by someone bent on discrediting his political associates or denigrating such a controversial figure as his son-in-law and fellow commander, the Earl of Manchester. No one has. Warwick's use of sea-power, like its instrument the navy, is left out of almost all the histories of the civil war, except for Clarendon's who spends five or six pages in bewailing Charles's carelessness in letting him succeed Northumberland in the first place, and then dismisses the matter from his narrative. Only in our own day have the researches of the Revd J. R. Powell and the writings of the best historian of the war, Dame Veronica Wedgwood, restored him to his place as one of the true architects of Parliament's triumph. His naval success transcends his not inconsiderable contribution to the political leadership in the late 1630s and early 1640s and to the formation of the Eastern Association, in which his son-in-law played so large a part and from which Cromwell and the New Model Army were to spring. The historian of the Eastern Association, Mr Clive Holmes, quotes words of his in recommending the replacement of local Essex gentry with professional officers that might serve as an epigraph to the self-affacing professionalism of his work as Lord High Admiral: 'the present occasion doth require men bred in warre'.

Chapter 7

The Outbreak of War

The state of affairs in July 1642 must have been highly gratifying to Pym and those who shared his view that a conflict was inevitable and had therefore best be undertaken on favourable terms. Except for the political warfare so adroitly managed by Clarendon the King had lost or blundered or failed all along the line. By withdrawing to the North he had left his powerful supporters in London and the Home Counties virtually without a rallying point. He had failed to secure Hull which might have compensated for a good deal. He had lost the navy. Apart from the very modest county magazines of the trained bands in those parts of England and Wales that the Royalists controlled, what arms had he to fight with? What money had he to buy them abroad? What ports did he control for which any arms-ship that ran the naval blockade could make? The answers were bleak indeed. On the other side Parliament controlled London, Bristol and all the prime sources of national wealth including every port of any size except Newcastle. They controlled the Tower of London and the main national magazines and dockyards. They were in the process of constituting armies that they were in a much better position to pay, to feed and to equip than anything the King could do. Faced with such complete superiority might he not after all concede the game?

It was a view widely held by foreigners and neutrals. But the King was both too facile in his optimism and too unshakable in his convictions to accept it. He met the challenge of Parliament's increasing power by issuing Commissions of Array, calling on his loyal subjects to meet him in arms at Nottingham where on 22 August 1642 he raised his standard. The war had officially begun. There had been several skirmishes already. In July Lord Strange had attempted to seize the local magazine in Manchester and had been beaten off after some confused street fighting. Later, as Earl of Derby, he was to earn an unpleasant reputation for atrocities in the Northwest and to be one of the few defeated Royalists to be executed. One of the charges against him was that of killing the first victim of the civil war. This unenviable distinction can never be established. All over England people were trying to seize the plate and horses of known sympathizers with the opposite party, to secure strong points such as forts and castles, to make sure of the magazines belonging to the militia or the trained bands. One of the first actions to be fought was at Marshall's Elm in Somerset where on 4 August a small party of Royalist cavalry is said to have routed a much larger body of Parliamentary foot. Cromwell gave a foretaste of the dash and thrust that win wars by seizing the plate that the Cambridge Colleges, mostly Royalist in sympathy, were preparing to send away to the King and followed it up by securing the county magazine. To men

A true and exact Relation of the manner of his Maiesties setting up of His Standard at *Nottingham*, on Munday the 22. of Auguſt 1642.

First, The forme of the Standard, as it is here figured, and who were preſent at the advancing of it

Secondly, The danger of ſetting up of former Standards, and the damage which enſued thereon.

Thirdly, A relation of all the Standards that ever were ſet up by any King.

Fourthly, the names of thoſe Knights who are appointed to be the Kings Standard-bearers. With the forces that are appoynted to guard it.

Fifthly, The manner of the Kings comming firſt to *Coventry*.

Sixtly, The *Cavalieres* reſolution and dangerous threats which they have uttered, if the King concludes a peace without them, or hearkens unto his great Councell the Parliament : Moreover how they have ſhared and divided *London* amongſt themſelves already.

Nottingham.

like him and Charles I, easily convinced of their divine mission, the war no doubt came as a relief from spiritual tension.

To others, the great majority, it was not so. Many on both sides could not see the issue in black and white but took arms more from personal loyalty or from a sense that it was ignominious to stand aside than from the whole-hearted exuberance of perfect faith. Clarendon records many such cases among his own acquaintances, most notably that of his closest friend Lord Falkland. But perhaps no instance is more telling than the dialogue between himself and Sir Edmund Verney, the King's standard bearer who was to be killed at Edgehill, the first battle of the war, at the very time that the King had raised his standard at Nottingham. It was a depressing moment. Recruits were slow in coming in. There were no arms. The weather was horrible. It was so wet and windy that setting up the standard itself proved difficult. During the night the wind increased to a gale and blew the standard down. So relentlessly did it rage that it was two days before it could be put up again. The significance of this omen was not lost upon those who were looking for guidance. Under these dire circumstances Clarendon told Sir Edmund how glad he was to see him 'in so universal a damp . . . retain still his natural vivacity and cheerfulness'. He replied smiling,

> My condition is much worse than yours, and different, I believe, from any other man's; and will very well justify the melancholic that, I confess to you, possesses me. You have satisfaction in your conscience that you are in the right; that the King ought not to grant what is required of him; and so you do your duty and your business together: but for my part, I do not like the quarrel, and do heartily wish that the King would yield and consent to what they desire; so that my conscience is only concerned in honour and gratitude to follow my master. I have eaten his bread, and served him near thirty years, and will not do so base a thing as to forsake him; and choose rather to lose my life (which I am sure I shall do) to preserve and defend those things which are against my conscience to preserve and defend.

Although the civil war did not divide society along the lines of class, or status to use a more accurately descriptive term, it did to some extent divide the political leadership of the country according to generation. The Parliamentary leaders were notably older than the Royalists. As Professor Lawrence Stone has pointed out,

> . . . of those peers under thirty-two years who took sides in the war, four out of five were Royalists and only one out of five Parliamentarians. In the Lower House, MPS in their twenties were Royalist rather than Parliamentarian in 1642 by a factor of 2 to 1; MPS in their fifties were Parliamentarian rather than Royalist by a factor of 2 to 1. This was more important politically than it would be today, since the high adult mortality of the period meant that young men obtained positions of responsibility very much earlier in their careers. Thus in 1640 about half the MPS were under the age of forty.

Professor Stone provides two suggestive lines of explanation: first that on the continent of Europe it was precisely with a centralized royal absolutism that the future lay, not with the seemingly clumsy, obsolete machinery of medieval representative institutions; and second that the older one was the longer was

The raising of the King's standard

Wife to a Royalist commander and sister to the Parliamentary commander-in-chief: Frances Devereux, Essex's sister, was married to the Marquis of Hertford

one's experience of Charles I's misgovernment. But whatever the reason, and these certainly are good ones, the fact provides additional evidence that the lines of division cut not only across friendship and neighbourhood but even through the closest of family relationships. It was not just that one might find oneself fighting one's cousins and in-laws: father and son, brother and brother, were very often on opposite sides.

A striking example of a family whom the civil war drove far asunder is that of the parson of Stanmer in Sussex, Stephen Goffe. Three sons were born to this puritan clergyman, Stephen, John and William. Stephen and John, the two eldest, both went up to Oxford and entered their father's profession, though with sympathies and opinions far removed from those in which they had been brought up. William, the youngest, was apprenticed to a drysalter in London, the wholesale provision merchants of the seventeenth century. Early in 1642 he was imprisoned by the Royalist Lord Mayor for presenting a petition to Parliament. It seems probable that so active a Puritan would have lost no time in joining the Parliamentary army in which he appears at once to have distinguished himself since by 1645 he had become a captain in the New Model. There, if not earlier, he caught Cromwell's eye. He rapidly became a colonel, was asked to sit as one of Charles I's judges and signed his death-warrant. He commanded Cromwell's own regiment at Dunbar, the hardest fought of all his victories, and a year later at Worcester. He was made Major-General of Sussex, Hampshire and Berkshire when Cromwell gave up his attempts at constitutional government in favour of direct military rule. As a member of Cromwell's intimate circle he was called to the Protector's death-bed to promise his support for the transfer of power to Richard. In the confusion that followed that short-lived expedient he was even tipped for the Protectorate himself, as the obvious successor to Cromwell's old second-in-command, John Lambert. Not bad going for the youngest son of an obscure Sussex rector. At the Restoration in 1660 he was, as a regicide and a zealous Cromwellian, a marked man. But he escaped to New England and in spite of the efforts of the home Government to bring him back to be hung, drawn and quartered he eluded all attempts at capture. Perhaps the old Ironside proved valuable to the people who sheltered him in their wars against the Red Indians. He died a free man nearly twenty years after he had left England.

William's success enabled him to befriend his second brother John who had been turned out of his living and even imprisoned for refusing to take the Covenant, imposed as a condition of the alliance with the Scots in 1643. In 1652 when the Scots and their Covenant had been sent packing the regicide obtained for the Royalist a country living not far from the one of which he had been deprived. John took no further part in politics. At the Restoration he got back his living but went no higher.

The eldest son, Stephen, enjoyed a career that in excitement and variety if not in distinction rivalled that of his third brother. After taking his degree at Oxford he became chaplain to the English regiment in the Low Countries, commanded by Colonel Vere, where so many of the civil war officers, including Sir Thomas Fairfax, the greatest of the Parliamentary generals, learned their trade. On his return to England he was made a chaplain to Charles I.

His learning and his contacts with foreign scholars, perhaps too his experience of life abroad, made him a natural choice as a secret agent. He was employed in Holland and France during the first civil war. After the King's defeat he came back to England and was imprisoned on suspicion of having helped the King to escape from Hampton Court. He himself managed to break out and was employed by Charles, now prisoner in the Isle of Wight, in his last hopeless intrigue with the Scots. After the King's execution he became a Roman Catholic, entered the Oratory at Paris of which he soon became Superior, dying years later in the Rue St Honoré not long after his youngest brother in the backwoods of America. Few Sussex parsonages can have bred a more strangely destined family.

At least the Goffe brothers did not find themselves in the terrible situation of trying to kill or maim each other. Indeed one was even able to help another in the general confusion. The real agony of the war was the violation of the dearest and most personal ties. Sir Henry Slingsby describes just such a case shortly after the outbreak of the war in Yorkshire:

A regicide who escaped to America: Colonel William Goffe

> ... at another part of ye town of York, Lieutenant Collonel Norton enters with his dragouns, Capt Attkisson encounters him on horseback, ye other being a foot; they meet; Attkisson misseth with his Pistol, ye other pulls him off his horse by ye sword belt; being both on ye ground Attkisson's soulgiers comes in, fells Norton into ye ditch with ye butt ends of their musketts; then comes Norton's soulgiers and beats down Attkisson and with blows at him broke his thigh bone, whereof he dy'd; after this scuffle they retreat'd out of ye town (a sore scuffle between two that had been neighbours and intimate friends) ...

The artless matter-of-fact account sets off the pathos of the scene perhaps because in eschewing eloquence it also eschews glamour. Here is no Victorian costume piece with splendidly mounted swashbucklers drinking healths to King Charles but the drabness, the crudity of a mugging, of the war as it was, as wars always were and always will be. It is in the opening scenes of the civil war, the dreadful moment when theory and practice collided, that the poignancy of recollection is sharpest. People never cease to astonish themselves and others by their capacity to adapt themselves to circumstances. After quite a short time mental adjustments are improvised by which sanity or at least stability is preserved.

Lucy Hutchinson's account of the period is among the most vivid passages in her sharp and strong narrative:

> Before the flame of the warre broke out in the top of the chimnies, the smoake ascended in every county. The King had sent forth Commissions of Array and the Parliament had given out Commissions for their Militia, and sent off their Members into all counties to put them in execution. Betweene these in many places there was fierce contests and disputes allmost to blood, even at the first; for in the progresse every county had more or lesse the civill warre within it selfe. Some counties were in the beginning so wholly for the Parliament that the King's interest appeared not in them; some so wholly for the King that the godly, for those generally were the Parliament's friends, were forc'd to forsake their habitations, and seeke other shelters: of this sort was Nottinghamshire.

Her father-in-law, Sir Thomas, was one of the members for the county. She and her husband had just settled in with their very young sons at the family house at Owthorpe and she was expecting the birth of another child. It was the hardest moment for a husband to abandon wife, family and estate, yet the solid Royalism of the nobility and gentry of the county, headed by the magnificent Earl of Newcastle and including John Hutchinson's first cousins, the Byrons of Newstead Abbey, ancestors of the poet, made it a dangerous place for a declared Parliamentary sympathizer. Another cousin, Henry Ireton, was the 'chief promoter of Parliament's interest in the country. But finding it generally disaffected, all he could doe when the King approacht it was to gather a Troope of those godly people which the Cavalliers drove out, and with them he went into my Lord of Essex his Armie; which he, being a single person, might the better doe.' Ireton was to marry Cromwell's daughter Bridget and to win his trust and respect to a degree unrivalled by anyone else. But it is clear that, at this stage, Lucy Hutchinson considered that her husband's private and domestic obligations justified him in trying, if he could, to sit tight. The war might, after all, be called off at the last moment. In any case few people thought that it could possibly last longer than a few months.

The fact that such a pair of zealots as Mr and Mrs Hutchinson could even have contemplated a policy of neutrality, or at least non-belligerence, shows how strong were the pressures, on both sides, against a resort to force. But civil wars and revolutions generate their own momentum. People are forced to choose, and, having chosen, to submit. There is no provision for contracting out. So it proved with the Hutchinsons. When the Mayor of Nottingham sent word to Owthorpe that the High Sheriff of the County was breaking into the magazine, John Hutchinson at once rode into the town to try and stop him. He was too late and was abused and threatened in the streets. Calling in at his father's house he found a Royalist quartermaster about to commandeer it as accommodation for the Earl of Lindsey, the commander-in-chief of the King's army. High words followed and Hutchinson, by his wife's account, bundled the officer out, although he had 'a Carabine in his hand', and locked the doors. Lord Lindsey then arrived and was a great deal more civil than his subordinate. A satisfactory arrangement was made but not surprisingly Hutchinson returned to Owthorpe a marked man.

Four or five days later a troop of Cavaliers plundered the houses of two Puritan neighbours and tried to arrest one who, like Hutchinson, was later to become a colonel and command a garrison but he escaped them by hiding in the gorse. They were making for Owthorpe with an order to secure its owner when night overtook them and they went back to Nottingham. Hutchinson, however, did not wait for them but went to a house in Leicestershire where two days later he sent for his wife to join him,

where she had not been a day but a letter was brought him from Nottingham, to give notice that there was a warrant sent to the Sheriffe of Leicestershire to seize his person. Upon this he determined to goe the next day into Northamptonshire, but at five o'clock that evening the sound of their Trumpetts told him a troope was comming into the towne; he stay'd not to see them, but went out at the other end as they came in, who, by a good providence for his wife (something aflicted to

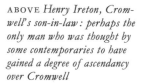

ABOVE *Henry Ireton, Cromwell's son-in-law: perhaps the only man who was thought by some contemporaries to have gained a degree of ascendancy over Cromwell*

be so left alone in a strange place) prov'd to be [commanded by] her owne brother Sir Allen Apsley, who quarter'd the next house to that where she was.

The encounter between brother and sister might not have been so happy if John Hutchinson had been less prompt in his getaway. But he managed his fugitive existence with great success. Not only did he deny his opponents his own horses and plate at Owthorpe, he even converted his Northamptonshire host from sending his to the King at Nottingham, persuading him instead to offer them to the Earl of Essex whose army was then in the county. Yet even at that point John Hutchinson did not take a commission, much as he would have liked to, 'but that he did not then find a cleare call from the Lord'.

If the great majority of upright, law-abiding, high-minded gentry went to war only after much self-questioning and distress, there were certainly those who welcomed the excitement, the destruction and the opportunities of fame and advancement. The rule of primogeniture meant that there were always a large number of rootless persons who had been brought up to look on themselves as entitled to noble or gentle status without enjoying the inherited wealth or the opportunities of earning necessary to underpin it. A good proportion of these men either attempted a professional military career in the

ABOVE RIGHT Soldiers who had any experience of war had usually gained it from service with Continental armies; such a scene is depicted in this predella from the portrait of Lord Vere, Fairfax's father-in-law

service of the Continental powers, especially the Dutch, or at least served for a campaign or two to learn the elements of soldiering. Even so swooning a young aesthete as John Evelyn underwent this apprenticeship, though in spite of strong Royalist principles he never took the opportunity offered by the civil war of practising the military art. The Earl of Warwick, as we have seen, recommended the employment of such officers to the Essex County Committee. On the Royalist side men like Harry Wilmot, a dashing young cavalryman from the Dutch service, were already prominent. Wilmot indeed had been one of the few officers to emerge from the first Scots war with some credit. And there were arrogant fire-eaters like Colonel Lunsford who wanted nothing better than a licence to set about the snivelling and seditious rabble. Above all there was Prince Rupert.

Prince Rupert

Rupert is the most glittering of all the military and political leaders thrown up by the civil war. Sir Thomas Fairfax has generally been rated a better commander; Oliver Cromwell combined talent for war with political and personal qualities of so extraordinary a nature as to make him look like Gulliver among the Lilliputians; Warwick, almost unnoticed by his contemporaries and by posterity, perhaps did as much to win the war as any; Charles I dominates the scene by tragedy and dignity as Clarendon does by intelligence and sympathy. But for what actors call star quality, the ability to attract every eye in the house from the first entrance, Rupert is supreme. He not only personifies the conception of the Cavalier, he transcends it. The fearless cavalry leader, the *grand seigneur* splendid in dress and style of life (though austere in avoiding self-indulgence), accompanied on campaign by his dog Boy (one of the many Royalist casualties at the battle of Marston Moor), the image of Rupert is part of everyone's apprehension of the civil war and perhaps even survived to inspire the portrayal of Ivor Claire in Evelyn Waugh's trilogy about the war of 1939–45. Reality does not fall short. Rupert's flawless courage on the battlefield was matched by a brilliance and boldness in strategy and tactics that no commander on either side surpassed, though both Fairfax and Cromwell were his superiors in the difficult art of maintaining some degree of tactical control once action had been joined. To his military gifts he added the marvellous good looks of his mother, the Winter Queen, and the distinction of royal blood. That his intellect was formidable is evident from his whole career as well as from the judgment of contemporaries, many of them hostile. On his previous visit to the country as a boy of seventeen he had impressed Archbishop Laud and others with the brilliance of his promise. Now on his return as a young man of twenty-three he had proved his courage in war and like Richard the Lionheart had caught the popular imagination by a romantic imprisonment. It was with all these advantages that he landed at Tynemouth in July 1642 and joined the King at Nottingham.

Charles at once made his nephew General of the Horse, leaving him a limited and characteristically imprecise independence of the commander-in-chief. This was to repeat the error of the first Scots war, but this time it was tragedy not farce. Dividing and obscuring the chain of command was a function of the King's mind. As in politics so in war: he was incapable of making a choice and sticking to it. Here in the initial appointment of his most successful commander can be seen the root of ultimate failure. The wheat and the tares are sown together. If the war were to be won, if in the state of things in August 1642 Parliament were not to enjoy a walk-over, it needed Rupert's fire and spirit to win it. Yet was it wise to entrust effective military responsibility to a brilliant young firebrand of foreign upbringing who knew or cared nothing of the issues for which men were venturing their lives and everything they valued? If there were to be a chance of peace Rupert would do his best to negate it. He had come to England for a war and a war he meant to have. No wonder that Clarendon and his friends distrusted and disliked him from the start. The irreconcilable elements in the situation arose from the radical duplicity of the King's mind. Was he really prepared to play the role that Clarendon and Falkland would have written for him? Or was he going for a military knockout? Was it to be compromise or no surrender?

Chapter 8
Edgehill

Sir Philip Warwick who charged under Rupert in the first big battle of the
civil war gives an account of how his arrival at Nottingham transformed the
drenching gloom in which Clarendon and Sir Edmund Verney were exchang-
ing their confidences:

> He found there a very thin and small army, and the Foot very meanly armed; and
> understanding in what forwardnes, and in what great numbers, and how well
> armed, Essex was advancing upon the King, advice is taken to retreat back to
> Shrewsbury, where in a little time new supplies coming out of Wales and other
> parts this Prince . . . so soon ranged and disciplined this small body of men, that
> engaging a good party of the Earle of Essex's under the command of Colonel
> Sandys near to the City of Worcester after a sharp dispute he there in person got a
> clear victory.

This was the skirmish at Powick Bridge which, as it was the first engagement
between the two main armies, carried a psychological value out of all proportion to the numbers involved or the object obtained. Small though the
action was there was no challenging the result. The Royalists had routed a
larger Parliamentary force.

The reception of the news reinforced the contrast in the public mind
between the characters of the two commanders. When the Earl of Essex set
out from London on his westward march he took with him his coffin and his
winding-sheet, hardly, one would have thought, an encouragement to his
troops. Prince Rupert, as Sir Philip Warwick well says, 'put that spirit into
the King's army, that all men seem'd resolved'. It would be difficult to define
the business of military leadership better.

But if Rupert was far superior to his opponent in all the arts of war, Essex
for all his *memento mori* approach was willingly accepted in his command by
his officers, his troops and his political masters. Rupert's manner was not
endearing. Clarendon and others speak of his roughness. Sir Philip Warwick
observes that

> a little sharpness of temper of body, and uncommunicablenes in society or council
> (by seeming with a pish to neglect all another said and he approved not), made him
> less grateful than his friends wished; and this humor soured him towards the
> Counsellors of Civil Affairs, who were necessary to intermix with him in Martiall
> councills. And these great men often distrusted such downright soldiers, as the
> Prince was, tho' a Prince of the blood, lest he should be too apt to prolong the
> warr; and to obtain that by a pure victory, which they wished to be got by a duti-
> full submission upon modest, speedy and peaceable terms, or by Addresses of the
> two Houses to the King.

In spite of the defeat inflicted on them at Powick Bridge it was Essex's men not Rupert's who occupied the strongly Royalist city of Worcester. The Parliamentary army was much too large for Rupert's small force to challenge in a set battle. But the King's strength was growing at a rate that made Essex think rather of defending the road to London than of arresting the King and bringing him back to Westminster, the orders he had originally set out to discharge. 'There cannot be too often mention', wrote Clarendon who was with the army at this time,

> of the wonderful providence of God, that from the low despised condition the King was in at Nottingham, after the setting up of his standard, he should be able to get men, money or arms, and yet within twenty days after his coming to Shrewsbury, he resolved to march, in despite of the enemy, even towards London; his foot, by this time, consisting of about six thousand; and his horse of two thousand; his train [i.e. artillery] in very good order . . . And though this strength was much inferior to the enemy . . . all thought it sufficient to encounter the rebels.

Clarendon and others believed that a great many of the Parliamentary soldiers would be only too glad to change sides once they saw that the King's was not a lost cause.

By mid-October both armies were marching towards London. The Royalists, starting from farther north and moving through steeper country with worse roads, could hardly have expected to catch Essex up if he did not choose to stand and fight. But the very fact that his army was larger and was

The Earl of Essex was pessimistically prepared for his funeral long before he died

equipped with a much superior train of artillery slowed down his movements. The King was travelling light, 'there being not one tent, and very few waggons belonging to the whole train'. This, as Clarendon makes clear, was not so much the practice of tactical virtue as an aspect of the general deficiency of weapons, stores and equipment of every kind. Body armour in particular was very short. On the other hand this was one of the rare moments in the war when there was enough money to pay the troops. Discipline, in consequence, was good. The briskness of the King's march reflected a certain *élan* as well as the conspicuous absence of impedimenta. Both armies were surprisingly careless about intelligence and reconnaissance, considering how many experienced officers were serving. And both were even more astonishingly incompetent in organizing the supply of food. The result was that they blundered into each other and into the first battle of the war in a state of unnecessary exhaustion.

It was not until late in the evening of Saturday 22 October when the bulk of the Royalist army had found quarters for the night in a string of villages to the north of Banbury that a party of Rupert's horse looking for billets in the village of Wormleighton ran into a smaller party of Parliamentarians doing the same. Their capture was the first intelligence the King had that the enemy were present in force within a few miles of him. Charles was quartered in the village of Edgecote a few miles to the southeast so that it was midnight by the time he heard the news. The bulk of Essex's army was quartered in or around Kineton, a little town just to the west, on the road towards Warwick. The King therefore had without knowing it put himself between Essex's army and London. But with an enemy believed to be considerably superior in force (in fact some of Essex's regiments were a day's march to the rear so that the two armies were probably about equal) so close on his heels, it would have been a wild gamble to march on the capital even if his own troops had been concentrated and provisioned for a forced march. Everything pointed to a battle in which luck and Rupert's rapid exploitation of it had given the Royalists the two great tactical advantages: they were astride the enemy's main line of communication and they were able to pick their ground.

Before sunrise Rupert had seized the heights above the village of Radway, the Edge Hill, as it was called, that dominates the country up to Kineton. He himself arrived there in the early morning. The King had confirmed his choice of rendezvous and all through the forenoon the foot regiments came in from the villages, some near, some a few hours away, in which they had spent the night. The weather was very sharp for October and few of the men mustering for battle had had much food or sleep. The delay, inevitable when men had to be marched in over varying distances, gave the Royalist commanders all too much time to squabble. Were they to fight that day or wait till the next? Were the infantry to be put in battalia in the Swedish fashion or the Dutch? This question concerned the deployment of the musketeers whose firepower was still in the mid-seventeenth century only subsidiary to the battle-winning push of the pike. The Swedish method as practised by Gustavus Adolphus meant thinning and extending the body of musketeers whose volleys would thus be greater in volume and, with proper training, more rapid in delivery. The King's general, the Earl of Lindsey, preferred the Dutch method that both

Edge hill   Battle

he and his opponent Essex had learned when they had served together under Prince Maurice and Prince Henry. Rupert, predictably, insisted on the more sophisticated, up-to-date technique perfected by Gustavus. In this he was supported by yet another general officer whom the King had added to the already top-heavy command structure. This was a veteran Scotch professional Patrick Ruthven, Earl of Forth, who had himself served in Gustavus's army. The King, too, came down on the side of Rupert. Lindsey, understandably infuriated, threw down his baton, saying that if he was not thought fit to perform the duties of a commander-in-chief he would charge as a private colonel at the head of his own regiment. He was as good as his word and, severely wounded, was captured by the Parliamentarians in whose hands he died next day. Naturally this did not endear Rupert to the native Royalist nobility who resented the arrogance and assertiveness of this alarming young foreigner.

On the Parliamentary side Essex reacted with the unexcited ordinariness that was both his strength and his weakness. It was not until he was on his way to church that he saw that the Royalists had seized Edge Hill and were going to offer battle. He did not want to fight that day if he could help it as there were other forces under his command at Warwick and Coventry that could be with him in a day at most, giving him what should have been a comforting superiority. As it was both sides probably numbered about 14,000 all told. The Royalists were proportionately stronger in horse and weaker in foot. Essex had a decided advantage in his artillery if he could make use of it. Seventeenth-century guns, in England at least, were too ponderous and difficult to manoeuvre to be much good in a fluid battle on open territory. Essex drew his forces up about a mile away from the Royalist position on the lower slopes of Edge Hill, concentrating them into a slightly narrower front, and waited.

Professor Austin Woolrych has pointed out in his excellent *Battles of the English Civil War* that the participants in those actions had to watch an opposing army, often for hours, at what in a modern battle would be a suicidally close range. Fire-arms were not the deadly things they have since become.

Pikemen and cavalry at the battle of Edgehill, from an early news-sheet

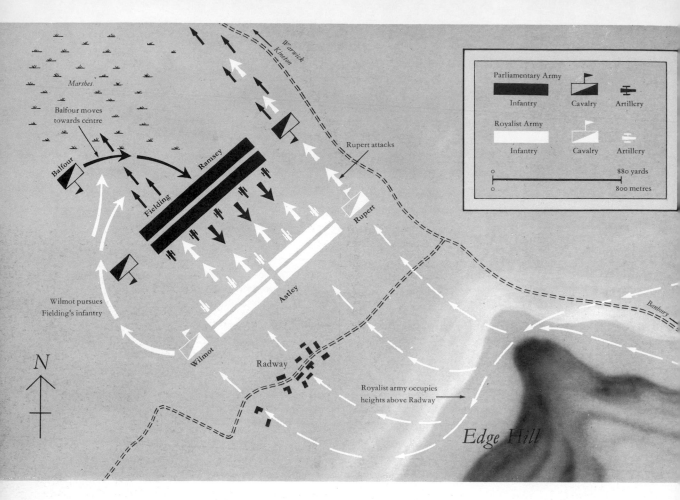

Parliamentary Army
Infantry   Cavalry   Artillery
Royalist Army
Infantry   Cavalry   Artillery

880 yards
800 metres

Marshes.

Balfour moves
towards centre

Balfour

Fielding

Ramsey

Rupert attacks

Rupert

Astley

Wilmot pursues
Fielding's infantry

Wilmot

Radway

Royalist army occupies
heights above Radway

Warwick
Kineton

Banbury

N

Edge Hill

*Plan of the battle of Edgehill,
1642*

In the opinion of Brigadier Peter Young, the foremost authority on the land fighting of the civil war, 'a skilled musketeer . . . would be lucky, taking deliberate aim, to hit a man sixty yards away'. Exposure was thus no great risk in itself. But the strain on the nerves of watching men talking, joking, chanting psalms, who might at any minute stiffen into battle order and try to kill one hand-to-hand must have been severe, especially on the unseasoned warriors of the opening battles. Even athletes, trained to compete, usually seem ill-at-ease when facing their opponents and waiting to begin. Winston Churchill has left a vivid account of the excitement he felt at Omdurman, an engagement superficially resembling the type of battle fought between Englishmen in the mid-seventeenth century. But, as the best modern account has emphasized, it was really nothing of the kind. The forces of a nineteenth-century European power faced those of the middle ages – and knew it from the start. The soldiers who have had to face the jeering, stone-throwing mobs in the Falls Road or the Bogside knowing that much nastier things may happen at any minute, come closer to the experience of their ancestors at Edgehill.

By the early afternoon it became plain that the Royalists were going to attack. The King who like Nelson at Trafalgar disdained making himself inconspicuous could be seen riding along his battle line accompanied by the Gentleman Pensioners. The Parliamentary artillery opened fire shortly before three o'clock and the Royalist guns responded. The plan of the battle shows a conventional pattern. On both sides the body of the foot are in the centre and the cavalry and dragoons on the wings, with some musketeers placed among the troops of cavalry. The dragoons, though mounted, were not usually expected to charge. Their horses were simply intended to give additional mobility in the immediate prelude to a battle, in which they generally fought on foot. Their characteristic function was to line the hedges and provide a defensive harassing fire on any flank attack.

On the Royalist side the cavalry on the right were commanded by Prince Rupert, those on the left by Wilmot. The body of foot in the centre came under the immediate control of the serjeant major-general, Sir Jacob Astley, a professional soldier who at sixty-three was almost of an age with his superior, Lord Forth, then nearing seventy. Jacob Astley fought right through the war, surrendering the last Royalist field army at Stow-on-the-Wold with the philosophic and, to his conquerors, prophetic words: 'Well, lads, you have done your business and may go play, except you will fall out amongst yourselves.' Liked and respected by officer and soldier, by friend and foe, he typifies the humanity and good sense that on both sides mitigated the passion and cruelty of war. If Edgehill were otherwise forgotten it would deserve to be remembered for the beauty and simplicity of his prayer before the battle: 'O Lord, thou knowest how busy I must be this day. If I forget thee, do not thou forget me.'

Across a mile or so of marshy ground the slightly shorter Parliamentarian line, shorter because the Dutch formation had been preferred to the Swedish, had Sir James Ramsey on the left marking Rupert while the right, under the nominal command of the Earl of Bedford, was effectively under Lord Fielding and Sir William Balfour, an experienced officer whose presence of mind was to save the day for Essex. Clarendon, who was present at the battle though not a combatant, draws attention to the social status of his officers: 'Of the nobility he had with him the lords Kimbolton, Saint-John's, Wharton, Roberts, Rochford and Fielding (whose fathers, the earls of Dover and Denbigh, charged as volunteers in the King's guard of horse) and many gentlemen of quality.' Essex had sited his front well, resting each wing on slightly rising ground, partly protected on the right by a wood.

The real battle opened, as in so many of the main actions of the war, with Rupert's charge. In this department of warfare forever associated with his name, Rupert introduced a new technique. Dutch cavalry tactics, in which most English officers had been trained, taught that the charge should be conducted at the trot. On reaching the enemy line the trooper would discharge his pistol, effective only at point blank, wheel to the rear and re-load while the ranks that followed performed the same evolution in their turn. Rupert's technique was much more drastic. The charge began at the trot, increased to the canter and finally, as the enemy line was reached, to the gallop. The troopers were to ride in close order, stirrup to stirrup, since there

William Walker, wounded in the arm at Edgehill when two horses were shot under him, died in 1736 reputedly aged 123, clearly the last survivor of the battle

was to be no wheeling to reload but, after the first discharge of the pistol, the crash of horse and rider into the enemy line and the cut of sword. Sir Philip Warwick, the young dandy who had critically noted the imperfections of Cromwell's turn-out as an MP, charged that afternoon under Rupert. He tells us that the King's Lifeguard, of which he was a member, had been nettled at being described as 'the *Troop of Shew*' and had demanded and received the post of honour on the far right of the line. How magnificently mounted they must have been can be gauged from his recollecting that 'when wee valued the estates of the whole troop, wee reckoned there was 100,000 l. *per ann.* in that Body'.

It was about three o'clock when this formidable attack was launched. Just before giving the order to charge Rupert was informed that Sir Faithfull Fortescue who commanded one of the troops under Sir James Ramsey intended to come over with all his men as soon as battle was joined and would fire his pistol into the ground as a signal. It was too late for Rupert to get word to all the regimental commanders and some of Fortescue's men were roughly handled before they managed to divest themselves of the orange tawny scarves or sashes which, in those days before troops wore uniform, served to distinguish Essex's men from those of the King. On came the Royalist horse, hardly slowed by the heavier going on the low-lying marshy ground, hardly bothered by the Parliamentary bombardment, clearing the few ditches and low hedges with the ease of men who had spent much of their lives in the saddle and knew their horses were up to their work. Only one officer, the King's cousin Lord D'Aubigny, was killed in the approach to the enemy and Clarendon hints at foul play by his Dutch lieutenant, resentful of a reprimand. The cannonading seems to have had little effect on the whole battle and none on Rupert's charge. Rattled by his apparently invincible advance the Parliamentary horse discharged their carbines prematurely, so that when the Royalists were on them they could offer no defence beyond bracing themselves to take the shock of nearly a thousand well-armed horsemen thundering towards them at the gallop. Even seasoned troops might have wavered. When they saw that some of their own side were deserting – and who at that heart-sinking moment could tell how many? – they turned and bolted, leaving their unfortunate musketeers to be cut down. Exhilarated by so easy a victory the Royalists galloped after them for glory and for plunder.

Much the same thing happened on the other wing where Wilmot led the charge. But here the Parliamentary lieutenant-general, Sir William Balfour, seems to have held a good part of his cavalry in reserve, so that as the Royalist left streamed off the field in pursuit of Fielding's regiment that had broken and fled, he was himself left in command of the only body of cavalry still formed up and ready to be committed to the battle. The Royalist foot under old Sir Jacob Astley had marched stoutly up to the numerically superior Parliamentarians and for a moment it seemed that their courage was to be rewarded, as the foot brigade on the Parliamentary left, raw troops demoralized by the total rout of the cavalry on their flank, turned and ran without firing a shot. Had Rupert's horse still been on the field, instead of pursuing the flying troops of Sir James Ramsey, the battle, and perhaps the war, would have

Although the two sides did not wear distinguishing uniforms, soldiers could tell friend from foe by different coloured sashes or armbands or by distinctive banners and standards

been settled in half an hour. But the two remaining Parliamentary brigades met the emergency with tactical adroitness and unshaken nerve. In the fierce fighting at push of pike they held their own, enabling Balfour to deliver an unopposed cavalry attack on the Royalist left flank. In a few minutes the situation was transformed. The main body of the Royalist foot were fighting for their lives. The standard was captured, though later retaken by the courage and dash of a single Royalist cavalry officer who found himself isolated in the confusion of the successful charge well to the rear of Essex's army. 'Captain Smith, Captain Smith, they are taking away the standard.' The shout of a boy taken prisoner drew his eye to the group and the flag. Its bearer, Clarendon's old friend Sir Edmund Verney had already, in fulfilment of his own prophecy, fallen in the thick of the fight after accounting for two of the enemy who had killed his old servant Jason. It was then too that the Earl of Lindsey fell mortally wounded and in spite of his son's heroic attempts at rescue was taken prisoner with him. Even the King was in great danger of capture, offering a second chance of ending the war in one afternoon, this time in the opposite sense.

Sir Edmund Verney's ring with a miniature of Charles I

Gradually the periphery of the battle began to react on the centre. Rupert's horse ran into some of the troops marching to reinforce Essex, including John Hampden's regiment, and found a check. Rupert himself had managed to retain control of three or four troops and to stop them ranging the countryside in a general chase. By the early evening some of the Royalist horse were beginning to drift back, unaware of the critical condition of their main army.

Grocers Hall in the City, which Parliament considered, but never used, as a safe retreat

Their arrival enabled the retreating foot to stabilize a position on the lower slopes of the hill, probably not far from that which they had advanced in the afternoon. By nightfall there was even talk of a second cavalry charge. But horses and men were too far spent: a night attack was a ticklish business even for experienced troops; and success, if obtained, could not have been exploited by the exhausted and ravenous foot. Both armies had fought to a standstill and, dead to the world, faced each other across the battlefield. The night was bitterly cold, a fact to which some of the wounded, stripped of the best of their clothes by prowling plunderers, were said to have owed their lives since the frost helped to stanch the flow of blood. In the morning, Essex drew off towards Warwick.

The road to London was now well and truly open. Had the King taken it the probability is that he would have reversed all the initial advantages with which Parliament had started. Both the population of London and the mercantile wealth of the City were by no means solid for Pym. Apart from the numerous active Royalists in London and the Home Counties, especially Kent, there was the great weight of those who wanted a quiet life and would support the side most likely to give it them. The navy with its bases and dock-yards in the Thames and Medway in Royalist hands would be almost certain to join the King. The trade, the wealth, the authority that London conferred on its possessor was almost enough in itself to decide the war.

The King, as we know, did not take it. Why? Perhaps because it was not in his character. If he had been the kind of man who could assess such a situation he would not have got himself into it in the first place. Instead he secured Banbury Castle and moved with the ceremony that belonged to his conception of kingship into what was to be his wartime capital, the loyal and learned city of Oxford.

Edgehill was a drawn battle; drawn, perhaps, in the Royalists' favour since losses were about equal and they were left in possession both of the field and of the strategic initiative. It has been described at some length because it epito-mizes so much of the first two years of the war. The Royalists begin and end by squabbling about command and by failing to choose a policy and sticking to it. The Parliamentarians with much superior resources and no inferiority of courage perform disappointingly. They do not win, or even look like winning. They survive by muddling through when they ought, given the balance of forces, to achieve a decisive advantage. In the actual fighting it is Rupert's energy and panache that stand out, but when the balance is struck the military pros and cons of having Rupert on one's side seem almost to cancel each other out. The battle exhibits no extraordinary military qualities in planning, direc-tion or control. Great opportunities are seized but inconsequently thrown away. There is plenty of courage, but perhaps not too much zeal; there is amateurism, huffiness, indiscipline and just enough professionalism to avoid total disaster. To pursue these elements through their frequent recombination in a detailed narrative of the battles of the civil war is not the purpose of this book. It has in any case been done well, recently and often in a number of other works. A more shifting, glancing technique may help to suggest the actual experience of civil war.

Chapter 9

Royalist High Tide

After a few days in Oxford the King marched out with his army towards London. In spite of the gift offered by his dilatoriness Essex had still not put himself between the two. So deeply alarmed was the Parliament that they recalled Warwick from the fleet to command the defence of London and sent offers of a treaty to the King. The messengers met him at Reading (he was coming down the Thames valley route) and, though well received, were not allowed to delay his advance. Essex, however, had at last put on a turn of speed and, travelling along the northern route over the Chilterns entered London a few days before the King, coming down the Great West Road, met the Parliamentary Commissioners formally at Colnbrook, near the present Heathrow Airport.

A short truce followed, broken almost at once by Rupert's storming of Brentford which two regiments of Essex's army had occupied. Parliament loudly accused Rupert of dishonouring the agreement, which he indignantly denied. Considering his punctilio in military matters it is difficult to believe that he acted in bad faith. What is certain is that his troopers behaved with the usual wanton destructiveness of victorious soldiers. Tearing up books, breaking open cupboards, ripping up mattresses, spoiling what they could not steal, they brought home to London what many owners of handsome country houses, Royalist and Parliamentarian alike, had already felt. The fact that on these occasions no distinction was drawn between the property of supporters and opponents stiffened the will to resist. London was much too rich and tempting to let a lawless army loose in. Essex's regiments and the trained bands knew as they faced the Royalists, much their inferiors in numbers, arms and supplies, that they had the whole resources of the capital at their command and the almost entire loyalty of its inhabitants, thoroughly alarmed at the prospect of a sack. The weather was drawing in (it was now the middle of November). There was only one thing left for the King's army to do and that was to march back to Oxford.

In the next few months the war crystallized into the pattern it was to follow till very near the end. Scotland was, for the moment, neutral but neutral on the Parliament's side. Ireland was in a state of confused atrocity in which the differences between Royalists and Parliamentarians were of secondary intensity. The real question was, would the King do a deal with the Papists and let loose those agents of anti-Christ, still reeking with the blood of Protestant innocents, on his blameless Englishmen? The answer, revealed when his secret correspondence was captured and published in 1645 after the battle of Naseby, was yes, in spite of his frequent and categorical denials. But characteristically he was pursuing this policy through such unreliable and ineffective people, while simultaneously pursuing others in direct contradiction of it that there was no great danger of it coming to anything. Except for propaganda purposes, particularly for justifying the cold-blooded slaughter of prisoners, Ireland played little part in the civil war. Some of her harbours were useful to Royalist privateers, even, when all was over, to the Royalist fleet that Rupert was to take into strange seas where the war between King and Parliament had never penetrated. But no action of any importance to the outcome of the war was fought in Irish waters or on Irish soil.

In England the King's failure to seize London was final. The Home Counties, the South and East, East Anglia and the greater part of the Midlands passed into and remained under Parliamentary control. In the North, both east and west, the Royalists soon confirmed their ascendancy, with the important exception of west and south Yorkshire where the Fairfaxes, father and son, provided a military nucleus for the clothing towns such as Leeds and Bradford whose sympathies were strongly Parliamentarian. In Cheshire and Lancashire, both mainly Royalist counties, Sir William Brereton did the same for Manchester. Wales and the Welsh marches were the heartland of Royalist recruiting. Bristol was at first, and by its nature, Parliamentarian. Somerset, Dorset and Wiltshire were in the beginning disputed territory but gradually passed into the Royalist sphere of influence as the result of the militant and effective Royalism of the two counties of the extreme Southwest, especially and conspicuously of Cornwall.

This was the more surprising because the western counties had a tradition of sturdy resistance to royal pretensions and courtier politics that stretched back to the Reformation. Peter Wentworth, the great champion of the Commons against even so popular a despot as Queen Elizabeth, had sat first for a Devon and then a Cornish constituency. Eliot and Pym, his successors, were West Countrymen who sat all their Parliamentary lives for West Country seats. In 1642 Pym's party was far better organized there and far more confident than the King's. So confident was it that it decided to proceed against the Royalist leaders at the Quarter Sessions at Launceston on charges of disturbing the peace. In the first demonstration of the bold and brilliant leadership that was to win the West for the King, Sir Ralph Hopton appeared in court to accept the indictment, produced his commission from the Marquis of Hertford, nominated by the King to command all his forces in the West, and argued, in the best Clarendonian terms, that 'he was sent to assist them in the defence of their liberties against all illegal taxes and impositions'. The grand jury acquitted him and, in the turning of the tables, accepted an indictment of riotous assembly against his opponents. Thus backed by the force of law he invoked the sheriff's power to call out the *posse comitatus*, the citizen body in arms, that stretches back to the Saxons and has been preserved for our historical consciousness by the classic Hollywood western. Hopton thus found himself at a stroke in command of 'three thousand foot, well armed'.

Cornish Royalism set an example of courage and humanity that brightens the early passages of the war. There is so little evidence of what the common, unlettered, country people thought that all assertion is unsafe but it does seem possible that the Cornish infantry believed in the justice of their cause. Their fighting quality was much admired and Clarendon explicitly notes that

> they were always more sparing than is usually known in civil wars, shedding very little blood after resistance was given over, and having a very noble and Christian sense of the lives of their brethren: insomuch as the common men, when they have been pressed by some fiercer officer to follow the execution, have answered 'they could not find it in their hearts to hurt men who had nothing in their hands'.

Sir Bevil Grenville, leader of the Cornish Royalists

What was certainly exceptional was the quality of the leadership. Hopton, a Somerset man, had been a popular member of the House of Commons, staying on in Westminster after most of the King's party had left. No Royalist general was better liked or trusted by his opponents as well as by his own men. His principal lieutenants, Sir Bevil Grenville and Sir Nicholas Slanning were men of the same type. Grenville indeed in his younger days had been closely associated with the Parliamentary opposition to the court and had supported its great leader Sir John Eliot against his own father. Both Hopton and Grenville had long been prominent in the life of their counties and both were entirely free from touchiness and jealousy. This enabled them even to defeat Charles I's characteristic scheme for ruining his own cause by dividing the command in the West between four officers equally, or, should this prove impracticable, by any two of the four. They agreed amongst themselves to vest the sole command in Hopton.

The results were dramatic. At the battle of Braddock Down on 19 January 1643 a Parliamentary army of equal or superior force was routed and the whole of Cornwall passed under Royalist control. Skilful Parliamentary defence nearly turned the tables on the Cornishmen when they invaded Devon and attempted both Plymouth and Exeter with insufficient forces. On 16 May the Parliamentary army which now outnumbered Hopton by two to one was defeated in one of the most astonishing actions of the war, at Stratton, just inside the border of Cornwall at its northeastern tip. All of Devon except the garrisoned ports of Plymouth, Exeter, Barnstaple and Dartmouth lay open to the Royalists. Unless prompt action were taken Hopton's men might join forces with the main army based on Oxford or at least with the troops that the Marquis of Hertford had raised in South Wales and which he had now brought across the Severn. This union was in fact achieved early in June at Chard in Somerset, but it was not without its disadvantages. In the first place to have induced the Cornish foot to march so far from their own county was a personal triumph for Hopton. How long it could be sustained was another matter. A cavalry captain in the force that met them records: 'These were the very best Foot I ever saw, for marching and fighting; but so mutinous withal, that nothing but an alarm could keep them from falling foul upon their officers.'

The Marquis of Hertford had himself been joined by Rupert's brother, Prince Maurice, with three regiments from Oxford. This mixture of commanders was not happily conceived. Maurice had all Rupert's faults of manner with none of his military flair. The Marquis of Hertford, an elderly aristocrat of scholarly and sedentary tastes, was not likely to put up with impertinence from an ignorant tough some thirty years his junior. Hertford had much in common with Essex, whose brother-in-law he was. Both men had been intimately connected with the royal family and both had been estranged through James I's interference with their marriages, involving one in humiliation and the other in tragedy. Essex had been married at James's instigation to Frances Howard, daughter of the Earl of Suffolk. As he was only fourteen at the time he was hardly in a position to argue had he wished to. While he was abroad completing his education his wife began an affair with James's young favourite Robert Carr. On Essex's return she refused to have marital relations with him and petitioned for nullity so that she might marry Carr. James himself presided over the hearing of the suit which found in favour of Lady Essex. When she was later convicted, and her new husband strongly suspected, of a poisoning in connection with the case, the scandal and mortification inflicted by the King's meddling were not easy for a proud, reserved man to forget or forgive.

Hertford's story is more romantic. While an undergraduate at Oxford he and James's niece, Arabella Stuart, had met and fallen in love. Their attachment became known and James, apprehensive of a possible dynastic threat to his own line, summoned them before the Council and extracted a promise not to marry without his consent. This was given but broken by a secret marriage. Again the secret was ill-kept. The pair were arrested and the bridegroom sent to the Tower. Both succeeded in escaping in disguise and in taking ship for the Continent but poor Arabella was caught by an English frigate off Calais. She was sent to the Tower and ultimately went off her head. The future Marquis lived abroad till her death and then made his peace with the King. But it is not surprising that, like his brother-in-law by a later, less storm-tossed marriage, he was not looked on in Parliament as one of the Court party. In fact his adherence to the King was yet another indication of how far the leading Royalists of the civil war were removed from the men who had been closest to the King in the years that had gone before.

Frances Howard, Essex's first wife

The presence of Hopton and his own happy relations with his subordinate commanders did much to make this over-generalled army effective. In two battles fought near Bath in early July the Parliamentary forces were decisively defeated. Neither action can be claimed as a triumph of the military art. In both cases the decision might easily have gone the other way. As so often in the civil war luck, individual heroism and personal leadership turned the trick.

In the first, the battle of Lansdown on 5 July, Hopton won a victory against his old friend and companion in arms Sir William Waller as hard-fought and dearly obtained as any in the war. The result was only clinched by Sir Bevil Grenville's leading his Cornish pikemen in a frontal assault up the steep hill on which the Parliamentary army stood. An officer in Prince Maurice's regiment saw them through the smoke: 'they stood as upon the eaves of a house for steepness but as unmovable as a rock'. The cost was terrible. To get there they had had to advance under the steady fire of a confident, experienced enemy and, when they had reached the top, to withstand three charges of cavalry. In the last of these Sir Bevil Grenville himself fell, a loss, as Clarendon says, that would have clouded any victory. Hopton himself was wounded in the fighting and badly hurt in an accident a few hours afterwards. He was close to an ammunition wagon that blew up, temporarily blinding him and inflicting severe burns and shock.

Waller knew how much the Royalists had suffered. He soon heard of Hopton's incapacitation and of the shortage of powder that was forcing them on to the defensive. By nature as active and confident as Essex was cautious and doubtful he reinforced his army from the garrison at Bristol and advanced. Up to this point Waller had been Parliament's star performer. In a series of sweeps up to the Severn and through the southern counties of Hampshire and

Sr WILLIAM WALLER Knight Sargeant
Maiar: Generall, of ye Parliaments army, and
a member, of ye Honoble House of Commons.

*Waller at the height of his
success in 1643*

Sussex he had captured towns and castles and defeated some not very formidable opponents commanding distinctly dubious forces in a series of actions to
which the word 'battle' had been somewhat promiscuously applied. The
numbers involved rarely amounted to a couple of thousand and it was the roll-
call of towns surrendered and distances covered that won him his early title
of William the Conqueror. Relations with his commander-in-chief were
notoriously bad: Essex was jealous of Waller's mushroom reputation,
Waller resentful of Essex's inert failure to reinforce success. With his opponents

he got on famously. Hopton, his old friend, had written to him after the first skirmish between their forces at Chewton Mendip suggesting a personal meeting. Waller's reply expresses that quality about the civil war that still has power to touch the imagination where the Wars of the Roses leave it unmoved:

> Certainly my affections to you are so unchangeable, that hostility itself cannot violate my friendship to your person. But I must be true to the cause wherein I serve. The old limitation, *usque ad aras* [as far as the altar], holds still, and where my conscience is interested, all other obligations are swallowed up. I should most gladly wait on you according to your desire, but that I look upon you as you are engaged in that party beyond a possibility of retreat, and consequently uncapable of being wrought upon by any persuasion. And I know the conference could never be so close between us, but that it would take wind and receive a construction to my dishonour. That great God which is the searcher of my heart knows with what a sad sense I go upon this service and with what a perfect hatred I detest this war without an enemy; but I look upon it as *Opus Domini* [the work of the Lord], which is enough to silence all passion in me. The God of peace in his good time send us peace, and in the meantime fit us to receive it. We are both upon the stage, and must act those parts that are assigned us in this tragedy. Let us do it in a way of honour and without personal animosities.

The Royalists, giving ground before him, were caught at Devizes, late in the afternoon of 9 July. Hopton, though still an invalid, was sufficiently recovered to preside at a Council of War and to take and enforce the bold decision that the cavalry under Maurice and Hertford should break out that night and call up reinforcements from Oxford. He would with far inferior forces hold on in a town that had no natural defensive features. Maurice and Hertford made good time to Oxford, riding in on the afternoon of 11 July. Unfortunately the main body of horse had left with Rupert and the King to meet Henrietta Maria who had landed on the Yorkshire coast earlier in the year and was now on her way to Oxford. With unusual efficiency the whole remaining body of cavalry marched out of Oxford late that night under the command of Wilmot and were sighted by the astonished Waller just as he was preparing to give Devizes the *coup de grâce* on the afternoon of the 13th. Those Royalist horse who had ridden with Maurice back and forth must have been near the limit of their effectiveness. Nonetheless Wilmot threw the whole weight of his force against the Parliamentary cavalry and routed them. The Cavalier charge at Roundway Down became one of the battle-honours of the King's army. Its effect was overpowering. Unprotected by their own horse, threatened on two sides by Wilmot's cavalry and Hopton's foot now advancing from Devizes, Waller's infantry either surrendered or fled. After an engagement nothing like so costly as Lansdown the army of Sir William Waller had been destroyed by a force much less than half its own strength.

Fierce recriminations followed. Essex was outraged that Waller had lost his army; Waller loudly asked what Essex had been doing to let the Royalists march their forces in and out of Oxford as they pleased. Had he had any inkling of such a possibility he would have been much brisker at Devizes. But before the Parliament had time to digest this disaster it was faced with one that reverberated across the noise and confusion of war. Rupert, after convoying the Queen to Oxford, joined the victors of Roundway Down before the strongly fortified city of Bristol. In spite of a mismanaged attack and a spirited defence in which Robert Blake, then a Captain of Foot, especially distinguished himself, the place was taken by storm on 26 July. The King now possessed the second port of the country with all its wealth and all its possibilities. He had even recaptured a few of his own warships which, together with some other vessels that could be fitted out as privateers, gave him a limited degree of sea-power and a base from which he could exert it. At the very least its nuisance value to the trade of London as it came up the western approaches to the Channel would be considerable. His cause had come a long way since the standard had been blown down at Nottingham less than a year earlier.

If the West had seen the most startling and complete reversal of fortune, the North too looked threatening to the general military situation of Parliament. The immensely wealthy Earl of Newcastle had brought his well-found, well-disciplined army south into Yorkshire, relieved the pressure of the Fairfaxes in York and through the agency of yet another dashing cavalryman, George Goring, inflicted a serious defeat on Sir Thomas Fairfax, the future Lord General of the Parliamentary forces, at the battle of Seacroft Moor between York and Leeds. This was at the end of March 1643. At the end of June Newcastle himself with much superior forces defeated both Sir Thomas and his father at the battle of Adwalton Moor. As a consequence the staunchly Parliamentarian towns of Leeds and Bradford had to surrender to the Royalists. Newcastle and his military advisers had not been slow to see how the North could be made to dominate the Midlands. As early as the middle of December he had secured and garrisoned Newark, a useful base from which operations could be mounted against Lincolnshire and of paramount importance as commanding the passage of the Trent on the main road from London to the North. The Royalists were to hold the town against the fiercest assaults and one of the most famous sieges until the King, himself a prisoner, ordered its surrender. It was this Royalist initiative that led Colonel Hutchinson to accept the commission he had earlier declined and, with his brother, to secure the other important crossing of the Trent at Nottingham before it too fell into the King's hands.

By the middle of 1643, therefore, Royalist success had touched high-water mark and the war had assumed the shape that it was to maintain in the long years of hard pounding that lay ahead. Parliament controlled London, the South and East Anglia, the Royalists the North and West with a salient, sharpening its point at Oxford, threatening London. The twin axes of the war were thus the main routes to the North and West. Whirling down the M1 and the A1, the M4 and the main lines from Paddington and King's Cross, a glimpsed place-name stirs an echo of Clarendon or Lucy Hutchinson. Left to themselves the Royalists might ultimately have co-ordinated their three areas of strength into three lines of attack on London. But two invisible barriers kept the apparently victorious Royalists at bay: the genius of Pym's political leadership and the Parliament's supremacy at sea. The second of these advantages was to be retained until the Royalists capitulated but the first was on a short lease. Pym was to die of cancer before Christmas.

A French representation of John Pym as a modern Herod. His lingering death was seized on by his opponents with unctuous zeal as an earnest of divine punishment

The year 1643 had opened with a powerful initiative from the peace party, so much the strongest in the House of Lords and far from negligible in the Commons, for a reconciliation with the King. In March a Commission of both Houses, headed by the Earl of Northumberland and including such well-disposed members of the Lower House as Bulstrode Whitelocke, was graciously received in Oxford under a flag of truce. This was, for Pym, a moment of intense danger. He dared not appear obdurate for fighting when there was an apparent opportunity of peace. But he knew that it was no good trying to do business with Charles I on a free and fair basis. If he hadn't reached that conclusion he would not have steered the country into war in the first place. But

May 1643: burning of Popish books and pictures and the executions consequent on the discovery of Waller's plot

here the correctness of his own analysis saved him when he would have been powerless to influence events. Whitelocke and Pierrepoint, two of the leading moderates among the Commissioners, got on so well with their old friends Falkland and Clarendon that they privately reached a complete agreement. The official terms demanding points, especially in Church matters, on which Charles was known to be immovable, could be disregarded. If he would make some concessions, notably in the militia, and re-appoint Northumberland Lord High Admiral, Northumberland himself and a good part of the Parliamentary party would adhere to him. At the very least he could seriously divide his opponents; at best he might end the war. Clarendon himself, long after the King's execution, remembered how he pressed and pleaded with him in private audience. Why did he not accept? Clarendon who knew him and loved him attributes his obstinacy to a promise he had given the absent Henrietta Maria, not to forgive any of his estranged ministers without her consent. Pym would not have needed such an explanation. Instead it was characteristic of the King to embark on a plot, concealed from his best advisers, for a rising in the city through the unreliable agency of Edmund Waller, the poet and cousin of Sir William, who was also a Commissioner. Its betrayal and Waller's abject saving of his own skin enabled Pym to profit from the deadly threat of the Oxford negotiations.

The Parliamentary Commissioners were not the only important visitors the King received that spring in his lodging at Christ Church. The Scottish Covenanters would have been glad to reinsure their Church settlement against any outcome of a war in which they were not as yet involved. Charles did not trouble to conceal his dislike of them. His cousin Hamilton had assured him of Scotland's neutrality. What had he to hope or fear from these tiresome people, in his eyes the cause of every subsequent catastrophe? They went on to London where Pym accorded them very different treatment. He was not himself anxious to accept their proposals for a uniform Covenanting Presbyterianism throughout the two kingdoms but there were much worse possibilities if the King should get the upper hand. With the series of military disasters culminating in the defeat of the Fairfaxes at Adwalton Moor, the loss of Bristol and the all but total collapse of the Parliamentary position in the West, this now seemed more than possible. With his last most perfectly timed act of political leadership Pym seized the moment to conclude an alliance with Scotland. He could not himself leave Westminster even if his health had permitted it. This most crucial negotiation was entrusted to the younger Sir Henry Vane, a man, in the phrase that epitomizes Clarendon's hatred both of the Scots and of Vane himself, 'chosen to cozen and deceive a whole nation which excelled in craft and dissembling'. Clarendon's anti-Scotch prejudices are as apoplectic as Dr Johnson's. But he is entirely right in asserting Vane's abhorrence of the Presbyterianism he was pledging to the Scots in exchange for their army. The members of the Long Parliament began to take the Covenant in September. Pym died early in December. The Scottish army crossed the Tweed late in January 1644.

Communication between Edinburgh and London was, at this dark hour for the Parliament, possible only by sea. But this service, substantial as it was, was

RIGHT *Robert Rich, Earl of Warwick, by Van Dyck. He was the outstandingly competent successor to the Earl of Northumberland as Lord High Admiral*

OVERLEAF *The Salusbury Family by an unknown artist. One of the King's strongest recruiting grounds was Wales, where Sir Thomas Salusbury was colonel of a regiment of foot raised in Denbigh and Flint*

the least of the advantages Parliament, now that its back was to the wall, drew from the navy. In both the great areas of England, the North and the West, that had now fallen under Royalist control there were strongly defended ports, Hull in the North and Plymouth in the West, that would have to be subdued if the King were ever to be able to withdraw his troops from them and concentrate them for an attack on London. Besides these two formidable bases from which any such move might always be taken in the rear there were lesser ports such as Scarborough and Lyme which in their turn might disconcert any concentration against Hull or Plymouth. This is the key to the underlying pattern of the war and to its surface transformations.

Charles's next move, on the morrow of his triumph at Bristol, is entirely consistent with such a reading of the situation. He decided to consolidate his control of the West by taking the one stronghold remaining to the Parliament in the Severn valley, the city of Gloucester. Since it was commanded by a professional soldier whose political sympathies, so far as they were known, were believed to be Royalist it was thought that the appearance of the army before the town in support of a summons from the King riding at its head might win a bloodless victory. On 10 August 1643 the summons was delivered but the answer was not at all what had been expected from an officer and a gentleman. Rather it provides the reader of Clarendon with one of the most vivid contemporary sketches from which the type-figure of Puritanism has been elaborated in Royalist propaganda:

> Within less than the time prescribed, together with the trumpeter returned two citizens from the town, with lean, pale, sharp and bald visages, indeed faces so strange and unusual, and in such a garb and posture, that at once made the most severe countenance merry, and the most cheerful hearts sad; for it was impossible such ambassadors could bring less than defiance. The men, without any circumstance of duty or good manners, in a pert, shrill, undismayed accent, said they had brought an answer from the godly city of Gloucester to the King; and were so ready to give insolent and seditious answers to any question, as if their business were chiefly to provoke the King to violate his own safe conduct.

This incident, as it happened, proved to be the turning point of the war. Opinion in the Royalist command had been divided as to whether to attempt Gloucester at all and as to what to do if the place did not submit. Was it to be stormed, like Bristol, or besieged, or left alone? An instant decision was made in favour of a siege (Prince Rupert conspicuously detaching himself to the independent command of the horse) and from that moment, we can see with hindsight, the general military fortunes of the Royalists began to go downhill. But to the attentive reader of Clarendon it is a turning point in a social and political as well as a military sense. Sir John Hotham and the King at Hull, Hopton and Waller in the West, Essex and Rupert in the Thames valley had communicated, even though one had thought the other a rebel engaged in acts of treason, in the language of courtesy and honour. Here in anger, in incredulity and in, perhaps, a degree of alarm is heard for the first time the note of holier-than-thou insubordination that was to swell to a crescendo after the second civil war.

The threat to Gloucester was a challenge that the war party at Westminster

The Sovereign of the Seas (detail), artist unknown. She was by far the largest and most beautiful English warship of her age

Essex at the height of his glory after the relief of Gloucester. All his victories are shown, including Edgehill, here described as Kenton (i.e. Kineton)

could not decline. Pym accepted it as an opportunity for restoring confidence in Essex as commander-in-chief and for demonstrating the power of the Parliament to march its army into Royalist territory. It was make or break. Bad news was pouring in from every quarter, from Ireland where Ormonde, the Lord-Lieutenant, had negotiated a truce that might liberate soldiers for the Royalist army, from Lincolnshire, where Newcastle's forces were carrying all before them. In this supreme crisis the London trained bands were called out, not to defend the city, but to march with Essex's army right across the southern Midlands to the Severn valley. Five regiments of them set off, escorted by part of Essex's army, on 24 August when the King had already been bombarding Gloucester and mining its walls for a fortnight. They kept to the north of the Thames valley, passing through Beaconsfield and Aylesbury before joining Essex's main body about twenty miles north of Oxford, the base from which Rupert's cavalry might be expected to attack. When he did a day or two later he was beaten off. On 5 September Essex reached the edge of Prestbury Hill, northeast of Cheltenham, from which, in the distance, he could see the great central tower of Gloucester Cathedral. He fired a gun and was answered from the garrison. They had only three barrels of powder left. Next morning Charles, not wanting to risk his army and its train between two forces, raised the siege. On 8 September Essex entered Gloucester unopposed.

The garrison commander had been lucky as well as brave. On the day the trained bands set out through Uxbridge a downpour had flooded the Royalist siegeworks and ruined the mines that were to have been exploded next day. The bad weather, the failure of a long siege, the denial of plunder that might have made up for want of pay cast something of a blight on the King's army as it drew off from Gloucester. But, as on the morrow of Edgehill, it found itself once again between London and London's army.

Chapter 10
The Impact of the War

The campaigns and battles of the civil war, remote as they seem to us, made, even in their own day, less impact on the consciousness of the nation at large than the fact of the war itself. As Hobbes so eloquently puts it in his great work of political theory directly inspired by these events of which he was a disenchanted spectator:

> For WAR, consisteth not in battle only, or the act of fighting; but in a tract of time, wherein the will to contend by battle is sufficiently known: and therefore the notion of *time* is to be considered in the nature of war; as it is in the nature of weather. For as the nature of foul weather lieth not in a shower or two of rain; but in an inclination thereto of many days together: so the nature of war consisteth not in actual fighting; but in the known disposition thereto, during all the time there is no assurance to the contrary. All other time is PEACE.

It is not only that the uncertainties and apprehensions enter into the relations, transactions and decisions of almost everybody. There are also immediate effects on trade and communication, on law and order, on education, and, most instantly and universally felt of all, on money and prices.

How did a country that even under Queen Elizabeth never financed its foreign expeditions or naval forces adequately manage to pay and feed and equip the armies of both sides for so long a period? The short answer is that it didn't. Soldiers and sailors were for the most part perennially short of provisions, boots, clothes and equipment. As for pay, the table printed by Dr Clive Holmes in his invaluable *The Eastern Association in the English Civil War* suggests that until the New Model was formed almost at the end of the war the armies of Essex and Waller were paid for rather less than half of the time served. Mutiny, indiscipline and desertion were only to be expected under such circumstances. The army of the Eastern Association, organized in the first place with characteristic efficiency by Warwick and his son-in-law Manchester, did a great deal better. We may be sure that the Royalist armies did worse, perhaps a lot worse. As early in the war as the winter of 1642 Clarendon wrote:

> the soldiery already grew very high, and would obey no orders or rules but of their own making; and prince Rupert considered only the subsistence and advance of the horse as his province, and indeed as if it had been a province apart from the army; and therefore would by no means endure that the great contributions, which the counties within command willingly submitted to, should be assigned to any other use than the support of the horse, and to be immediately collected and received by the officers.

Clarendon here touches on a feature common to both armies. The cavalry, in a good position to help themselves, were not so dependent on the pay-master and the commissariat as the foot regiments. Certainly on both sides there seems to have been much less difficulty in recruiting for this arm. A party of horse, foraging, scouting, raiding, must have been a much more common sight than the laborious passage of an army:

> The wanton troopers riding by
> Have shot my fawn and it will die.

When Rupert was raiding down the Thames valley after Edgehill a detach-ment of his men under Sir John and Sir Thomas Byron, neighbours and cousins of Colonel Hutchinson, occupied Fawley Court, near Henley, the country house of Bulstrode Whitelocke. The Byrons behaved properly, giving orders that the house was not to be damaged. But once they had gone the troops got on with it. Curtains were torn down, cushions and mattresses slashed, books destroyed, manuscripts used to light pipes; in the outbuildings a hundred loads of hay and corn were spoilt in a night. Miss Spalding, White-locke's biographer, paints a vivid and detailed picture of a kind that would have become recognizable in most parts of England before the war was over. Theft and destruction are infectious pleasures. Those to whom the issues of the war meant little might yet see that it offered an incomparable opportunity for indulging in them. Personal safety and the rights of property did not in the seventeenth century enjoy the universal respect that some nostalgic historians, Clarendon among them, have sometimes implied. Life for the poor was harsh. Death by starvation was not so uncommon as to shock the con-science of society. Duelling amongst the aristocracy was accepted as a civilized practice. The standards of an age are hardly likely to improve in war.

What the cavalry did often, the infantry would do with a sharper appetite when they got the chance. The taking of a town that had refused to surrender was universally recognized as an opportunity for unlimited plunder. Where a town had surrendered, where troops had been given terms specifically allowing them to march out with their possessions, honour contended, not always successfully, with indiscipline. No one was a greater stickler for the proprieties than Rupert. Yet after the surrender of Bristol he was unable to stop his own men from pillaging the Parliamentarians to whom he had granted safe conduct. Very few European states paid their troops punctually. Until they did, looting could hardly be brought within bounds.

The other long-remembered and deeply resented general infliction of the war was Free Quarter. There were no barracks to put the soldiers in. Some-times a castle, or in the case of a Parliamentary army, a cathedral could be pressed into service. But if nothing else was available the citizens might be called upon to provide board and lodging. Oxford was fortunate in possessing colleges and university buildings that could accommodate the Court and a good number of soldiers. Even this was not without its griefs. John Aubrey who went up to Trinity just as the civil war began wrote of the octogenarian head of his house:

> 'Tis probable this venerable Doctor might have lived some years longer, and finisht his Century, had not those civill warres come on; which much grieved him,

that was wont to be absolute in the colledge, to be affronted and disrespected by rude soldiers. I remember being at the Rhetorique Lecture in the hall; a foot soldier came in and brake his hower-glasse.

Since England had no system of public finance of the scale required, both sides at first attempted to pay for the war by 'voluntary' contributions (of which Clarendon speaks so euphorically in the passage recently quoted) and by sequestrating the estates of opponents. Neither side found these sources of revenue adequate. The King had at his disposal a wider range of traditional fiscal instruments than the Parliament. But at the crisis of the war Pym crowned his work by passing the Excise Ordinance – Parliament legislated by ordinance since a statute required the Royal Assent – which enabled it to impose a purchase tax on any commodities it liked. 'A hateful tax', fumed the High Tory Dr Johnson, defining it in his *Dictionary* more than a century later. It was a notable and permanent contribution to the art of war finance. Parliament's control of London and the bulk of the nations's commerce made such an expedient particularly valuable.

People who lived in parts of England whose control was disputed or which changed hands might find themselves dunned by both sides in turn. This bore particularly hard on farmers. Their produce and their animals might suffer double depredation, and the economic margins of a seventeenth-century economy were apt to be narrow at the best of times. Ruin must have been a common consequence for those so unfortunately placed. But the crudity and harshness of the system was often tempered by consideration and good sense. Juxon, Laud's especial protégé, who had succeeded him as President of St John's and was to attend Charles I on the scaffold, was Bishop of London at the outbreak of war. Unlike the archbishop he was renowned for the gentleness of his temper and the courtesy of his manners. So much was he liked and respected that he was allowed to live at his palace at Fulham throughout the civil war and was not even deprived of the temporalities of his see, that is, houses, lands and the revenue arising from them, until 1649. Juxon possessed tact of an exceptional order. In 1636 Charles had enraged anti-clerical opinion by making him Lord High Treasurer, an office that had not been held by a Churchman since the Reformation. As Fuller points out in his *Worthies*, 'few spake well of bishops at that time (and lord-treasurers at all times are liable to the complaints of a discontented people)'. Yet in spite of this, 'petitioners for money (when it was not to be had) departed well-pleased with his denials, they were *so civilly languaged*'.

Next to the population of those counties particularly exposed to the requisitions of armies, the section of society most immediately affected by the war was the educated class, that is, the lawyers and the clergymen. In both professions structure and operation was suddenly and drastically transformed. In the case of the lawyers it was to amount only to an interruption, but it was serious enough while it lasted. Clarendon, a future Lord Chancellor, records Parliament's ordinance late in 1642 forbidding the judges to go on assize and points to 'the example of judge Mallet, who . . . had been forcibly taken from the bench by a troop of horse'. He had in fact been drawing up a petition at

Maidstone assizes against Parliamentary control of the county militia. But in any case, as Clarendon goes on to point out, 'the records, upon which the legal proceedings were to be, were at London; and so the exercise of the law ceased throughout the kingdom, save only in some few counties, whither the king sent some judges of assize, and into others, his commission of oyer and terminer . . .' The difficulty was accidental, a derailment, as it were, of the regular train of the Common Law. No one, as yet, had suggested pulling up the tracks.

With the clergy it was a very different matter. The conflict between the Laudians and the Puritans was one of the central issues of the war. The Irish

Laud's dream. Pornographic detail and the imputation of atrocities lend spice to this vivid piece of propaganda against the archbishop

The Souldiers in their passage to York turn unto reformers pull down Popish pictures, break down rayles, turn altars into Tables

Parliamentary soldiers reforming the Laudian church

revolt invited Parliamentary propagandists to identify the archbishop and his policies as popery sailing under false colours. Few Laudians in Parliament territory were treated with the indulgence shown to Juxon. And Puritans, even a-political Puritans, in Royalist counties had a very thin time of it. On both sides they were ejected from their livings and often threatened with violence. Richard Baxter, according to his own account, only escaped lynching because he happened to be out for a walk when his churchwarden at Kidderminster was found attempting to comply with the Parliamentary order for the destruction of all images and statues of the Persons of the Trinity or of the Virgin Mary. A few days later when the King's Declaration (the Commission of Array) was read in the market place the 'violent country gentleman' who read it, 'seeing me pass the streets, stopped and said, "There goeth a traitor"'. Baxter retired to Gloucester but, with some courage, returned a month later. He 'found the beggarly drunken rout in a very tumultuating disposition' and left Kidderminster for the rest of the war, eventually serving for two years as a chaplain to Whalley's regiment in the New Model Army.

The experiences of the Royalist clergy were often equally unpleasant, and, as the war went against the King, more and more widespread and prolonged. But the social effects of the displacement and dispersal of a great part of the most educated and educating element of the nation were felt far outside the rectories and deaneries from which they were ejected. In the first place there was the actual fact of their being bundled out: the first great rent in the age-old fabric of society as it was known from one end of England to the other, not, like King and Parliament, mysterious, remote entities to the vast bulk of the population but everyday personifications of a familiar, established order of things. Foundations were shaken. And then there was the question of replacement. The old monopoly of the universities was challenged. Men would be found to preach and expound the Gospel whose formal education was small or non-existent but whose natural abilities might be formidable. A way was being opened to things as yet dimly descried but even in that state powerfully alarming or exhilarating, according to one's point of view. The process begun at the Reformation was being carried who knew how many steps further. The epigram in which the great lawyer, John Selden, the friend alike of the Parliamentary leaders and of Falkland and Clarendon, had summed up the first great convulsion was to prove its truth in the events he himself witnessed in the close of his long life: '*Scrutamini scripturas* [Search the scriptures]. These two words have undone the world.'

Archbishop Williams exchanges his mitre for a helmet

Just because the Church of England monopolized the supply and provided virtually the only market for higher education, the disruption of so many clerical careers was another fact of some importance. At the universities themselves some of those who had not yet taken holy orders fought in the Royalist army. John Dolben was to end his days as Archbishop of York, a city in whose defence he had been severely wounded only a few days after he had carried the standard at the battle of Marston Moor. William Beaw who was ninety when he died as Bishop of Llandaff in 1705 had left his Fellowship at New College to fight at Edgehill, taking twelve of his pupils and friends with him. He fought right through the war and, expelled from his Fellowship, earned his living as a colonel in the Russian service. Even the great William Chillingworth, author of *The Religion of Protestants*, that most powerful defence of the Anglican position against the Roman, and an admired member of the Great Tew circle, turned from theology to experimenting with bombs. Archbishop Williams of York, who had been so bitter an opponent of Laud as to seem at one time an ally of the Parliamentary opposition, had, somewhat surprisingly, assumed a quasi-military position at Conway where he endeavoured to secure the passage of English troops from Ireland for the King.

But it is not in such direct contributions to the Royalist war effort that the upsetting of the clerical hive produced its most conspicuous results. The idea of the Church, in its higher echelons at least, as the natural, the only, career open to the scholar had still a couple of centuries' life left in it.

> Make me, O Sphere-descended Queen,
> A bishop, or at least a Dean

wrote a precocious Winchester schoolboy as late as 1800 in an ode on the Progress of Learning. But the turning out of doors of a great part of the nation's educated talent did shift the learned world away from the strictly clerical. Many of the great intellectual lights of the age that succeeded the civil war and the Protectorate were, as they always had been, bishops, deans, clerical heads of Oxford or Cambridge colleges. But many were not: Isaac Newton and Christopher Wren, to take but two instances. It is true that there were plenty of educated laymen before the civil war: one has only to think of circles such as those of Selden or Falkland. But the identification of the leading clergy with the world of learning was close and natural. Looking at a clerical *corps d'élite*, the dean and chapter of St George's Chapel in Windsor Castle, who were ejected at the very beginning of the war, one can see how wide such a body stretched their net. The dean, Christopher Wren, who refused to give up

the keys of his chapel to the Roundhead captain sent to secure the castle, was the father of the greatest bearer of his name and the brother of one of the most hated and intransigent Laudian bishops, Matthew Wren. Among his twelve canons was another bishop, Godfrey Goodman, Bishop of Gloucester, who had been chaplain to the King's mother, and who made no secret of his agreement with the Church of Rome on many matters that made Puritan hair stand on end. Prynne had petitioned against him for adorning the town cross at Windsor with a crucifix. Laud deeply disapproved of his independence and

Dobson's painting of Prince Rupert with Colonel William Murray and Colonel John Russell, probably painted at Oxford about 1644, is traditionally said to represent Rupert's and Murray's success in persuading Russell to renew the commission which he had decided to resign

had prevailed on Charles I to reverse his translation to the richer see of Hereford after Goodman had moved his furniture into the Bishop's palace. Of the other canons three were Fellows of Eton and one was vice-provost, two had been *habitués* of Great Tew, four were Royal chaplains, most had been Fellows of Oxford or Cambridge colleges and one had been Regius Professor of Greek. One, as we have already seen, was the neighbour and friend of John Hampden. The ejection of such a body may suggest something of the changes that could be felt and seen under the first impact of the civil war.

That prices should rise, that labour should become scarcer will come as no surprise to a twentieth-century reader. The nominal pay of a foot soldier on both sides may be taken as roughly equivalent to that of a farm labourer – a generalization that it would be impossible to defend in detail since pay rates varied at different times and in different units during the war, and agricultural labourers then and much later earned different wages in different parts of the country. Dragoons and cavalrymen were paid, in theory at least, much higher rates to cover the keep of horse and equipment. Whatever else, this must have meant that wages and prospects of employment tended to improve. As for commodities the interruption of trade and the demand of the soldiers naturally made goods scarcer and prices higher. But except for the cutting off of London's coal supply for the greater part of the war while Newcastle was in Royalist hands, shortages and substitutes did not, in contrast to the two wars of our century, make more than a local and temporary impression. Clarendon describes with some amusement the arrival of the Parliamentary Commissioners at Oxford in February 1643:

> These commissioners brought with them a great quantity of provisions, even of bread and beer, as well as of beef and mutton and fowl, sufficient to feed the whole company that came with them, during such time as they believed they should stay there; of which they were ashamed as soon as they entered Oxford, and saw the great plenty in the markets, not only of the usual common fare, but of those choice fowl, of pheasants, partridge, cocks, snipes, in that abundance as they were not so well furnished in London; besides the best fish and wild fowl, which was brought in every day, from the western part, in such plenty that it can hardly be imagined.

Such Pickwickian abundance was, even in peacetime, only for the well-to-do. And the Oxford that Clarendon was describing was not under siege. The presence of the Court attracted the luxury trades. The artist, William Dobson, whose portraits are among the most accomplished ever painted by a native Englishman, found plenty of commissions there.

The hardships endured by the people of England as a result of the civil war were nothing in comparison to the famine, the devastation and the plague that the Thirty Years War brought to their contemporaries in Germany. In some ways indeed the civil war actually improved the quality of life for common people. It greatly enlarged opportunities of employment. It offered to the young, the adventurous and the ambitious an exciting prospect of continuing and growing change. It brought public affairs within the reach of anyone who cared to listen or had learned to read.

The propaganda battles of the civil war are the seed-bed of the national

Mercurius Rusticus, the Royalist newspaper. The scenes depict Parliamentary misdemeanours or humiliations in the opening days of the war

press. Both sides began to publish newspapers early in 1643. The word 'journalist' was not to appear in the language until 1665 but the phenomenon so described had already made a brilliant début. Sir John Berkenhead, the Royalist editor, was, says Aubrey, 'exceedingly bold, confident, witty, not very grateful to his benefactors; would Lye damnably'. Could Lord Copper himself have asked for more? His antagonist, Marchamont Nedham, was worthy of his steel. Besides the newspapers, pamphlets poured from the press, no longer inhibited by fear of Star Chamber, so that the literate Londoner was better equipped than any of his forebears to understand and take part in the great controversies of his day. Overt Royalism was obviously dangerous. But no Government, not even Cromwell's with its highly efficient intelligence and counter-intelligence service, could put a stop to the printing and circulation of opinions it objected to.

By far the most popular and effective of political media on the Parliamentary side was the pulpit. Here the Royalists being, so to speak, a People of the Book were at a disadvantage. But those who had substituted extempore prayer for the ordered liturgy, who gave the sermon pride of place in all acts of public worship, had an instrument denied to their opponents. At the highest level of policy making it could be used to prepare the public mind for the latest manoeuvre, as Professor Trevor-Roper has so clearly demonstrated in his essay on the sermons preached before the Long Parliament on the officially appointed Fast Days. But over a far wider field it enabled the unlettered to formulate and express their political and religious opinions. In the Parliamentary armies, particularly in the Eastern Association from which Cromwell was to fashion the New Model, officers and soldiers were often preachers: and often their chaplains were men of advanced radical opinions in Church and State. Herein lay the ferment that was to turn rebellion into revolution. This was far from being a merely military experience. In every town and village where Parliamentary sympathies prevailed, the frequency and promiscuity of preaching changed the pattern of life.

No survey of the impact of the civil war, however cursory, could leave out of account those who either were or wished to be neutral. At the outbreak of the war there were serious and prolonged attempts by the gentry in parts of England as far divided as Yorkshire and Devon to devise some kind of non-aggression pact that would keep the war at a distance. There were noblemen whose chief anxiety was not to run into any kind of danger. Clarendon says scornfully of the Earls of Salisbury and of Pembroke, 'that though they wished they [i.e. the Parliamentarians] might rather be destroyed than the King, they had rather the King and his posterity be destroyed, than that Wilton should be taken from the one of them, or Hatfield from the other; the preservation of both which from any danger they both believed to be the highest point of prudence and politic circumspection'. The Earl of Arundel, the great connoisseur who had commanded the King's army in the First Bishops' War, had withdrawn to Italy well before the raising of the standard at Nottingham. The same acid judge observed that Arundel 'had no other affection for the nation or the kingdom, than as he had a great share in it, in which, like the great leviathan, he might sport himself'.

The clerical journalist who produced Mercurius Rusticus, Bruno Ryves. At the Restoration he was rewarded with the deanery of Windsor

On the other side Lucy Hutchinson, equally contemptuous of 'a man of great wealth and dependancies' who clung to his neutrality, tells the cautionary tale of the Earl of Kingston. Called on by an emissary of the Parliamentary Committee to declare himself he did so in the most solemn manner:

> 'When,' said he, 'I take armes with the King against the Parliament, or with the Parliament against the King, let a Cannon Bullett divide me betweene them.' Which God was pleas'd to bring to passe a few months after; for he, going into Gainsborough and there taking armes for the King, was surpriz'd by my Lord Willoughby and, after a handsome defence of himselfe, yielded, and was put prisoner into a pinnace and sent downe the river to Hull, when my Lord Newcastle's Armie marching allong the shore shot at the pinnace, and being in danger the Earle of Kingston went up upon the decks to shew himselfe and to prevaile with them to forbeare shooting, but as soon as he appear'd a Cannon bullett flew from the King's Armie and devided him in the middle, being then in the Parliament's pinnace, who perished according to his owne unhappie imprecation.

To stand neutral was, in a person of consequence, considered an evasion of responsibility. A magnate or a member of Parliament owed it to his country to make up his mind and, having made it up, to serve the cause he had chosen. But it was not thought discreditable to withdraw, like a batsman retiring hurt, before the innings was closed. Denzil Holles, one of the five members whom Charles had tried to arrest and a veteran leader of the Parliamentary opposition, had raised his own regiment and had commanded it with distinguished courage at Edgehill and against Rupert at Brentford. Yet early in 1643 he withdrew from the army and spoke and voted thenceforward with the peace party in the Commons. Late in the war a Royalist turncoat anxious to curry favour with his new friends accused Holles of collusion with the King when sent as a Parliamentary Commissioner to treat for peace. Even then he was cleared by vote of the House of Commons. Clarendon makes the distinction plain in the following judgment of the Earl of Chandos, so very different from the verdicts passed on his brethren of Arundel, Pembroke and Salisbury:

> [He] was a young man of spirit and courage; and had for two years served the King very bravely in the head of a regiment of horse, which himself had raised at his own charge; but had lately, out of pure weariness of the fatigue, and having spent most of his money, and without any diminution of affection, left the King, under pretence of travel; but making London his way, he gave himself up to the pleasures of that place; which he enjoyed, without considering the issue of the war, or shewing any inclination to the parliament . . .

The neutrality of those who, not being members of the political nation, did not consider themselves to be involved was a different matter. It might be violated under the necessities of war; men might be conscribed against their will to make good the casualties and desertions of some attenuated regiment; but no one censured them for their lack of enthusiasm in not volunteering in the first place. Their moral right to contract out was recognized if not always respected.

Nor was it considered in any way disgraceful for the common soldiers to re-enlist in the opposing army on the morrow of a lost battle. After Edgehill the Parliamentary garrison at Banbury, surrendering to the King's much superior force, supplied him with a good number of recruits. In the later stages of the war when it was the King's turn to suffer defeats exactly the same thing happened. Fairfax remarked that the Royalist foot were the best troops that he ever commanded.

What would never be tolerated was any attempt to assert the right of neutrality by force. Towards the end of the war the farmers and country people of the West, exasperated by the exactions of both sides, began to form a movement known as the Clubmen with just such a purpose in view. The Parliament by then had victory almost within its grasp. The Royalists, too

The gardens of Wilton – seat of the Earl of Pembroke – on which so much care and money had been lavished. The exquisite formality then in fashion lends point to Marvell's military imagery: 'When gardens only had their towers, And all the garrisons were flowers . . .'

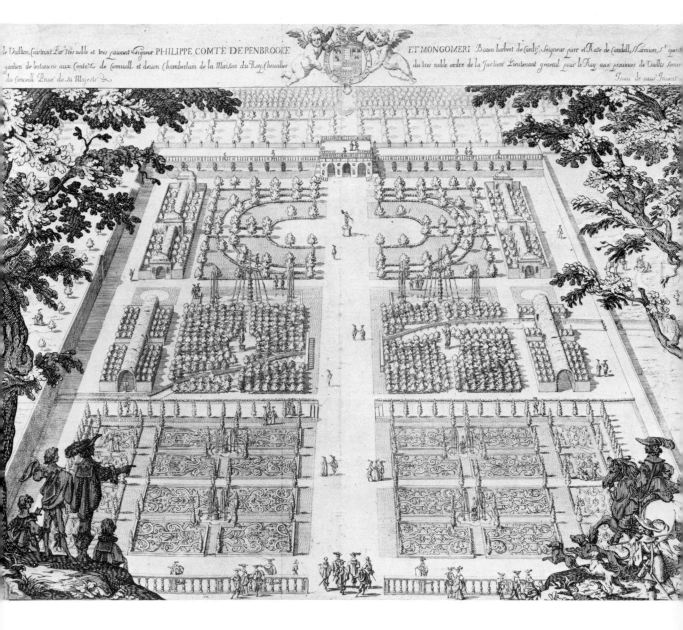

hard pressed to neglect any expedient, attempted with some success to influence the movement in their favour. But the intolerable conduct of what Clarendon called 'a dissolute, undisciplined, wicked, beaten army' swung them to the Parliamentary side. Nonetheless Cromwell had in the end to scatter them at Hod Hill. The Parliament would soon have enough to do to control its armed forces without permitting the growth of any rivals.

Chapter 11

The Scots and
the Eastern Association
Turn the Scales

When the King broke up the siege of Gloucester the general position of the Royalists still looked highly favourable. Charles with his main army, now rejoined by Rupert's horse, was between Essex and the capital. In the North, Newcastle had overrun Lincolnshire and appeared to be threatening the Eastern Association. In the West Prince Maurice had taken Exeter and had even inflicted some losses on the ships that the Parliament had relied on to maintain the city's resistance. But Exeter, unlike Hull and Plymouth, was not a deep-water port offering safe anchorage at all states of the tide. As a further consequence of the victories in the West many of the towns and strongholds of the near South and Southwest, Hampshire, Wiltshire and Sussex, had passed into Royalist control.

There were, however, disquieting signs of what was to come. The successes that had culminated in the taking of Bristol had been dear bought. The Cornish foot, the real battle winners, had suffered heavy casualties. Worst of all they had lost, except for Hopton, the outstanding leaders who alone could manage so fiery a fighting force. Like all units whose strength lay in the fierceness of their local patriotism, the further their victories took them from home the less could they be relied on. Cornwall was a long way from Bristol for a man who could not write or receive letters and had no means for allotting his pay, even supposing it were not months in arrears, to the wife and children he had left behind. And what about their jobs, their smallholdings, their every day-to-day concern? Matters were not made better by the characteristic and public squabbling of the High Command. On the capture of Bristol the Marquis of Hertford had appointed Hopton governor of the city. Rupert, however, had other views and had written to the King asking for the appointment himself. This Charles had immediately granted in ignorance of what Hertford had already done. Had anyone less disciplined and unselfish than Hopton been concerned this imbroglio might have had serious consequences. As it was, the King felt it necessary to go to Bristol in person and settled the matter by allowing Rupert to retain the title on the clear understanding that Hopton was to be lieutenant governor with full enjoyment of the authority, privileges and rewards of the governorship. To avoid similar collisions Hertford was invited to attend on the King as one of his Council, a function he was by temperament and ability much fitter to discharge than that of a commander in the field.

The army with which Charles manoeuvred to intercept Essex was, in the matter of infantry, not therefore that of the spring and summer. In the middle of September 1643 he brought Essex to battle on terms very similar to Edgehill eleven months earlier. Once again the forces were about equal in number, once again the Royalists had proportionately more and better cavalry and rather less foot, once again the King held both the strategic and tactical advantages of being astride his opponents' line of communication and of having been able to choose his ground. He even had adequate artillery. But this time it was the Parliamentarians who had decidedly the better of a drawn battle. They took advantage of features the Royalists had neglected and skilfully used the lanes and hedges to minimize the potentialities of cavalry action. Unable to charge, the Royalist horse suffered severely and, poorly supported by their foot, achieved no proportionate gain. Essex's army marched on to Reading and London in good order and good heart.

The first battle of Newbury, as this action is called to distinguish it from another fought just over a year later, claimed some notable victims on the Royalist side. One in particular demands to be recorded in Clarendon's imperishable words:

> . . . a loss which no time will suffer to be forgotten, and no success or good fortune could repair. In this unhappy battle was slain the lord viscount Falkland; a person of such prodigious parts of learning and knowledge, of that inimitable sweetness and delight in conversation, of so flowing and obliging a humanity and goodness to mankind, and of that primitive simplicity and integrity of life, that if there were no other brand upon this odious and accursed civil war than that single loss, it must be most infamous and execrable to all posterity.

The elogy that Clarendon goes on to pronounce is one of the most famous in English literature. The loss he felt was that of his dearest friend. But the loss to the cause of moderate and intelligent Royalism was not less sharp. It was not that the King was particularly inclined to listen to Falkland or felt any special ease or intimacy in his company. Rather the reverse. Clarendon himself clearly enjoyed in a much higher degree both his trust and his affection. But the very fact that Charles kept such a man, to whom he was not personally close, in such a position did set some limits to what Rupert or the Queen, his politically disastrous intimates, might prevail on him to attempt. The replacement of Falkland as Secretary of State by the egregious Earl of Bristol weakened the forces of wisdom in the royal councils.

Contemporaries and historians have compared the loss of Falkland at Newbury to that of John Hampden at Chalgrove Field. Early in the summer of 1643 a brave and talented but totally unscrupulous Scotch professional soldier, John Urry, arrived in Oxford with a great deal of valuable intelligence about the disposition and movements of the Parliamentary army he had just deserted. In particular he brought news of a Parliamentary pay train that was shortly to pass over the Chilterns with urgently needed money for the armies of Essex and Waller and he was able to pinpoint the quarters of all the troops between Oxford and Stokenchurch where it was hoped to surprise the convoy as it came down the hill towards Lewknor. The code of honour that permitted a gentleman to betray such a trust is not easily intelligible, but Charles I who could be fastidious enough in such matters found no difficulty in immediately knighting Urry and giving him a command in the party of horse with which Rupert at once set off to capture the enemy treasure. With inexcusable carelessness the Parliamentary commanders had made no change in the disposition of their forces and had ordered no alert, though Urry, perhaps to satisfy military punctilio, had not attempted to disguise the fact that he had gone over to the other side. Rupert achieved complete surprise, slaughtering a good number of troopers in their beds. He raided deep into Parliamentary territory with impunity and success, except that the pay train did not come his way. As he was returning to Oxford with a rich booty of captured arms and horses he ran into a party of Parliamentary troops who tried to cut him off from his line of retreat across the Thame at Chiselhampton where his advance party had already secured the bridge. In a sharp skirmish outside the village of Chalgrove Rupert routed the inexperienced Parliamentary cavalry although they outnumbered him. But they were supported by a foot regiment commanded by John Hampden who put up a stiff fight until he was badly wounded in the shoulder. As he rode off the field towards Thame the Royalists noted that his head hung down, though legend has it that he turned to look towards the hills where his fine estate lay a few miles away. He died a few days later in Thame, after great suffering. Clarendon in relating the incident exults over the death of so formidable an enemy but Sir Philip Warwick, a reliable and well-placed witness, tells us that when the King heard of Hampden's wound he wanted to send his own surgeon to him at Thame.

By the end of 1643 the impetus of the war is beginning to take charge. Of the men who wanted or who could have attempted negotiation Falkland, Hampden and Pym were dead. The influence of Clarendon on the Royalist side sank as that of Rupert rose. Holles and the peace party at Westminster had been weakened by the defection of six peers to the King at Oxford. The Covenant and the Scots army not only strengthened the war party: they added a new and dangerous complication – foreign intervention. The adventurers, the extremists and the revolutionaries each had their hand strengthened. The moderates were the universal losers. Nonetheless they still at this point occupied the chief positions. On the Royalist side nobles such as Hertford and Newcastle had military commands or political influence that not even the Queen or Rupert could override. In the Parliamentary army the principal commands were still held by Essex and Manchester, men of much the same outlook as their two opponents just mentioned. In Parliament itself Pym had outmanoeuvred the earliest avowed leader of an anti-monarchical party, Henry Marten, and had had him sent to the Tower. A year later things were to look very different. On the Royalist side Rupert was to appear a moderate compared with reckless adventurers like Wilmot and Goring who seemed to accept no political and little military limitation on their activities. Wilmot indeed had gone too far and had lost his command. But the transformation of the Parliament and its army had been even more complete. Cromwell and the younger Vane had come into their own.

Besides the Scottish alliance and the relief of Gloucester, the year 1643 brought one more great boon to the hard-pressed Parliament: the development of the Eastern Association into a military force from which the New Model Army was to issue. Every writer on this subject will, for a long time, stand in debt to Dr Clive Holmes's seminal work to which a crude summary

Henry Marten, wit, republican and regicide. His luxurious and far from strict private life was the cause of great scandal to the Puritans and had earlier alienated him from the King

can hardly do justice. The core of the Association was formed by Essex, Cambridgeshire and Suffolk. Norfolk at first was tepid in its enthusiasm for the Parliamentary cause: there were strong Royalist elements and, in the early days of the war, an overwhelming desire to maintain the unity and the peace of the county against the political divisions of the nation. But the facts of geography reinforced by the energy of East Anglian Parliamentary leadership, particularly that displayed by the Earl of Warwick, his son-in-law Manchester, and the whole nexus of family and business connections institutionalized in the Providence Island and Massachusetts Bay Companies turned the scale. The Mountagu family, of which Manchester was the head, dominated Huntingdon. Hertfordshire was an early recruit to the Association though it sent no representatives to the meeting at Bury St Edmunds in February 1643 at which the first attempts were made to consolidate the Association from a limited local defence arrangement between neighbouring counties into a more positive, even aggressive, military organization. Sealed off from any contact with Royalism it was inevitable that Norfolk should be absorbed.

From the first the Eastern Association bore the impress of Warwick's style, combining ideological combativeness with an undoctrinaire concern for military necessities. Although Warwick himself was called almost at once to exercise his talent for war as Lord Admiral (the title was in fact conferred on him by a vote of both Houses on 7 December 1643 in recognition of his effective discharge of the functions belonging to the post since the beginning of the war), his early insistence on professional military competence in the officers and on the necessity of securing the means of paying and equipping the troops were fully understood by his colleagues and successors. No one had grasped them quicker than Oliver Cromwell, the restless, intense Huntingdon squire whose elemental force of personality had made so deep an impression on a young Court dandy. In the regiment that he raised for the Association his own troop was equipped by the central Parliamentary treasury and the other four by the funds of the Association. Contemporaries noted that as his discipline was stricter so were his men better armed and better mounted than the common run. Many of them rode their own horses or had helped themselves from the stables of Royalists. In tastes and prejudices a typical country gentleman of the early seventeenth century, he knew and loved horses. Towards their riders his attitude displayed the same robust acceptance of conventional wisdom, scorning the 'decayed serving-men and tapsters' who, in his view, had been too indiscriminately enlisted into the Parliamentary army. Ideally he would have liked to command a regiment officered by gentlemen and recruited from the young sons of freeholders, self-respecting, independent, habituated to an active life. But behind the contortions of his public utterance, sometimes stuttering into passionate incoherence, sometimes luxuriating in the easy rhythms of contemporary Biblical cant, was a hard, lean realism unequalled in English history. If he could not get them, he would make do without.

A siege helmet (TOP) *and a lobster-tail helmet*

I had rather a plain russet-coated captain that knows what he fights for and loves what he knows than that which you call 'a gentleman' and is nothing else. I honour a gentleman that is so indeed . . . It may be it provokes some spirits to see

Sir Thomas Fairfax. This lead bust by an unknown artist is by far the most striking portrait of the great commander

such plain men made captains of horse. It had been well that men of honour and birth had entered into these employments – but why do they not appear? But seeing it was necessary the work must go on, better plain men than none.

Cromwell's political and social utterances are not often so crystalline in their clarity or so entire in their candour. Like Charles I he was a man of profound personal religion, personal in the sense that the conviction was neither painless nor secondhand. Like Charles I, and most serious-minded contemporaries, he saw history as the gradual unfolding of God's inscrutable purposes. His politics, like the King's, derived from his religion. Richard Baxter who incurred his severe displeasure by declining his offer of a regimental chaplaincy records that: 'He had a special care to get religious men into his troop; these men were of greater understanding than common soldiers . . . and making . . . that which they took for public felicity to be their end, they were the more engaged to be valiant.' Cromwell's regiment from its beginnings thus manifested the characteristic qualities of the Eastern Association: a superiority of men and material backed by a strong individual commitment to the cause for which the war was being fought. Would Essex and Waller, one wonders, have passed Colonel Cromwell's selection board? Did they know what they fought for and love what they knew? The phrase suggests a more whole-hearted enthusiasm, a fundamentalist readiness to smite their opponents hip and thigh, a less critical approach to the validity of solving political difficulties by killing one's fellow countrymen than one can detect in those two high-minded and sincere servants of the Parliament. Certainly neither of them encouraged among their own troops the ideological ejaculations that became so marked a feature of the Eastern Association.

In the first half of 1643 the differences between the Association on the one hand and Parliament and its main army under Essex on the other were not merely doctrinal. The counties of the Eastern Association were paying for their army: was it reasonable or practical to expect them to contribute to that of Essex? There were, as Dr Holmes shows, frequent conflicts of jurisdiction between the general requisitioning powers of the commander-in-chief and those of the County Committees of the Association. Parliament at Westminster was in any case increasingly suspicious of the local and defensive nature of the Association. The tide turned with Newcastle's advance into Lincolnshire in the summer, at the very moment when the efforts of the central Parliamentary organization were concentrated on relieving Gloucester. The only hope of checking Newcastle was the army of the Eastern Association. So desperate was the situation for the Parliament, so confident the Royalists that even in Norfolk the King's party rose and seized King's Lynn. Had Newcastle struck across the Wash and supported them he would have obtained a harbour of great strategic value. Instead he decided to break the power of the Fairfaxes by reducing Hull into which they had retreated with the remains of their army. It was one of the worst military blunders of the war. Hull was much too tough a nut to crack and Sir Thomas Fairfax much too enterprising and inspiring a commander to sit tamely behind the fortifications. Newcastle's army was discomfited by frequent sallies and ultimately balked by the flooding of their siege works. Meanwhile Fairfax had used the Parliament's command of the sea to ship most of his cavalry across the Humber. When the gallant Royalists of King's Lynn had been forced to surrender and Newcastle was making no headway with the siege, he himself crossed the river and, joining forces with the Eastern Association, defeated the Lincolnshire Royalists at Winceby, near Horncastle, on the southern edge of the wolds. On the same day, 11 October 1643, his father, Ferdinando, Lord Fairfax, led a sortie against Newcastle's forces outside Hull that finally decided him to break up the siege.

Winceby was a landmark in the history of the war. It was the first battle in which Fairfax and Cromwell fought together, though they did so only in the sense of being present on the same field. Cromwell as a Colonel of Horse was in any case subordinate to Manchester, to whom the chief credit for the victory was given by contemporaries. Cromwell's horse was in fact shot under him early in the fight and it is difficult to see on what ground, other than his subsequent performance, he can be supposed to have had much share in the direction of the battle. But it was also the first action in which the Parliamentary horse had routed Royalist cavalry, and for that, as a trainer of troops and as a fighting leader, Cromwell certainly deserves recognition. What cannot be doubted is that Winceby transformed the position of the Eastern Association. It had re-established for the Parliament the whole position in the Eastern Midlands. In return it was put on a sound financial footing and by an Ordinance of 20 January 1644 Manchester was entrusted with its central military and

This print of the Parliamentary commanders dating from the end of the first civil war shows how minor was Cromwell's standing at the time

The Portraturs of the Comanders in Cheife of the Parlyments Forces by Sea and Land

Sr Tho: Fairfax Gen: of
the Army and Cunstable
of the Tower of London

Lord Fairfax

Ma: Gen: Skipon

Leivt: Gen: Cromwell

Robt El of Essex late Gen:
of the Parliamt Army

El of Warwick Admi-
rall of the Narrow Seas

Alex: Lasley
Gen: of the Scots

Earle of
Manchester

Printed & sould by P. Stent

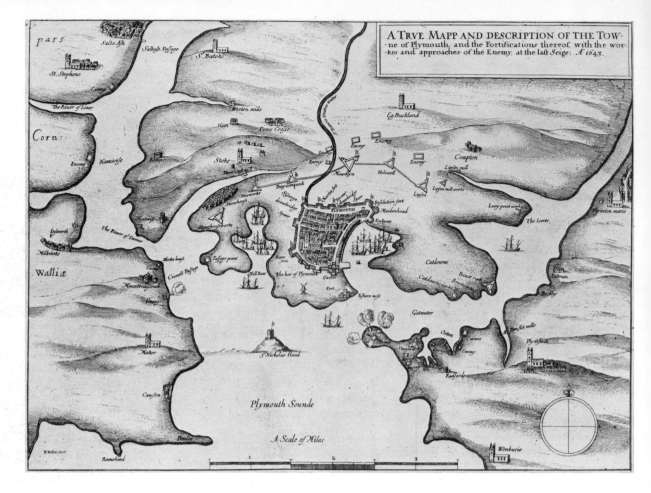

Plymouth during the siege of 1643. Without control of the sea, the city, already all but encircled, would have had no hope

financial control. Few decisions in the whole course of the war paid such rapid and substantial dividends.

If the victory at Winceby and the imminent appearance in the field of a large Scotch army had put Parliament in a position to go over to the offensive in the North, the initiative in the West still lay with the Royalists. After the surrender of Exeter the only bases left to the Parliament in the Southwest were Plymouth and Lyme. And Plymouth throughout the autumn and early winter was closely besieged by Prince Maurice. Both here and at Hull there had been a plot to betray the place. In both cases it had been sea-power that had enabled Parliament to retain control and to bring the commanders responsible, in the case of Hull the governor, Sir John Hotham, and his son, to London for trial and execution. Hull had set a pattern that even the dullest could recognize. If Newcastle had felt himself free to press on southward, reinforcing himself with the Royalists in Lincolnshire and the counties under Parliamentary control as he went along, could even the Eastern Association have stopped him? It was a question that Warwick had made sure was not to be put to the proof. Parliament recognized the correctness of his judgment by accepting his demand for a vast increase in effective naval strength. The Winter Guard for 1643–4 was to consist of twenty-two warships and twenty-four armed merchantmen as against a bare half-dozen of each for the preceding winter. The Southwest was only one of the claimants for a share of sea-power. The port of Newcastle had still to be blockaded until the Scots took it the following October; the threat of Royalist sea-power based on Bristol had to be met; the danger that Ireland might be brought in with its limitless supply of troops could only be countered by control of the sea passages, a control that by the end of 1643 had been partly lost.

Nevertheless, it was in the Southwest that the war-winning quality of Warwick's strategy was most signally demonstrated. Plymouth was so effectively supported from the sea that just before Christmas Maurice raised the siege. Following on the King's failure at Gloucester this was hardly a tonic for drooping spirits. In April 1644 he appeared before the little town of Lyme, a steep, awkward place but undefended by anything more formidable than turf ramparts and blockhouses and garrisoned by a mere five hundred soldiers against his own five thousand and a train of artillery. Inside, however, was the only military leader produced by either side whose claim to genius can hardly be contested. Nelson, no unqualified judge in such matters and never inclined by modesty, false or otherwise, to undervalue himself in comparison with others, has left his opinion on record: 'I do not reckon myself equal to Blake.' The great admiral of the Commonwealth and Protectorate who was to lead English fleets to victory against the Dutch, till then the greatest naval power of the century, and against the Spaniards and who was to lay the foundation of England's three centuries of power in the Mediterranean was then a colonel in the army. As a captain at the storming of Bristol he had distinguished himself by a vigorous defence. Once again at Taunton he was to show what can be done by holding on against vastly superior odds and with little prospect of relief. But his achievement at Lyme, glorious as it was as a feat of arms, outstanding as an example of leadership, since it was not only soldiers or sailors but a civil population that he contrived to inspire, would not have been possible without the vigorous and enterprising support of the navy. In the very first assault two Parliament ships over the horizon beyond Portland heard the furious cannonading of Maurice's guns and altered course for Lyme, arriving just in time to replenish the garrison's supply of match and bullet and to land some seamen to help in the defence. Food and reinforcements came at timely intervals culminating in the appearance of the Lord High Admiral himself at the head of a powerful squadron. The failure to take what Clarendon scornfully describes as 'a little vile fishing town, defended by a small dry ditch' drove Maurice to a constant succession of heavy attacks. His own reputation was at stake. It became increasingly clear that he was going to lose it. At last on 14 June, after forty-six days' close siege in which he had lost well over a thousand men, Maurice drew off. He had certainly heard that Essex, in a military blunder as disastrous as his own, had decided to disregard his orders and march to the relief of Lyme. But a deserter from his army had already told Blake that he was preparing to abandon the siege. It had so weakened his force that he was now no longer able to carry out the plan of joining the King,

A detail from a Dutch engraving of an engagement between Blake and Tromp in May 1652

who was on the march to the west of Oxford, and had to retire to Exeter.

The year had begun badly for the Royalists. In Cheshire where Sir William Brereton had managed to maintain a nimble Parliamentary force in a county largely Royalist, Byron, John Hutchinson's Royalist cousin, had been given an army sufficient to deal with him. This was the more important because the Cessation, as the truce in Ireland was called, that the King's Lord Deputy, Ormonde, had negotiated with the rebels in September 1643 liberated a number of English regiments who could be shipped across the Irish Channel. Byron had Brereton's small force shut up in Nantwich and all but at his mercy, a quality conspicuous by its absence in his conduct of this campaign, when Fairfax marched to the relief with a ragged, starving, job lot of troops. His skill, Byron's ineptitude and a fortunate cloudburst enabled him to inflict a crushing defeat. This was at the end of January. Two months later Waller at last won an outright victory against his old friend Hopton at Cheriton near Alresford in Hampshire. Alarmed at the possibility of being cooped up in Oxford by superior forces the King decided to call in some of the garrisons such as Abingdon and Reading that protected it so that he would have troops enough for a field army. Oxford was strongly defended and could be left to take care of itself. But before setting out he appointed Rupert his lieutenant-general with headquarters at Shrewsbury. Come what might, the Welsh recruiting grounds and the route to Ireland must be made sure.

Hardly had Rupert arrived at the seat of his new command before he received an urgent summons to relieve the hard-pressed garrison at Newark. Winceby and Newcastle's discomfiture before Hull had put the Parliament on top at the crossroads of England where North and Midlands meet. If Newark fell the way would be open for direct communication with Scotland. At the head of an army a good deal smaller than the Parliamentary forces outside Newark Rupert marched with his usual speed and manoeuvred with even more than his usual brilliance so that the town was not only relieved but the besieging army forced to surrender at negligible cost. As so often, many of the losing side re-enlisted under the winner and the whole armament of a well-found body of some seven thousand men fell to the Royalists. Coming at about the same time as the news of their defeat at Cheriton this elegant victory did a great deal to cheer them up.

Suddenly the clouds began to part for the Royalists. The Scotch invasion had not destroyed their whole position in the North. The city of Newcastle, far from falling an easy prey as in the Bishops' War, had beaten them off and Sir Marmaduke Langdale, head of an old Yorkshire recusant family, had surprised their quarters at Corbridge in a highly successful cavalry raid. When Rupert returned from Newark to his proper sphere of activities in the Northwest, he captured a string of towns, Stockport, Bolton and Liverpool. His brother's endeavours at Lyme were not, as we have seen, equally attended with success. Still, considering the size and number of the armies ranged against them the Royalists were not doing badly. Even better things might be expected from the disarray of the Parliamentary high command. Essex, bitterly resentful of the financial arrangements made with Manchester, jealous of the popularity and reputation of Sir William Waller, would not obey orders to combine with them and plunged off westward, first to the relief of Lyme and then to Plymouth which was perfectly well able to defend itself without his assistance.

This was an unlooked-for boon. Charles had expected to spend the summer playing hide-and-seek along the Severn valley, avoiding action with an army that far outnumbered him and yet keeping close enough to Bristol to threaten any who threatened it. Now with Essex out of the way he had no reason to decline action if it were offered. It soon was. Waller, shadowing the King's army along the opposite bank of the Cherwell near Banbury, saw a chance for a quick stroke dividing an opponent who had let his order of march extend too loosely. But the Royalist commander, too, showed initiative and quickness of eye in restoring the situation and emerged undoubted victor from the confused set of skirmishes collectively known as the battle of Cropredy Bridge. It would not normally have been more than a nuisance to the losing side. But Waller's army was on the verge of disintegration through lack of pay and general weariness of the war. A victory might have held them together for a few more weeks. As it was they deserted in droves. On his return to London their unlucky commander pointed out in forceful language to the Committee of Both Kingdoms (the body that had been created to co-ordinate the Scotch and English conduct of the war) that an army composed of local levies, trained bands and other such flotsam and jetsam simply would not do. 'Till you have an army merely your own that you may command, it is in a manner impossible to do anything of importance.'

The army of the Eastern Association offered the pattern on which such a force might be built. After Rupert's stunning blow at Newark, Lincolnshire had again passed under Royalist control. Manchester and his army reconquered it, storming Lincoln early in May, and moving on to join the Fairfaxes and the Scots at the great siege of York. The Earl of Newcastle had fallen back on the northern capital in the middle of April not so much because of the direct pressure of the Scottish army, of which, as Clarendon gleefully points out, he got the better in several actions but because the Fairfaxes were operating in his rear. The two armies made several attempts on the city but made no impression. But no large inland town, even if well provisioned as York was, can hold out indefinitely. The King would either have to send an army to its relief or lose the North for good. For this reason a concentration of the three Parliamentary armies was prudent.

So intellectual a soldier as Rupert could be counted on to foresee and to analyse so logical a development. And he must also have known that to him must fall the task of relieving York, supported by whatever other forces the Royalists could muster in the North. Newcastle had sent most of his cavalry out of the city before the siege was formed so that the Prince had in addition to his own the horse commanded by Goring and Sir Marmaduke Langdale, both of them cavalry generals of proved quality. In spite of the reputation for recklessness and mere bravado that his detractors, contemporary and post-humous, have tried to fasten on him – a misrepresentation that convinces the more easily through his fearlessness and dash on the field of battle – Rupert was a strategist. The entrance of the Scots had made the Irish counterweight an object to be secured at any cost short of endangering the main Royalist

position in the North and West. This was what he was engaged on in Lancashire. As soon as that had been attended to he would concert his plans for the relief of York and, as at Newark, turn a defensive necessity into an opportunity for attack. No one, friend or foe, could question Rupert's readiness to strike when the time was ripe. What is sometimes forgotten is that he had

The Earl of Newcastle accepts
the genuflexion of his horses

restrained the King from premature offensive action with inadequate forces
that very spring.

It is in the light of this that we must consider a letter from the King to his
nephew. It was written on 14 June in great distress and agitation. The Queen,
whom Parliament had lately impeached for High Treason, had been sent for

safety to Exeter. She was on the point of giving birth to a daughter and her pregnancies, always difficult, seem to have lost nothing in the telling. To the appalling symptoms that Sir Theodore Mayerne, courteously abandoning his London consultancy to attend his old patient, dismissed as hysterical were added the fears of what she might be subjected to if she fell into the hands of Parliament. And with Essex between her and the King's none-too-powerful army, with Warwick's frigates patrolling the Channel, was not this all too possible? It was not until a few days later that the King suddenly recognized Essex's division of the main Parliamentary army for a heaven-sent opportunity. He moved over to the offensive with the results so disastrous to Waller already described. As he did so he heard the good news of the safe delivery of his daughter. The cloud had lifted.

But Prince Rupert, that strange cross between chivalric legend and computer-dom, was both by temperament and situation excluded from a share in his uncle's emotions and from his day-to-day intelligence. For all he knew he might at any moment have to race southward to rescue him from Essex and Waller. Such at any rate was a perfectly reasonable inference from the letter on which he had to act. The material parts of it read as follows:

> I must give you the true state of my affairs which . . . is such as enforces me to give you more peremptory commands than I would willingly do . . . If York be lost I shall esteem my crown little less . . . But if York be relieved and you beat the rebels' army of both Kingdoms which are before it, then (but otherwise not) I may possibly make a shift . . . to spin out time until you come to assist me. Wherefore I command and conjure you by the duty and affection which I know you bear me that, all new enterprises laid aside, you immediately march according to your first intention with all your force to the relief of York. But if that be either lost, or have freed themselves from the besiegers, or that, for want of powder you cannot undertake that work, that you immediately march with your whole strength directly to Worcester to assist me and my army.

Rupert received the letter at Liverpool on 18 June. He at once set about assembling every scrap of strength he could muster. Even when that was done his forces barely totalled 15,000 against the 25,000 of the three armies outside York. On 30 June the besiegers heard that he had reached Knaresborough about fifteen miles to the west. Leaving their guns and stores before the town so that they could carry on where they left off they laboriously ranged their armies across the road from Knaresborough and Wetherby on the open heath near Long Marston. To concentrate their strength they built a bridge of boats across the Ouse, thus making a passage for the troops ringing the northern side of the city. The Ouse is formed by the junction of two rivers, the Ure and the Swale, which meet just south of Boroughbridge, a few miles northeast of Knaresborough. In a characteristically swift and brilliant manoeuvre Rupert swung his army northeast, crossed the Ure at Boroughbridge, the Swale at Thornton Bridge and then turned southeast down the Ouse to York, having sent a patrol to surprise the party guarding the bridge of boats. He was able to relieve the city without the enemy so much as holding him up for five minutes, his flank protected by the river. Even from the victor of Newark it exceeded expectation.

Newcastle was, of course, delighted and expressed his pleasure and gratitude in the civil and generous terms proper to a great nobleman. But Rupert was not interested in the manners or the personalities of the country whose quarrels he had chosen to fight in. Winning battles was his business, not conciliating people's feelings. Did he even perhaps in his heart resent the position accorded to great nobles in the direction of a war that he was doing more to win than they were? The damage caused by his high-handed treatment of the Marquess of Hertford over the governorship of Bristol had not been forgotten or forgiven. Yet barely a year later he repeated his mistake: and this time it proved irreparable. Without replying in kind to Newcastle's courtesies he sent him a brusque order to join him outside the city with his army at four o'clock next morning.

From a field commander's point of view Rupert's urgency was unquestionably right. The enemy had been outgeneralled and found themselves in a position that they could not possibly have allowed for. To strike at them while they were still in a muddle was to exploit the advantage already achieved. If they were given time to regroup, their superior numbers would make a battle much less inviting. Confused, as they were, their very size was an encumbrance. All this is true. But it would not have been less true if Rupert had condescended to the virtue of tact or to knowledge of the world. Newcastle had raised and maintained an excellent army at enormous personal expense. He had commanded in the North with considerable success and, what he perhaps valued more, the respect of friend and foe. He and his officers and men had just reached the triumphant conclusion of a long and hard siege in which they had given a very good account of themselves. The men, who had not been paid for some months past, were busy looting the camp of the besiegers. And, most unlucky of all, Lord Eythin, the professional soldier on whom Newcastle relied as chief of staff for all military decisions, had a rankling grudge against Rupert over his own misconduct of the action in Germany at which the Prince had been taken prisoner. It was not therefore surprising that when four o'clock came Rupert found no sign of Newcastle's army at the rendezvous.

Rupert brought his own army across the bridge of boats and marched them up to Marston Moor. The Parliamentary allies had concluded that he was more likely to lunge past them to the Midlands and were therefore withdrawing southwards towards Tadcaster to protect what they thought was the threatened area. By nine o'clock in the morning they realized that Rupert was forming up his whole army on the moor and that if he delivered an immediate attack they were beaten men. Frantic messages were sent to halt the column of march and to reform line of battle but the van had already reached Tadcaster and it was early afternoon before the allies were in any posture to receive an attack. Luckily for them the huffing and puffing of the Royalist commanders had lost the chance of a quick and deadly victory. Newcastle arrived with a party of gentlemen about nine and was at least civil. Eythin arrived some hours later and was not. Their troops were not in position till four in the afternoon.

Marston Moor, the most important battle of the Great Civil War, exhibits all the characteristics with which the reader will now be familiar. As a show-piece of the military art it leaves much to be desired. On the Royalist side Rupert had botched a brilliant conception by mishandling colleagues. Having done so he should either have taken the huge gamble of carrying out his original plan alone or called it off. Goring who commanded the cavalry on the left charged home with his usual success, totally routing the rather poor, untrained horse that Fairfax had under him that day. But as at Edgehill, a battle which Goring must have known about though himself absent, the victors galloped gaily off the field looking for loot and enjoying the hunt. On the Royalist right Byron, facing Cromwell and the renowned cavalry of the Eastern Association, lost the advantage of his ground by advancing to meet that terrible charge and taking his own horse into the soft going that would otherwise have slowed the attack. In the centre the Royalist foot almost out-fought their much more numerous opponents. Both Lord Fairfax and Lord Leven, the Scots commander, could not get their men to stand and themselves fled the field, bearing the news of a Parliamentarian disaster. The day was saved by the Eastern Association, though even Manchester, left to bear the brunt of the Royalist infantry, is said to have been on the point of retreat when Cromwell's horse, controlled as ever in victory, suddenly fell on their un-protected flank and rear. The battle was not yet quite decided. Enough of Goring's horse had returned from their pursuit to form up, facing Cromwell, on the ground from which four or five hours earlier they had driven the Parliamentarian right. Cromwell charged again and that was the end of Royalist power in the North.

It was not quite the end of the fighting. Newcastle's Whitecoats, the famous North Countrymen he had raised and issued with the undyed woollen sur-coats that gave them their name, refused repeated offers of quarter. They were cut down where they stood, an example of courage without hope that won the admiration of their fellow soldiers on either side.

The casualties of Marston Moor had been heavy, especially on the Royalist side. Under a full moon the soldiers stripped the bodies of the dead and those who had been left for dead. In York the scene was harrowing. The terrified fugitives who had escaped the pursuit – and after Goring's men broke at the end of the day they had been pursued up to the city walls – had difficulty in getting in, 'for at ye barr none was suffered to come in but such as were of ye town, so that ye whole street was throng'd up to ye barr with wounded and lame people, which made a pitiful cry among them'. Thus wrote Sir Henry Slingsby whose regiment had been in York throughout the siege, shut up so tightly that he could not get news of his children, a few miles away. He stayed on in the city after the battle. Rupert who had only entered it shortly before midnight marched out next morning 'with ye remaining horse, and as many of his footmen as he could force'. Poor footmen! They had marched twenty-two miles on 1 July, stood to arms from two o'clock in the morning of the 2nd, marched out to the Moor and fought as hard a battle as any of the civil war, and now on the 3rd they were required to march north again towards Rich-mond. Newcastle and Eythin were not of the party. The earl who had fought bravely considered that the result might expose him to ridicule, an altogether intolerable thought, so he and his chief of staff were off to Scarborough 'where they took shipping to go beyond sea'. Neither of them took any further part in the war. It was left to Sir Thomas Glemham, the governor of the city, to make the best terms he could for its surrender. This he did,

> and upon that day fortnight ye battle was, we yield ye town: and that upon very good conditions if they had been kept; for we were to march out with our arms, and with flying colours, to have convoy till we came within 12 miles of ye prince; those that would, might tarry in ye town: those that would not, might have carts provided to convey such household good stuff as they had in ye town; to have protection and enjoy their estates. Upon these articles we march out, but find a failing in ye performance at ye very first, for ye soulgier was pilleg'd, our Wagons plundered, mine ye first day, and others ye next. Thus disconsolate we march, forc'd to leave our Country, unless we would apostate, not daring to see mine own house, nor take a farewell of my children, altho' we lay ye first night at Hessay, within 2 miles of my house.

Fortunately for us one important clause of the treaty forbidding any deface-ment of churches or images within them was kept. The visitor to the Minster, the Chapter House and All Saints, North Street, has cause to remember Sir Thomas Glemham and to be thankful that that kindly, gentle Yorkshireman, Sir Thomas Fairfax, was among the victors of Marston Moor.

Chapter 12

From Marston Moor to Naseby

After Marston Moor an outright Royalist victory was scarcely thinkable. To divide, to disturb and to frustrate the enemy rather than to defeat him was the utmost of rational ambition. There were optimists of Panglossian calibre, such as the Earl of Bristol, for whom the total overthrow of the Parliamentary forces, no matter how superior, was a matter of day-to-day expectation. And there were men such as the Earl of Antrim and the Earl of Montrose with schemes for raising the Highlands and bringing over Irish clans to join them that might, if successful, alter the balance of the war. Montrose had visited the King when he was besieging Gloucester in the summer of 1643 and had obtained his commission. He joined Rupert at Richmond two days after Marston Moor but the Prince was more in need of the few men Montrose had scraped together from the Borders than able to supply him with troops for the invasion of Scotland. A month later he crossed the Lowlands in disguise to embark on the brilliant military adventure that has made his memory immortal.

But the results of the victory extended beyond the position of the two main contestants *vis-à-vis* each other to the structure of the coalition called Parliament. The Royalists had indubitably lost the battle but who had won it? We have, said the Scot Dr Baillie in the interminable, self-righteous, patronizing drone that his English colleagues in the Assembly of Divines at Westminster had already begun to find irritating. Royalist and Parliamentarian alike testify to the inglorious performance of the Scots army. If Clarendon is to be believed the headlong flight of its general, Sandy Leslie, Earl of Leven, was ludicrously checked by a village constable. 'Give glory, all the glory to God', Cromwell had written from the battlefield. To such unexceptionable sentiments everyone must nod agreement, though Dr Baillie might feel some reservations as to the doctrinal purity of their immediate source. It was Cromwell's name that was on everyone's lips, not least on those of the men who had fought against him. 'Is Cromwell there?', Rupert had eagerly asked a prisoner from the Eastern Association captured a few hours before the battle: and it was the same good judge who later in the day coined the name Ironside by which history knows his troopers. Whatever the Scots might say, whatever the moderate, pacific party in both Houses might feel, everyone recognized that it was the army of the Eastern Association, and especially the horse, that had won the day.

What threw Cromwell's role into even higher relief was the virtual renunciation of the fruits of victory by the Earl of Manchester. There is, of course, no comparison between the historical stature of the two men. But Manchester has the better claim to be regarded as the creator of this great military instrument and was in fact its commander. A much milder, better balanced man than Cromwell he seems to have been sickened by the slaughter and by what he saw when he entered York after the battle. He made no attempt to assert any claim. He hardly seemed to want to go on with the war at all. It is possible that a visit paid to the camp before York by the younger Sir Henry Vane, Cromwell's close Parliamentary associate at this period, may have given him an alarming insight into the revolutionary ferment that was beginning to work. Vane's ideas consistently tended to alarm people, ending with Cromwell himself. As the man who had negotiated the alliance with the Scots and yet was increasingly known as the Parliamentary leader of the movement, so strong in the ranks of the Eastern Association, for a greater liberty in religion than the Scots would allow, he might hold the key to a settlement of that crucial question. And might not that key unlock the door to the deposition of the King and to the calling in question of social and political obedience? Whatever Manchester's feelings were on the morrow of Marston Moor they had crystallized four months later into the classic definition already quoted of the whole Parliamentarian dilemma. Arguing with Cromwell and others at a Council of War after the indecisive second battle of Newbury, he said, 'Gentlemen, I beseech you let's consider what we do. The King need not care

Parliament triumphant over its foes in 1645–6. Note Strafford, as Lord Deputy, off-handedly discharging a blunderbuss at the sacred vessel

how oft he fights, but it concerns us to be wary, for in fighting we venture all to nothing. If we fight a hundred times and beat him ninety-nine times, he will be King still. But if he beat us but once, or the last time, we shall be hanged, we shall lose our estates, and our posterities will be undone.' 'My lord, if this be so,' replied Cromwell, 'why did we take up arms at first? This is against fighting ever hereafter; if so let us make peace, be it never so base.'

Both positions are logically faultless. And both are shadow boxing. With the King's defeat now probable, if not imminent, what was going to happen? Were politics and religion to be forced back into recognizable channels or was the whole nation to say good-bye to its past and embark on a voyage to heaven knows where? Manchester and his like had everything to lose by eccentric political experimentation. And quite apart from material self-interest they understood the old machinery of government and were confident of their ability to make it work. In the public quarrel that followed the exchange quoted above, Cromwell accused Manchester of military incompetence and political pusillanimity. Manchester replied by charging Cromwell with subversive doctrines. He was alleged to have said that 'he hoped to live to see never a nobleman in England' and to have told his commanding officer to his face 'that it would not be well till he was but Mr Montagu'.

This, as we have seen, was not at all what the men who had led the Parliament into the war, the Great Contrivers as Clarendon calls them, wanted. The men who did want to do away with aristocracy and a good deal more had, except for Vane and Cromwell, come forward during the war itself. And was Cromwell in fact anti-aristocratic? It seems at best doubtful. His prejudices in favour of the gentry – his own class – have already been made plain. In the years of his Protectorate he professed an undoctrinaire social conservatism: 'a nobleman, a gentleman, a yeoman, that is a good interest', as he said to one of his Parliaments. One of his daughters married a peer but there is no evidence to suggest that Cromwell was either elated or chagrined by such a connection. On the other side, however, there is a story of a domestic chaplain aspiring to her hand and getting very short shrift.

Whatever his own views Cromwell's chief associates were men of radical opinions. Vane's fellow New Englander, Hugh Peter, the voluble army chaplain, and Harrison, the bold cavalry officer whom Cromwell honoured by sending him to Westminster with the official dispatches of Marston Moor, were beginning to make a name for themselves. Henry Ireton, Colonel Hutchinson's cousin, was another young officer who was to come to have a unique influence on Cromwell. He was serving with him at this time and was no friend to mild, middle-of-the-road policies. But amongst the troops these men commanded, the freedom and excitement of preaching and controversy were stirring sleeping giants. In his quarrel with Manchester Cromwell even had the unusual experience of finding himself supported by John Lilburne, 'Freeborn John', the most fearless, most irrepressible political agitator of that turbulent time.

The radicals in the army were further strengthened by Essex's disappearance into the abyss. After relieving Lyme he continued indecisively westwards, partly intending to relieve Plymouth, partly to attempt the capture of the

OPPOSITE *The Earl of Manchester by Sir Peter Lely*

BELOW *Hugh Peter, one of the most famous and effective of radical army chaplains as a preacher and pamphleteer*

James Graham, Marquis of Montrose, in a pre-war portrait

Queen at Exeter. This she forestalled by escaping to France, after fighting off one of Warwick's ships. So on Essex went to Plymouth, taking Taunton and Tavistock on his way. The Royalist commander raised the siege at his approach and retreated into Cornwall. By now it was the last week in July. The King had heard the terrible news from the North as he was moving west in pursuit of Essex but saw nothing to be gained by abandoning his quarry. Essex now had no convincing strategic objective left. He could go on into Cornwall in the hopes of disrupting the tin exports that paid for so much of the Royalist import of munitions, or he could turn round and either fight the King or slip past him. Against his better judgment, it is said, Essex went on. The King moved fast and purposefully. At the end of August the Lord General and all his main army were hopelessly bottled up at Lostwithiel, above Fowey. Neither relief nor evacuation was possible, a crowning incompetence in so sea-girt a county. By great luck and the criminal carelessness of Goring the Parliamentary horse under Sir William Balfour got away. Essex escaped in a rowing boat. The whole of his foot and artillery were left to surrender.

At almost the same moment as the tottering Royalist cause was revived by this resounding victory at the far southwestern tip of Britain, it was scoring an even more extraordinary success in the northeastern Highlands. Montrose, alone and without resources, had found the few hundred wild Irishmen who had been landed to wander through the Highlands just as they were about to blunder into a force of Covenanters. Subjected to Montrose's stirring eloquence the Covenanters joined him and together they defeated a more sizable and professional force at Tippermuir outside Perth. They took the town, the next in importance after Edinburgh and Glasgow. Success brought in recruits. By mid-September Montrose appeared before Aberdeen, a town well fortified and strongly held. His summons was contemptuously refused and the drummer who carried it shot. The Covenanters came out to give battle and against all the odds were beaten. The town was sacked with a savagery that made the war in England appear tame. Argyll and the authorities in Edinburgh took energetic counter-measures. But Montrose had the will-o'-the-wisp genius of the born guerrilla leader and they could not catch him. Meanwhile as the news of his exploits filtered down to England the Royalists and the radicals were on a flowing tide. The Scots Commissioners who had hoped to impose their approved system of Church government on England and the moderates who had hoped for a peace before things got even further out of hand were alike dejected.

While Charles had been absent in the West his depleted garrison at Oxford had won the admiration of their opponents by one of the most daring and skilfully executed operations of the whole war. By universal consent the whole credit belongs to a professional soldier of high intellectual quality – Clarendon describes him as 'a very good scholar in the polite parts of learning, a great master in the Spanish and Italian tongues, besides the French and the Dutch, which he spoke in great perfection; having scarce been in England in twenty years before' – Sir Henry Gage. Gage owed his Continental education to the fact that he came of a stoutly recusant family to whom the professions in England were largely closed. He had studied philosophy at an Italian uni-

Popish Recusants disarmed, for the greate Securi-tr of the kingaome,

Confiscating arms from re-cusants: the popular prejudice against Roman Catholics remained inveterate in the century between the Armada and the Glorious Revolution

versity before entering the Spanish service in Flanders at the age of twenty-three as a pikeman. As he rose in the service and in his intervals of unemployment he read widely in the theory of war, translating books from Latin into English and English into French. He was liked and respected at the archiducal court in Brussels where his diplomatic gifts were recognized. He was a natural choice for the negotiations between Strafford and the Spaniards over the proposal for English naval protection against the Dutch in exchange for a subsidy. It was only late in the war that he obtained leave from his Spanish employers to take service with the King. He arrived in Oxford in the spring of 1644 and being, according to Clarendon, 'indeed a man of extraordinary parts, both as a soldier and a wise man', was much consulted by the King's council 'whilst they looked to be besieged, and thought Oxford to be the more secure for his being in it'. This infuriated the governor of Oxford, Sir Arthur Aston, another Catholic professional soldier whose arrogance and brutality made him one of the most unpopular commanders on either side. It is characteristic of the King's conduct of the war that he should have made such a man commander of the Oxford garrison to please the Queen and should lack the strength of mind to replace him by a subordinate of such obvious superiority.

The frustrations of such a position made Gage the readier to undertake a mission that, however small the chances of success, would at least take him where Sir Arthur Aston could not interfere. Basing House, two miles outside Basingstoke, the seat of the Marquis of Winchester, the richest nobleman in England, was a great palace, protected by a double line of fortifications, that dominated the main road to the Southwest. Repeatedly attacked by Parliamentary forces it had beaten off every assault and, like Donnington Castle outside Newbury, stood above the high-water mark of inundations that covered all the surrounding counties. It was so huge in extent and so complete in its facilities that it served as a base for raiding parties large enough to play havoc with the trade between London and the Southwest. Basing had been under close siege by the combined levies of Hampshire and Sussex amounting to some three thousand horse and foot throughout the whole summer. The Parliamentary commander, knowing that the garrison was running out of ammunition and food and that there had been a severe outbreak of smallpox, called on the marquis to surrender 'to avoid the effusion of Christian blood'. The reply marked 'Hast, hast, hast, post hast' reads:

Sir,

It is a crooked demand, and shall receive its answer suitable. I keep this House in the Right of my soveraigne, and will do it in despight of your Forces. Your letter I will preserve in testimony of your Rebellion.

Winchester

Even the King who had hoped to relieve the place when he left Oxford but had not thought it prudent to delay his march to the West is said to have advised surrender, only to be told by its owner 'that under His Majesty's favour, the place was his, and that he was resolved to keep it as long as he could'. Nonetheless he had sent a message to his wife in Oxford that unless he received help within ten days – this was after seventeen weeks of close siege – he would have to capitulate. Since he, like Gage, was a Roman Catholic he expected the conditions to be harsh.

Sir Arthur Aston considered the appeal at his council and regretfully decided to refuse. Basing was forty miles away. The Parliament had strong garrisons of horse and foot at Abingdon and Reading both of which sent out regular patrols. There was also another force of enemy cavalry at Newbury. The chances of reaching Basing were small, of getting back to Oxford minimal. Gage accepted that the service was 'full of hazard' but offered to lead a picked party of gentlemen volunteers and their servants, mounted on their best horses, together with the remains of an infantry regiment that had recently arrived in Oxford from one of the perimeter garrisons.

They marched out on a Monday night, four hundred foot escorted by two hundred and fifty horse. By morning they had reached the wood near Wallingford where Gage intended to lie up while his men had some rest. From there he sent a messenger to Sir William Ogle, the governor of Winchester, who had promised to make a hundred horse and three hundred foot available for any attempt to relieve Basing. Gage worked out an ingenious plan whereby the besiegers should be attacked from two sides while the marquis led a sally from the house. About noon he set off again to march by side roads to the village of Aldermaston, far from any centre of activity. Just in case their movements were noticed by the country people they were wearing the orange tawny scarves and ribbons of the Parliament. By bad luck Gage's advance party ran into a Parliamentary troop in the village. Several were killed but some escaped to raise the alarm. The plan to get some sleep at Aldermaston had to be abandoned and the march was resumed at eleven that night, the horsemen and the infantry taking it in turns to ride. Between four and five on the Wednesday morning they halted within a mile of their objective.

Here was an even nastier surprise. A message from Sir William Ogle awaited them to say that the strength and regularity of the enemy's cavalry patrols made it quite impossible for him to send any forces at all. Gage was on his own, against a well-officered, well-found force between four and five times his own strength. He at once discarded his original plan and decided to bunch his force for a concentrated attack. So close did he expect the action to be that he made all his men tie white tapes or handkerchiefs round their upper arm so that they could tell friend from foe. Then placing his cavalry on his flanks and himself commanding the foot in the centre he gave the order to march. They came up a rise to find five troops of horse waiting for them at the far end of a field whose hedges were 'lined very thick with musketeers.' The attackers stood the fire well and then charged. It was no easy victory but after two hours' stiff fighting the Parliamentary forces retreated and Gage was able to bundle in the twelve barrels of powder and twelve hundredweight of match which was all so light and fast a force could bring. However, he lost no time in sending a detachment to the village of Basing while marching his main body to Basingstoke where he found enough provisions to keep the garrison for two months 'together with fourteen barrels of powder and some muskets, and forty or fifty head of cattle with above one hundred sheep'. Carts were commandeered and the rest of that day and the next were spent in transporting all this into the garrison. The party detached to the village of Basing had caught the enemy off their guard and in a smart action had taken a number of prisoners, including the eldest sons of two of the Parliamentary commanders. These were handed over to the marquis as likely to be more than worth their keep.

Gage had done all that he came to do. The problem of getting back now that every Parliamentary force for miles knew where he was and where he would be making for was the most challenging of all. He gave out that he was going to squeeze the neighbourhood and sent orders to the two or three nearest villages that they should deliver so many loads of corn to Basing House by noon next day on pain of being burned to the ground. In fact he marched that very night at eleven, crossed the Kennet at a ford close to a bridge that the enemy had destroyed, and next morning forded the Thames barely a mile from Reading without interference. In crossing the rivers the cavalry took the foot soldiers on the cruppers of their horses and swam them across. They camped at Wallingford that night and entered Oxford on the Saturday morning. His total casualties were eleven killed and about forty wounded.

With this unexpected run of Royalist successes it seemed that Marston Moor had scotch'd the snake not killed it. Accordingly every effort was made to catch the King's army on its way back from the West to its winter quarters in Oxford. Essex, who had been brought by sea to Southampton, and Waller, who was at Farnham, were ordered to concentrate the left-overs of their respective armies and rendezvous with the army of the Eastern Association. Manchester's disinclination to move and to do anything to precipitate matters led to the indecisive action at Newbury from which the King derived the moral and tactical advantage of relieving Donnington Castle and slipping his artillery train inside it out of harm's way. His army got safely away to Oxford where he shortly rejoined it, having made a detour to Bath to see Rupert now raising a new army and promoted, at last, to succeed the aged, deaf and gouty commander-in-chief.

Military changes of a much more far-reaching character were gestating at Westminster. The public quarrel between Cromwell and Manchester, the disintegration of Waller's army, the catastrophe at Lostwithiel spelled the end of the Old Guard. The success of the Eastern Association showed the Parliament the way 'to an army merely your own that you may command'. The genius of Cromwell's leadership pointed to the man. But the Old Guard were still well entrenched in the two Houses of Parliament, which had after all chosen them and supported them through thick and thin. And Cromwell's was a name at which the Scots grew vehement. The disgraceful irregularities of religious observance under his command were the next worse thing to papacy and prelacy. Essex sided with the Scots, and since Manchester was the object of Cromwell's direct attack both he and his father-in-law Warwick must have appeared as obstacles to the military new deal. On 9 December Cromwell dropped his personal campaign, conceded that all commanders made mistakes from time to time, and pleaded for national unity against the common enemy of the realm. He was followed by a speaker who proposed, as an extension of Cromwell's plea, that Parliament should pass a 'self-denying ordinance', making military command incompatible with a seat in either House. This would for ever put a stop to lobbying and political back-biting among the High Command. Unity would be restored at the centre and the armed forces would accept Parliament's purified authority with even greater enthusiasm.

It was a dazzling stroke by the Cromwellians, too dazzling for Cromwell's large and awkward mind. Those who see in it the hand of Sir Henry Vane are surely in the right. Beneath its unexceptionable surface of simple patriotism was concealed an ingenious device. In the first place, as the French Resident was quick to observe, it put the peers at a grave disadvantage. Members of the Lower House like Waller and Cromwell could resign their seats if they wished to retain their commands. Essex, Manchester and Warwick could not. And in the second place once the measure had gone through there was nothing to stop amendments or exceptions being voted. The lords saw that they were being corralled and trumpeted their alarm by throwing the measure out. But there were too many issues interlocking, notably the proposal for the creation of a New Model Army of 22,000 men together with the appointment of its commander-in-chief and subordinate officers, the charges, still outstanding, of Cromwell against Manchester and Manchester against Cromwell, and the hair-trigger issue of religion. Against so skilful a hunter as Vane, the lords of the forest had little chance. By the beginning of the spring they had so enmeshed themselves that they voted for the Self-Denying Ordinance, and Essex, Manchester and Warwick gave up their commissions.

Throughout this period of delicate political manoeuvre Cromwell gave no opening to his enemies. He had championed the appointment of Fairfax as commander-in-chief of the New Model and was one of the tellers in the vote that achieved this. To all appearances he was placidly accepting the end of his own military career. He made no move to resign his seat. The main armies on both sides were inactive. He was, however, recalled to service in a subordinate capacity when Goring's activities in the West necessitated the relief of Weymouth and Taunton. Waller was ordered to go to their help, taking Cromwell's

The Walker portrait of Cromwell

regiment with him. The regiment gave dangerous signs of refusing obedience and Parliament quickly ordered Cromwell to march at its head. The victor of Marston Moor was to serve as a regimental officer under the unlucky commander of Cropredy Bridge. It is not more surprising that Cromwell accepted the appointment without a murmur than that Waller, a fiery and quarrelsome man, found him an unexceptionable subordinate: 'Although he was blunt, he did not bear himself with pride or disdain. As an officer he was obedient, and did never dispute my orders, or argue upon them.' Taunton was in fact relieved from another quarter and both Waller and Cromwell had no urgent call of duty to prevent their laying down their commissions during the month of April as the newly passed ordinance required.

Cromwell reported to Fairfax's headquarters at Windsor to do this on 19 April 1645. The very next day a letter from the Committee of Both Kingdoms required him to take command of a brigade of horse and prevent the King, who was preparing to leave Oxford, from joining with Rupert. He caught and defeated some outlying detachments of Royalist cavalry and summoned Bletchingdon House, one of the perimeter strongholds, which was, to his surprise, surrendered. The unfortunate commander had the house full of guests, many of them women, and felt that his hospitality should not expose them to the horrors of a storm. He was court-martialled and shot in Oxford the next afternoon. But Cromwell's strength could only impede, not prevent, the King's movements. On 8 May Charles and Rupert joined forces at Stow-on-the-Wold. At a Council of War it was decided to carry out an offensive sweep through the northwest Midlands towards Chester. Rupert's conquests of the previous year had one by one fallen to the Parliament and control of the Irish traffic was again imperilled. Goring was given an independent command in the West and returned to resume his efforts against Taunton, still held for the Parliament by the indefatigable Robert Blake.

Parliament's first response to the King's motions was to order Fairfax and the New Model to march down to the Southwest. This was what Rupert and the King had been banking on. But as soon as the Committee of Both Kingdoms realized that the Royalist army was heading north they recalled Fairfax to threaten Oxford, having first detached some regiments to relieve Taunton. Rupert countered by recalling Goring: at least that is what he tried to do. But Goring, having at last got his own independent command, was in no hurry to come. The Royalist central direction of the war, never strong, had been weakened in the spring of 1645 by the King's decision to send the Prince of Wales, now rising fifteen, to form his own court in the West with Clarendon, Hopton and Culpeper as the chief members of his council. Partly this was to insure against the possibility of both King and Prince being captured as the result of one unlucky battle, as Simon de Montfort had captured King Henry III and his eldest son. Partly there were not a few about the King who, for very different reasons, wanted Clarendon out of the way. And the West seemed to promise great things: it was the only part of England where Parliament was still very much on the defensive and where the Royalists controlled a major port and from time to time enjoyed local supremacy at sea. In fact, as Clarendon found when he got there, the whole position was rotten. The atrocious Sir

Richard Grenville, unworthy brother of Sir Bevil, had already initiated the gangster regime that was to make Royalism wither in its most fertile soil. Goring's intemperance and indiscipline spread rapidly through the army he commanded. Nothing was to be looked for from the West in the spring of 1645 that could help the Royalists in the centre.

The King and his army, however, were in good heart. News of yet more extraordinary victories in the Highlands was coming in. Lord Bristol's unquenchable optimism was always on tap. Clarendon's sober confrontation of unpleasant realities, his tiresome disinclination to countenance a double game in Ireland or elsewhere, were out of sight and out of mind. The campaign too was opening well. On 30 May Leicester was summoned to surrender. Meeting with a refusal Rupert stormed and sacked it. The loss of so rich and important a town was a heavy blow to the Parliament. For the Royalists it turned out much worse. Hardly ever had the soldiers had such an opportunity of looting and the army was much weakened, as Clarendon points out, 'by the running away of very many with their plunder, who would in few days have returned'. Clearly the Parliament could not let the King's army rampage through the Midlands. Fairfax was at once ordered to leave Oxford, where in any case he could do little good as he had no siege train with him, and march against the King. He set out on 5 June and a week later not far from Market Harborough his patrols were in contact with the Royalists who had no suspicion of his presence or how strong he was. His intelligence on the other hand was excellent and he had intercepted a letter from Goring explaining his inability to comply with the King's order to join him. And Fairfax had also on 10 June petitioned Parliament that Cromwell might be appointed his lieutenant general as he was without a cavalry commander. The request was at once granted. On 13 June Cromwell was cheered as he rode into the camp of the New Model at Kislingbury bringing with him six hundred horse from the Eastern Association. On 14 June the battle of Naseby was fought. It was a well-timed entry.

Naseby was the last great set-piece battle of the civil war to be fought on English soil. Its course follows the pattern set nearly two years earlier at Edgehill and traced out further at the great victory of Marston Moor. Neither side had any marked advantage from the ground, as Streeter's engraving, published three years after the battle, makes clear. What the artist disguises is the enormous numerical superiority of the Parliamentarians, nearly two to one in the infantry and more in the cavalry. As at Marston Moor the God to whom Cromwell so rapturously ascribed the victory had revealed himself to the big battalions. Not that the Royalists had any misgivings as they formed up in magnificent array that summer morning. The King as at Edgehill was a conspicuous figure, splendidly mounted, his gilt armour glittering in the sun. Again as at Edgehill old Sir Jacob Astley commanded the foot in the centre, and Rupert had the place of honour on the right wing. The Royalist left was commanded by Sir Marmaduke Langdale and the backbone of it was his Northern Horse, still, though sadly reduced in numbers, as good cavalry as any on the field. Facing Langdale was Cromwell, with a much larger force, and opposite Rupert was Ireton, newly promoted commissary general, more for

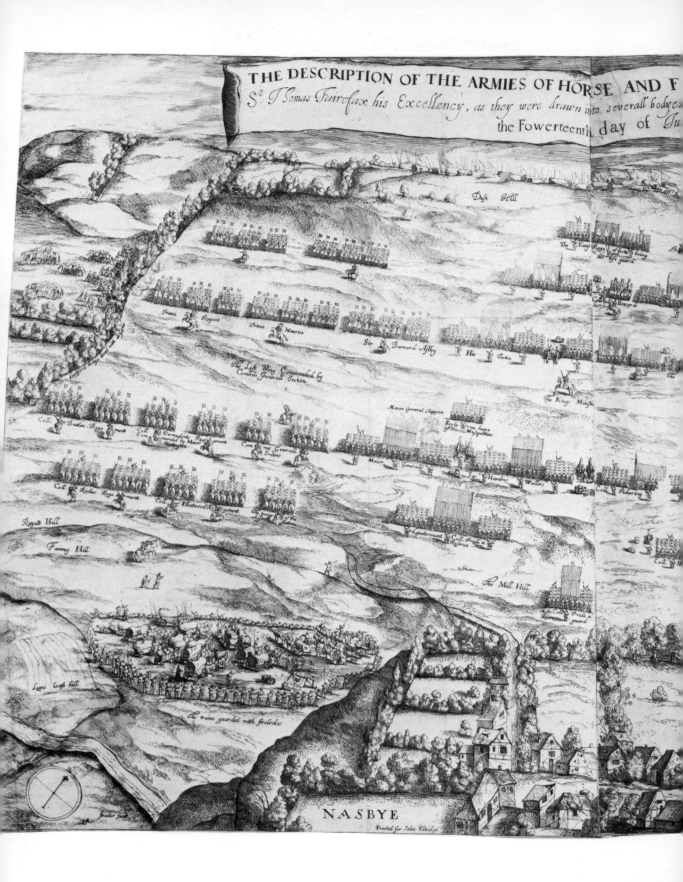

THE DESCRIPTION OF THE ARMIES OF HORSE AND F

S.ᵒ Thomas Fairefax his Excellency, as they were drawn into severall bodyes

the Fowerteenth day of Ju

Dust Hill

The Kings Reg.ᵗ of horse being for the guard

Prince Rupert

Prince Maurice

Sir Barnard Astley

His Tertia

The King Maiesta

The Left Wing Commanded by
Comiss: Generall Ireton

Coll. Brutton Reg.ᵗ

Coll. Vermudens Reg.ᵗ
Com: Generall Major Huntley

Com̄iss: Generall Ireton

Maior General Skippon

Coll. Hamond
Erle of Manchest:

Maior
Generall

Coll. Richer Reg.ᵗ

Coll. Fleetwood Reg.ᵗ

Maior Hardres
Wallers

Coll. Pickering

Lieutenant Coll. Pride etc.
Reserve

Coll.

Reput Hill

Fanny Hill

The Mill Hill

The Coll. Pride
guard

The traine guarded with forelockes

Long closs hill

NASBYE

Printed for John Patridge

Within the engraving:

OF HIS MAJESTIES, AND

Battayle at NASBYE;

Streeter's engraving of the battle
of Naseby from Sprigge's
Anglia Rediviva shows the
Parliamentary right commanded
by Cromwell; Rainborough's
regiment forms part of the
reserve directly below the hill on
which a knot of rustics have
gathered to watch. Streeter's
beautiful representation skilfully
conceals the inequality between
the two armies

his all-round abilities and force of character than for specific military talent. Skippon, the veteran who had licked the London trained bands into military shape and had subsequently served Essex as general of the foot, had the centre.

The battle began about eleven in the morning with Rupert's charge sweeping like an Atlantic roller up the hill, overrunning Colonel Okey's dragoons that lined the hedges and putting Ireton's cavalry to flight notwithstanding the dogged courage with which he, though wounded, tried to rally them. Rupert, who had strongly advised the King not to offer battle, had almost put him in a position to win it. Cromwell's charge against Langdale was not so instantaneously successful. But the Royalists gave ground and at last began to break. The King with characteristic courage turned his horse's head towards the point of danger. But one of the Scottish nobility who was riding in his bodyguard snatched at the reins and dragged the King's horse round, shouting with two or three full-mouthed Scottish oaths, 'Will you go upon your death in an instant?' The sudden movement of so eye-catching a figure could not be mistaken, but could be misunderstood. The horsemen near him imagined that some fresh movement was intended and took up the cry to move to the right. Since this was away from the direction of the enemy charge and from the hard-pressed Northern men who were retreating before it, the idea of flight seized hold. In a moment the Royalist position disintegrated. Rupert, returning to the field with his victorious but disordered troops, quickly saw that he would have his work cut out to save his uncle falling into enemy hands. He managed to rally enough men to protect the King's retreat first to Leicester and then further northwest to Ashby de la Zouch. But the person of the monarch was all that was saved. His foot and guns were all captured, as were such of his cavalry as were not killed in the pursuit except for the pitiful force that still attended him.

Worse, if anything could be worse, the victors captured and published all the King's secret correspondence. *The King's Cabinet Opened* proved to anyone whose mind was still ajar to evidence that Charles could not be trusted. Far more valuably it documented every assertion of his readiness to intrigue with Papists and Irishmen, whose name was anathema to all right-minded Englishmen of the time. Such revelations no doubt helped to justify the brutalities to the women and children of the Royalist soldiers that disgraced the first victory of the New Model Army. It was alleged that they were Irish. C. V. Wedgwood's suggestion that they were Welsh (and therefore in that age Welsh-speaking) is far more probable, since Rupert had largely recruited on the Welsh borders. But the Puritan God of battles reigns in the Old Testament, not the New. Its uncritical but selective readers could find there divine warrant for acts as cruel and wanton as those with which the dissolute Royalists of the Southwest like Grenville and Goring relieved the tedium of existence. The war in England was lurching unpleasantly towards the horrors familiar in less favoured lands. The decisiveness of the King's defeat at Naseby was a boon for the country.

Chapter 13

Twilight of the Cavaliers

After Naseby rational belief in a Royalist victory was only possible to those who, like Montrose in the Highlands, were ignorant of the event. In the first half of July he won two more brilliant victories at Alford and Kilsyth. Early in May he had defeated a force sent against him under the experienced Sir John Urry, now temporarily back on the side he had originally deserted. The extraordinary run of Montrose's success could only fortify the belief of his royal master that God would not, in spite of appearances, allow him to lose the war. That he was being chastised for his sins Charles could readily accept: and that further and deeper humiliation might be in store for him he was forced to recognize as probable. A few days after the battle he wrote a letter to his son in the West Country that none of his councillors knew about till many months later.

Hereford the 23rd of June 1645

Charles,

My late misfortunes remember me to command you that which I hope you shall never have occasion to obey; it is this: if I should at any time be taken prisoner by the rebels, I command you (upon my blessing) never to yield to any conditions that are dishonourable, unsafe for your person, or derogatory to regal authority, upon any conditions whatsoever, though it were for the saving of my life; which in such a case I am most confident, is in greatest security by your constant resolution, and not a whit the more in danger for their threatening, unless thereby you should yield to their desires. But let their resolutions be never so barbarous, the saving of my life by complying with them would make me end my days with torture and disquiet of mind, not giving you my blessing, and cursing all the rest who are consenting to it. But your constancy will make me die cheerfully, praising God for giving me so gallant a son, and heaping my blessings on you; which you may be confident (in such a case) will light on you. I charge you to keep this letter still safe by you, until you shall have cause to use it; and then, and not till then, to shew it to all your council; it being my command to them as well as you; whom I pray God to make as prosperously glorious as any of the predecessors ever were of

Your loving father, Charles R.

When that letter was written the King was still far from conceding military defeat. The most hopeful plan was to concentrate his forces in the southwestern peninsula. But as Rupert repeatedly emphasized the success of such a scheme depended on speed of execution. Unless the King was quick about bringing his forces over the Severn to Bristol or Bridgwater Cromwell and Fairfax would get there first and smash the last remaining Royalist army. Charles at first accepted this and actually arrived at Chepstow from where he was to embark his forces. But his reluctance to chew on unpalatable truths was too ingrained a habit. He had lost a battle but, with the insouciance of the Earl of Bristol to inspire one, what was a battle here or there? Wales was the country from which he had recruited his last army. Why not recruit another before joining Rupert and the others in the western redoubt? Besides he had found in the fastnesses of South Wales a retreat that combined the impregnability and the magnificence of Basing House with the *douceur de vivre* of Oxford or even the pre-war splendours of his great palace at Whitehall. This was Raglan Castle, the seat of another great Roman Catholic nobleman, the Marquis of Worcester. In the ordered, peaceful days regulated by the ceremonial rhythm of life in a great house, it was possible to forget the ugly and essentially meaningless clatter of external reality – *l'histoire événementielle* in the making – and to hear again the underlying harmonies of the divine purpose. The King played bowls and went to church, talked and read on subjects that interested him. It was like wearing a suit of his own clothes after years in a uniform that didn't fit.

He was, however, still the executive head of a Government demoralized and enfeebled by faction and defeat. The earlier antagonism between Rupert and the moderate core of the Royalist party, Clarendon, Hopton, Culpeper and the rest, was brotherly love compared to the fierce mutual dislike, the open contempt, between Rupert and the Earl of Bristol. This disastrous rivalry had reached its climax on the day before Naseby when Bristol had been for fighting and Rupert for avoiding action until there was less disparity in numbers. That the King should have overridden the military advice tendered by a commander-in-chief whose most relentless critics never accused him of excessive caution showed how the scales of royal favour were weighted. That Rupert in spite of his own superb performance on the field had been utterly justified by the event can hardly have eased relations in the Royalist supreme command. That Bristol should still be retained as, to all appearances, the King's closest and most trusted adviser was argument enough that total defeat could not long be postponed.

To a scientific general such as Rupert, careless and indifferent as to the issues over which Englishmen were agonizing, the deduction was perfectly clear. He had been against making peace at Oxford in the spring of 1643 when there were powerful parties on both sides making for it. He had not interested himself in the negotiations between the Commissioners at Uxbridge late in 1644 which were hardly more than a propaganda exercise on the part of the Parliament. But in a lost war the terms of peace grow rapidly steeper. Rather than write directly to the King, Rupert communicated his thoughts to their common cousin, the Duke of Richmond. Charles replied at once in a letter whose eloquence and grandeur show how it was possible for so untrustworthy a man to command the love and loyalty of good men who were not fools.

Cardiffe, Aug. 3 1645

C.R.

Nephew, this is occasioned by a letter of yours which the duke of Richmond shewed me yesterday . . . Now as for your opinion of my business and your counsel thereupon, if I had any other quarrel but the defence of my religion,

crown, and friends, you had full reason for your advice. For I confess, that speaking as a mere soldier or statesman, I must say, there is no probability but of my ruin; yet as a Christian, I must tell you, that God will not suffer rebels and traitors to prosper, nor this course to be overthrown: and whatever personal punishment it shall please him to inflict upon me, must not make me repine, much less give over this quarrel; and there is as little question that a composition with them at this time is nothing else but a submission, which, by the grace of God, I am resolved against, whatever it cost me, for I know my obligation to be, both in conscience and honour, neither to abandon God's cause, injure my successors, nor forsake my friends. Indeed I cannot flatter myself with expectation of good success more than this, to end my days with honour and a good conscience; which obliges me to continue my endeavours, in not despairing that God may yet in due time avenge his own cause. Though I must aver to all my friends that he that will stay with me at this time, must expect and resolve either to die for a good cause, or (which is worse) to live as miserable in maintaining it as the violence of insulting rebels can make him.

Having thus truly and impartially stated my case unto you, and plainly told you my resolutions, which by the grace of God I will not alter, they being neither lightly nor suddenly grounded, I earnestly desire you not in any wise to hearken now after treaties, assuring you, that as low as I am, I will do no more than was offered in my name at Uxbridge. Confessing that it were as great a miracle that they should agree to so much reason, as that I should be within a month in the same condition that I was immediately before the battle at Naseby. Therefore, for God's sake, let us not flatter ourselves with these conceits: and believe me, the

Raglan Castle, where Charles I enjoyed a last few weeks' respite from the war. It was one of the many castles later slighted, or made indefensible, by Cromwell, leading William Gilpin to write in the eighteenth century: 'What share of picturesque genius Cromwell might have had, I know not. Certain however it is, that no man, since Henry the eighth has contributed more to adorn this country with picturesque ruins' very imagination that you are desirous of a treaty will but lose me so much the sooner. Wherefore, as you love me, whatsoever you have already done, apply your discourse hereafter to my resolution and judgment. As for the Irish, I assure you they shall not cheat me; but it is possible that they may cozen themselves; for be assured, what I have refused to the English, I will not grant to the Irish rebels, never trusting to that kind of people (of what nation soever) more than I see by their actions. And I am sending to Ormond such a despatch as I am sure will please you and all honest men; a copy whereof, by the next opportunity, you shall have. Lastly, be confident I would not have put you nor myself to the trouble of this long letter, had I not a great estimation of you, and a full confidence of your friendship too.

Part of a monument to Sir William Penn who served in the Parliamentary navy and rose to be General-at-Sea under the Commonwealth. Note his armour and the land ordnance and barrels of powder. Penn took part in various combined operations, notably against Bunratty Castle in Ireland

The omitted sentence at the beginning of this letter shuffled off Rupert's complaint at having heard only at second hand of the King's sudden intention to march north into Scotland to join the victorious Montrose. Such a scheme bore all the hallmarks of Lord Bristol's wild optimism. How readily it evoked a similar response from the King this letter clearly shows. Clarendon does not exaggerate when he describes it as 'so lively an expression of his own soul, that no pen else could have written it . . . a part of the portraiture of that incomparable King . . .' Inextricably mixed with a profound and humble resignation to the will of God is a conviction that, as in the case of Job, the Lord will bless the latter end more than the beginning and give him twice as much as he had before. And again this compound of serene faith and Micawberish optimism is tempered by a strangely objective forecast of the likely course of events, itself mysteriously dissolving into the quasi-realism of supposed political expedience, such as believing that he can outwit the Irish Catholics and make them serve his purposes. *Sancta duplicitas!*

By the time these letters were exchanged it was already clear that the Western position was gravely compromised. Fairfax and Cromwell *had* got in first. Not only had Taunton been relieved at its last gasp but Goring's army that had threatened it had itself been heavily defeated at Langport. Worse still, Bridgwater, long regarded as impregnable and used therefore as the chief arsenal of the West, had fallen in an afternoon. Bristol itself was now cut off from the remaining Royalist territory in the far southwest. Everywhere else the absence of a field army left Royalist strongholds to be picked off at leisure. On the border Carlisle at last yielded; in Yorkshire Pontefract and Scarborough surrendered. If the King were to march north he would find few secure places beyond Newark. Nonetheless he set off, perhaps not sorry to be on the move. If Raglan had been a blessed interlude of calm, the Principality had not been as entire in its obedience as he had expected. The gentry were squabbling among themselves and refusing orders; Archbishop Williams at Conway had lost none of his talent for setting everybody by the ears; the Parliamentary navy, even without Warwick to direct it, had lent its power to an uncomfortably effective combined operation in Milford Haven.

Leaving the Welsh border, the King marched by way of Lichfield to Doncaster which he reached on 18 August. His total force probably amounted to a bare 2000 so that when he heard that the Scotch army was approaching from the West and Colonel Poyntz, the Parliamentary commander-in-chief at York, from the north, retreat was the only possibility. With the destruction of Royalist power in the North after Marston Moor and at the centre after Naseby the Committee of Both Kingdoms had reasonably withdrawn its forces from the Eastern Association to concentrate every available man on the reduction of the Southwest. The Parliamentary heartland was thus unexpectedly open and the chance of plundering an as yet unplundered country seconded the invitation. It was while so occupied in Huntingdon, Cromwell's own home town, that the King's men heard on 24 August of Montrose's crowning victory at Kilsyth, a village in the gap that runs between the Forth and the Clyde. The main Covenanting army was routed and Argyll himself took ship to Berwick for safety. Edinburgh submitted to the conqueror, releasing the prisoners and paying the money he demanded. On 18 August he entered Glasgow in triumph, prudently leaving his wild Irishmen encamped several miles away. His force in any case would not admit of his garrisoning either city.

To Charles the news no doubt suggested that the divine plan was already manifesting itself. To the Scotch cavalry that had headed him south from Doncaster it was clear that they must march home at once and deal with Montrose before he broke into England and raised the North for the King. In high hopes Charles moved westward to relieve the city of Hereford, besieged by the Scotch infantry, whom he had not felt strong enough to challenge when he tiptoed northward up the Welsh border only three weeks earlier. He was in fact no stronger now, but he had in him the certitude of victory that can disconcert the most rational forecast. His faith was, apparently, confirmed by the event. The Scots, mutinous for want of pay, alarmed by reports from home, daily conscious of the hatred and resentment of the people they were among, drew off at the King's approach. He entered Hereford in triumph on 4 September. From there he moved on to Raglan to plan the consummation of the work Montrose had so nobly begun. The first, most pressing problem was the relief of Bristol where Fairfax had been besieging Rupert since 21 August.

Unfortunately there remained what Henry James in another context called 'the dear little deadly question of how to do it'. Bristol was immensely strong but Rupert's garrison of a mere 1500 was insufficient to man such extensive fortifications. And where was the army that could raise the siege? Langport and Bridgwater had shattered the only possible nucleus of such a force. The grandiose promises of its titular commander, George Goring, now by all accounts in an advanced state of alcoholism, could hardly inspire much confidence. Yet Rupert's surrender of Bristol on 10 September seems to have come on the King like a thunderclap, startling him out of calm and hope. That the terms Rupert had obtained were generous, that he and his men had more than justified their reputation in the eyes of such opponents as Fairfax and Cromwell, that they had fought until sheer weight of numbers had carried the day and there was no alternative but pointless slaughter and the horrors of a sack, carried no weight with the visionary of Raglan. The divine plan had been thrown out of gear. With a most uncharacteristic failure of self-restraint the King gave way to despair, to anger and to shrillness. Rupert's pigeons so long on the wing came home to roost. All the spite, the jealousy and the justified resentment that he had contemptuously accumulated among the leading Royalists from the light-headed Bristol to the sagacious Clarendon told against him at last. As Clarendon himself points out, the terrible letter that the King wrote him was not the reaction of an instant but the product of reflection. Rupert had surrendered on the morning of the 10th. The news must have reached Raglan within forty-eight hours, probably less. On its receipt the King returned at once to Hereford, from where he dates this famous letter 14 September 1645:

Nephew,

Though the loss of Bristol be a great blow to me, yet your surrendering it as you did is of so much affliction to me, that it makes me forget not only the consideration of that place, but is likewise the greatest trial of my constancy that hath yet befallen me; for what is to be done, after one that is so near to me as you are, both in blood and friendship, submits himself to so mean an action? (I give it the easiest term) such – I have so much to say, that I will say no more of it: only, lest rashness of judgment be laid to my charge, I must remember you of your letter of the 12th of August, whereby you assured me, that if no mutiny happened, you would keep Bristol for four months. Did you keep it four days? Was there anything like a mutiny? More questions might be asked, but now, I confess, to little purpose: my conclusion is, to desire you to seek your subsistence, until it shall please God to determine of my condition, somewhere beyond seas; to which end I send you herewith a pass; and I pray God to make you sensible of your present condition, and give you means to redeem what you have lost; for I shall have no greater joy in a victory, than a just occasion without blushing to assure you of my being

Your loving uncle, and most faithful friend, C.R.

The wheel had come full circle. Without Rupert's energy and professionalism the war would have been lost before it had begun. Without his victories, his panache, his tactical flair, his strategical grasp there would have been little chance of winning it. Not content with dismissing him in disgrace and ordering him into exile, the King sent further instructions to the members of his council in Oxford, where Rupert had marched his troops under Fairfax's safe conduct, for the arrest not only of the Prince himself but of the governor, Colonel Legge, who was known to be his close friend. Rupert's cause had not been helped by the antics of his elder brother, the exiled Elector Palatine Charles Louis, a spiritless womanizer, who had been living in London trying to enlist Parliament's diplomatic and financial support. His efforts had been crowned with success in the shape of a vote for a pension of £8000 at almost exactly the same moment as Fairfax was laying siege to his brother in Bristol. Was the sudden surrender part of a plot by the Palatine family to supplant their uncle and his posterity on the throne of England? The simpler and more obvious explanation of sheer military necessity was not more likely to commend itself to Charles because it was clearly true. Motives were more real to his mind than facts, particularly facts of power. The divine motives had been revealed to him: Rupert's insufficient strength, his unblemished record of loyalty and honour, were but as dust in the balance: and the ready plausibility of Lord Bristol could supply any deficiency in this, or any other, argument. Sir

Thomas Glemham, the gallant officer who had served with such distinction as governor, first of York and then of Carlisle, was sent to succeed Legge at Oxford. The King once more headed north, hoping for a junction with Montrose and intending to relieve Chester and thus secure the Irish passage.

The contrast with his earlier wartime progresses or even with the state so recently kept at Raglan was bizarre enough to be amusing. The Royalists were on their beam ends. Sir Henry Slingsby who marched with the King 'thro ye almost unaccessable mountains of Wales' has left a vivid account of the conditions they encountered:

> In our Quarters we had little accomodation: but of all ye places we came to, ye best at old Radnor, where ye King lay in a poor low Chamber, and my L^d of Linsey and others by ye Kitching fire on hay; no better were we accomodated for victuals; which makes me remember this passage; when ye King was at his supper eating a pullet and a peice of Cheese, ye room without was full, but ye men's stomacks empty for want of meat; ye good wife troubl'd with continual calling upon her for victuals, and having it seems that one cheese, comes into ye room where ye King was, and very soberly asks if ye King had done with ye cheese, for ye Gentlemen without desired it.
>
> But ye best was, we never tarry'd long in any place, and therefore might ye more willingly endure one night's hardship, in hopes ye next might be better.

On 23 September the King entered Chester, escorted only by his lifeguard and the handful of infantry he had with him. The bulk of his cavalry under Sir Marmaduke Langdale were left some miles outside the city with orders to cross the Dee further to the south and then to swing round and fall on the besieging army encamped to the north. This movement would synchronize with a sally from Chester itself, taking the enemy between two fires. Unfortunately no one on the Royalist side knew that the energetic Colonel Sydenham Poyntz balked of his prey at Doncaster a month earlier had been moving swiftly across to catch the King on his second northward march. Soon after crossing the river Langdale encountered this unexpected enemy and at once attacked. At first he had the better of it but when the besieging army came to Poyntz's aid Langdale was hard pressed. An urgent message to the force inside Chester was misinterpreted. Ignorant of Poyntz's presence the Royalists thought that this was the signal to carry out the original plan. The King climbed up one of the towers of the city wall to watch the battle but it was already lost. The Royalist horse had broken and the lifeguard, riding out to take the enemy in the rear, lost themselves in a melée of fugitives making for the safety of Chester and a far larger number of victorious pursuers.

The loss of life was heavy and what touched the King closest was the death of his young cousin, Lord Bernard Stuart, Earl of Lichfield, who had ridden in his Guard since Edgehill. The first casualty in that first battle had been his elder brother; another brother had fallen in the course of the war. But Bernard had been the dearest to the King, dearer perhaps than anyone except his Queen, now far away in France. It was at this moment of bereavement and defeat that Slingsby records his

> wonder at ye admirable temper of ye King, whose constancy was such that no

perills never so unavoidable could move him to astonishment; but that he still set ye same face and settl'd countenance upon what adverse fortune soever befell him; and neither was exalt'd in prosperity nor deject'd in adversity; which was ye more admirable in him, seing that he had no other to have recourse unto . . . but must bear ye whole burden upon his shoulder.

The King's personal safety was now paramount. If he fell into the hands of the Parliament and the Prince of Wales were to be taken in the Southwest, no victories of Montrose, no reinforcements from Ireland could help. On his way to Chester and the melancholy battlefield of Rowton Heath the King had paused at Chirk Castle to send urgent instructions to his son's council in the West:

Chirke Castle 29th Sept. 1645

Colepepper,

I have seen and considered your despatches; and for this time you must be content with results without the reasons, leaving you to find them: lord Goring must break through to Oxford with his horse, and from thence, if he can find me out, wheresoever he shall understand I shall be; the region about Newark being, as I conceive, the most likeliest place. But that which is of more necessity, indeed absolute, is that, with the best conveniency, the most secrecy, and the greatest expedition, prince Charles be transported into France; where his mother is to have the sole care of him, in all things but one, which is his religion; and that must still be under the care of the bishop of Salisbury; and this I undertake his mother shall submit unto: concerning which, by my next despatch, I will advertise her. This is all.

Short and emphatic as the letter was the King drove the point home again in a postscript:

C.R. For lord Goring's business, though I wish it, I cannot say it is absolutely practicable; but for my son's, that is of necessity to be done; yet for the way, I leave it to your discretion, having already with you, as I conceive, as much power in paper as I can give you. France must be the place, not Scotland, nor Denmark. C.R.

Nobody, as it happened, acted on these categorical instructions. The only breakout that Lord Goring contemplated was a voyage to France to recruit his health when he had drunk the West of England dry. As for the Prince's council the last thing they wanted was to put their chief source of strength and hope in the hands of Henrietta Maria. And France under Cardinal Mazarin was in Clarendon's settled judgment the inveterate enemy of the King's interest. In any case the Prince was in no immediate danger. Fairfax had hardly moved west of Exeter, which was still held by the Royalists, and the chops of the Channel swarmed with Royalist privateers as well as a few King's ships, should a hurried departure become necessary. Once the Prince was known to be moonlighting the whole West would collapse.

That the King should even have contemplated the possibility of the Prince sailing to Scotland shows how tenaciously he clung to the illusions implanted by his cousin Hamilton and to the hopes that had flowered with Montrose. By the time he reached Newark in the middle of October 1645 it was no longer

George Digby, K G, 2nd Earl of Bristol, by Justus van Egmont. The Earl of Bristol's brilliant vivacity so dazzled the King and Queen that the disastrous consequences of taking his advice seem to have passed unnoticed

possible to doubt the reports that Montrose had put his fate to the touch and lost it all. At Philiphaugh in the Scottish borders he had been defeated, not without some treachery on the part of the canny border nobility, and his Irish infantry horribly massacred after their surrender had been accepted.

> I have asked grace at a graceless face
> And there is none for my men and me.

The pitiless traditions of the border found their champions in the Covenanting clergy. Montrose had only with difficulty been prevented from plunging in to be butchered with the men who had marched and fought so gallantly. He escaped, in spite of the price on his head, and made his way back to the Highlands.

Part of the reason for the King's move to Newark was a vague hope of a junction with Montrose. The other part was that Oxford was almost the only other choice left open, and Oxford would mean a confrontation with Rupert. This Lord Bristol was particularly anxious to avoid. In egging the King on to dismiss his best general he had overreached himself. Rupert was not the only member of the King's circle to have made enemies. When he complained of the manifest injustice he had received and demanded to be tried by court-martial, Bristol's critics and opponents supported his claim. Newark separated from Oxford by a hundred miles of hostile territory seemed safely out of range. But Rupert was never a man to be easily deterred. As soon as he knew where the King was making for he set off together with his brother Maurice at the head of a hundred horse. News of his approach was received by the King and his Secretary of State with as much consternation as if it had been Cromwell. It was hastily decided that Lord Bristol should volunteer to lead the northern horse under Sir Marmaduke Langdale to support Montrose in Scotland. All went well as far as Doncaster. There Bristol heard of a Parliamentary regiment newly raised in the neighbourhood and at once sought it out and scattered it. Halting at Sherburn-in-Elmet he heard that the Yorkshire horse were preparing to attack him a mile or two outside. Without waiting to collect his main strength he at once galloped out of the town at the head of a few troops and charged the Parliamentarians. According to Clarendon, who never could resist the ludicrous aspect of his old friend's activities, the enemy broke and fled towards Sherburn. The main body of the Royalist horse, seeing cavalry in headlong retreat towards them, concluded that all was lost and that it was high time to melt away. The victorious Secretary of State thus returned from battle to find his army gone. Sir Henry Slingsby, who stayed with the King at Newark but whose part of the country this was, gives a more prosaic and probable account of the defeat. All agree that Bristol and Langdale and a few others managed to reach Skipton Castle and from there actually got as far as Dumfries before the Scottish horse caught them. Even then Bristol's astonishing luck held. He and Langdale escaped to the Isle of Man where Lord Derby and his massive French countess were long to defy the Parliament.

At Newark the King saw for himself something of what his unfortunate subjects had to endure from a military force that was no longer sustained by any sense of purpose. 'He betook himself', says Clarendon,

A painted window at Farndon Church commemorating the King's supporters at the siege of Chester

to the regulating the very great disorders of that garrison; which, by their great luxury and excesses, in a time of so general calamity, had given great scandal . . . The garrison consisted of about two thousand horse and foot; and to those there were about four and twenty colonels and general officers, who had all liberal assignments out of the contributions [i.e. the locally enforced taxation], according to their qualities; so that . . . there was very little left to pay the common soldiers, or to provide for any other expenses.

The officers who lost their pay and allowances were naturally disgruntled so that it was in no atmosphere of undying devotion that the King heard of Rupert's arrival at Belvoir Castle a few miles off. Charles sent him a sharp note forbidding him to move until further order and reproving him for his disobedience in having come. Rupert took no notice. Next day he entered the town, having been met outside with some ceremony by its governor, Sir Richard Willis. It was after all only eighteen months since he had relieved the place by one of the most celebrated victories of the war. Coming into the King's presence he told him without beating about the bush that 'he was come to render an account of the loss of Bristol and to clear himself from the imputations which had been cast upon him. The king said very little to him; but meat being brought up he went to supper; and during that time asked some questions of prince Maurice, without saying anything to the other.'

Rupert, after his dismissal from his command. This eloquent portrait (detail), painted by Dobson at Oxford, was left unfinished when the Prince set out to demand a fair hearing from the King at Newark

Both parties retired to bed without saying any more. But the King seems to have realized that sending his most successful commander to Coventry in front of a body of officers who largely took his part could hardly enhance either his dignity or his authority. Next day he ordered a hearing before a council of war. The verdict unmistakably vindicated Rupert, finding nothing worse proved against him than indiscretion. The King was not pleased. But news of the approach of Parliamentary forces left him little time to reassert the authority that he felt had been challenged.

On the morning of the day he meant to start for Oxford he summoned Sir Richard Willis to his bedchamber and told him that in view of his distinguished service he proposed to make him captain of his horseguards, a post vacant by Lord Bernard Stuart's death at Rowton, and to replace him as governor by Lord Bellasis, a local nobleman. Willis at once asked to be excused. He was not rich enough for so expensive an appointment and his removal from his governorship would be taken as a mark of disgrace. The King politely poohpoohed his objections and, as it was a Sunday, went to church. At his dinner immediately after the service, Willis, accompanied by Rupert, Maurice and twenty others burst in. Willis protested that what the King had told him in private was the common talk of the town: he had been publicly dishonoured and he demanded satisfaction. Rupert said that Willis was being punished for being his friend and others denounced the absent Bristol as the traitorous cause of all the trouble. Pale with fury, the King ordered them all out of his presence. That evening a petition was presented for Willis, like Rupert, to have his case tried before a court-martial. There was no question now of a night march. The town was in an uproar. But the King was not to be cowed. Facing the mutinous elements drawn up in the market place next morning he coldly offered release from his service and passes to go beyond sea to such as

*Charlotte, Countess of Derby.
This redoubtable Frenchwoman
held her husband's Isle of Man
against the Parliament in the
closing year of the first civil war*

would not accept his orders. Willis, the two princes, and two hundred others accepted the offer somewhat lamely and rode off to Belvoir. Short of offering violence to their sovereign there was not much alternative.

The delay to Charles's departure had made a precarious journey a great deal more dangerous. Strong Parliamentary patrols had now been established round the garrison, particularly to the west and south. The King determined to break out of the trap in one quick dash. He kept his plans to himself, only ordering the troops to march an hour after the gates had shut for the night. He left Newark at eleven o'clock on the night of Monday 3 November with four or five hundred horse. By three in the morning they had reached Belvoir where the governor, who had had strict orders not to tell the princes of his movements, met them with guides and escorted them till daybreak. They

Basing House towards the end of the war

passed close to Burleigh-on-the-hill where the Parliamentary garrison cut off some stragglers. At six in the evening the King stopped at a village near Northampton to catch four hours' sleep. Marching through the night they had passed Daventry before day broke and reached Banbury, where a cavalry escort from the Oxford garrison was waiting for them, before noon. The whole party reached Oxford in safety later that day.

The King had done now with marching and councils of war. He was safe enough in Oxford for the winter but he could hardly expect to hold out in the spring. Once Fairfax and Cromwell had mopped up the West they would sit down outside Oxford and that would be that. No stronghold could stand for long without any hope of relief. Even Basing House had been stormed at last amid horrid scenes of murder and destruction. The exhibitionist Harrison had

F BAZINGE HOVSE

BATTERED DOVNE. D. THE KINGES BREAST WORKS. E. THE PARLIAMENTS BREAST WORKS.

killed a defenceless actor, urged on by the bloodthirsty pulpit eloquence of Hugh Peter, and this was by no means the only victim. The aged Inigo Jones was lucky to be stripped only of his clothes and left to shiver. So vindictively thorough was the sack that the house was never rebuilt and the sale of its treasures, looted by the soldiers, kept the London dealers down there for some time. The aged Marquis of Winchester, observed by the ineffable Peter surveying the ruins of his splendid house, replied to his glib impertinences with the wish 'that the King might have a day again'. It was to be granted: but it would be another king and a very different sort of day.

Inigo Jones in old age, by Dobson

Chapter 14

The End of the First Civil War and the Birth of Army Radicalism

The winter of 1645–6 gives historical substance to Oxford's claim to be considered the home of lost causes. For the last time – and surely in a part of that mind, divided like a submarine by strengthened bulkheads and watertight doors, he recognized that it was the last time – the King kept his court. The paradox of finding liberty in a condition of imprisonment was not fanciful. He was not free to leave Oxford but he was free from all the main influences and pressures, good or bad, loved or hated, that had shaped his performance and his understanding of his duties. The Queen was in France, Clarendon in the West, Bristol a fugitive. There were no armies to command, no generals to listen to, no diplomacy to conduct. The Parliament at Westminster had shown at the Uxbridge negotiations, when the Royalist armies were still in being, that they were no more disposed to compromise than the King himself; indeed before the Commissioners met they had underlined their resolution by beheading Archbishop Laud, for nearly four years a prisoner in the Tower. Hamilton who had misjudged the Scottish scene so disastrously and had been so bitter an enemy to Montrose was a prisoner of the Royalists in a Cornish castle. Such initiatives as were open were all remote. Encouragement to Montrose on the run in the Highlands; schemes of the Queen's for a French-supported Irish invasion of England; negotiations with the Pope through the Earl of Bristol's versatile kinsman Sir Kenelm Digby to the same end; flirtations, vicariously conducted through a French diplomat, with the Scotch army in England; flies cast over the separate factions that were already beginning to appear in the English Parliament and its army. Nothing was direct, nothing first-hand. The King was isolated from the current of events.

For a man of his tastes Oxford was no bad place to be isolated in. Its treasures and beauties can hardly have known a more appreciative guest. Magdalen Tower he pronounced the most absolute building in Oxford. The court added its patronage to the riches of architecture and painting, carving and stained glass that it found there. William Dobson, the greatest English portraitist between Nicholas Hilliard and Samuel Cooper, was active in Oxford up to the end of the war. Sir Henry Slingsby who had spent much of the preceding winter there with the King gives a thumb-nail sketch of his daily course of life:

> . . . he . . . would himself once or twice a week take horse and go about ye town, to view both within and without ye works, and be among his ordinance where they stood upon their carryages: he kept his hours most exactly, both for his exercises and for his dispatches, as also his hours for admitting all sorts to come and speak

ABOVE *Archbishop Laud*

THE HIGH BORNE PRINCE IAMES DVKE OF YORKE.

borne October = the 13. 1633.

Sould by Tho: Ienner at the South Entry of the Exchange.

RIGHT *The young Duke of York at tennis, a game also enjoyed by his father; this picture was probably engraved in London when the Prince was in the custody of Parliament*

with him. You might know where he would be at any hour from his rising, which was very early, to his walk he took in ye Garden, and so to Chapple and dinner; so after dinner, if he went not abroad, he had his houres for wrighting and discourcing, or chess playing, or Tennis.

(The tennis Charles I played was the indoor, winter game.)

The picture of life in that long, hard winter when many rivers froze solid is less agreeable in the other few beleaguered garrisons that still held out for the

The cold, not cruelty makes her weare
In Winter, furrs and Wild beastshaire **Winter** *For a smoother skinn at night,*
Embraceth her with more delight.

Winter fashion during the first civil war. Newcastle, from which London drew its coal supply, was in the hands of the Royalists

King, and much harsher for the unfortunate population of the far West subjected to the lawless depredations of the Royalist rabble as well as the exactions of the New Model. But elsewhere things were returning to normal. London's coal supply was restored; the trade along the great western routes was no longer throttled by the garrisons at Donnington and Basing House. Hugh Peter, changing from the gruesome to the pastoral, celebrates the healing return of economic life to its familiar channels:

The final siege of Newark,
6 March–8 May 1646. Note the
protective earthworks
immediately adjacent; the one
directly to the southeast, lying
alongside the southern arm of the
Trent, known as the King's
Sconce, is still in an excellent
state of preservation

A Section or Profile
of the Dimensions of
the Forts and Redouts
upon the Line

Peter Lovell fecit

Oh, the blessed change we see that can travel now from Edinburgh to the land's end in Cornwall, who not long since were blockt up at our doors. To see the high-ways occupied again; to heare the Carter whistling to his toiling team; to see the weekly Carrier attend his constant mart; to see the hills rejoycing, the valleys laughing.

The spring had melted the last of the Royalist snow. Chester had surrendered early in February 1646. Hopton, restored too late to the command in the West, had surrendered to the chivalrous and humane Fairfax in March. Later in the month Sir Jacob Astley who had miraculously scraped together 3000 recruits on the Welsh borders was surrounded and forced to surrender at Stow-on-the-Wold as he marched to join the King at Oxford. The capitulation of Oxford, Exeter, Newark, and the castles such as Raglan, Harlech and Pendennis could only be a question of time.

The King, toying with the possibilities of escaping to France or Denmark, of joining Montrose in the Highlands, of boldly putting himself in the hands of Sir Thomas Fairfax, eventually opted for the Scotch army. He left Oxford in the small hours of 27 April disguised as a servant to the two men who accompanied him, John Ashburnham, a groom of his bedchamber, and Michael Hudson, one of his chaplains. The governor himself unlocked the East Gate and watched them ride over Magdalen Bridge in the direction of London. No one on either side knew where they were going. But after roaming the country incognito for a week, an activity for which the King was by temperament and cast of mind not nearly so well fitted as his eldest son, he rode into the Scots' camp at Southwell. The standard of the defeated Royalist party now waved over the court of his son.

So rapid and complete had been the Royalist collapse in Devon and Cornwall that the young Prince of Wales had been lucky to get away. In the generally demoralized state of his supporters it is not surprising that there seems to have been a plot to betray him. Culpeper and Hopton got wind of it and warned their young master who by good fortune had left his headquarters at Truro to spend a day or two as the guest of the governor of Pendennis, the all but impregnable castle that dominated the western entrance to Falmouth harbour. Almost entirely surrounded by sea it was connected with the mainland only by a narrow isthmus. Its walls were strong and in good repair; the heart of its septuagenarian governor was stout in proportion, as he showed in the splendid answer he returned to Fairfax when called on to surrender a fortnight after the Prince had left:

Sir,

The Castle was committed to my government by His Majesty, who by our laws hath the command of the Castles and Forts of this Kingdom, and my age of seventy summons me hence shortly. Yet I shall desire no other testimony to follow my departure than my conscience to God and loyalty to His Majesty, whereto I am bound by all the obligations of nature, duty and oath. I wonder you demand the Castle without authority from His Majesty, which if I should render, I brand myself and my posterity with the indelible character of Treason. And having taken less than two minutes resolution, I resolve that I will here bury myself before I deliver up this Castle to such as fight against His Majesty and that nothing you can threaten is formidable to me in respect of the loss of loyalty and conscience.

Your servant, John Arundell of Trerice

Could the Prince be safer than in the hands of so lion-hearted a castellan? Some of his council thought not. The King had already approved their reasoned objections to his earlier and explicit instructions that his son was to be sent to France forthwith. Before leaving Oxford he had given them discretionary power over the Prince's movements provided always that they should run no risk of his falling into the hands of the rebels. In spite of the detection of the plot (if plot there was: the evidence is not conclusive) the risk was still acute. It was finally agreed at a council at Pendennis on 2 March that the Prince should sail that night, but not for France. He should make either for the Scillies or the Channel Islands depending on the direction of the wind.

Both these places were alive with Royalist privateers. The very completeness of Warwick's success in securing the navy for the Parliament at the beginning of the war had meant that when, as a result of Hopton's victories in the West, the King acquired ships and bases there was no question of forming a fleet to challenge Parliament to battle. Instead the Royalists used their sea power in the strategy that all the major enemies of the Royal Navy except the Dutch were to employ in the succeeding centuries: that of the *guerre de course*. Unlike pitched battles which are likely to be bloody and certain to be expensive the *guerre de course* offers the prospect of fast, easy and enormous wealth. There were plenty of mongrels in the kennels of Dunkirk and the Breton ports eager for a licence to fall on the fat sheep of England's trade entering the Western Approaches or coming up the Channel. This the King's letter of marque provided. Its holder and his crew were entitled to the same legal and personal rights as those who served in a properly constituted navy. The effect was to legalize piracy. At the height of Royalist sea power Warwick calculated that he had two hundred and fifty ships to deal with and that about a third of these were Dunkirkers or Bretons.

It was in one of these vessels that the future Charles II had his first taste of naval life. The frigate that bore him from Pendennis to the Scillies belonged to Jan van Haesdonck, a Dunkirker who controlled a small fleet of privateers. She was commanded by Baldwin Wake, one of the three or four captains of the Royal Navy who had escaped to join the King when the fleet was taken over by Parliament. The discipline, however, appears to have been that of a privateer. The distinguished passengers were plundered and their baggage rifled by Haesdonck's ruffians on the short and stormy passage to Scilly. The royal party disembarked on the afternoon of 4 March and were little pleased by what they saw. The Scillies were ideal as a base for commerce raiding, but they were not much good for anything else. Accommodation was primitive; communications were bad. As the news gradually came in of surrender after surrender, it became plain that the Scillies might prove a trap. With all the Cornish bases and ports in their hands Parliament could soon establish local command of the sea. Sure enough on 12 April nine ships commanded by William Batten, Warwick's vice-admiral who had succeeded him on the passing of the Self-Denying Ordinance, were sighted in the offing. Fortunately for the Prince and his party a violent storm blew up almost at once and drove the fleet off its station. The moment the wind fell enough to permit a ship to put to sea, the Prince and his party sailed for Jersey in Baldwin Wake's own frigate *The Proud Black Eagle*, arriving safely the next day, 17 April.

With the King a prisoner and the Prince in the Channel Islands there was no motive for continued resistance to the victorious Parliament beyond gallantry and honour. The Scillies, the Channel Islands, the Isle of Man, the West Indies, could maintain their independence either on their own resources or as privateering bases. Most of Ireland if not friendly to the King's cause was passionately hostile to Parliament; the southern ports were still firmly Royalist. In Wales and Cornwall the castles of Raglan and Pendennis, defended by two very brave old men, held out till August. Harlech, too strong to be worth attempting, did not capitulate until March 1647. But everywhere else the war was over by May or June 1646. Of the rich and important towns Exeter surrendered on 16 April, Oxford on 24 June. In both cases posterity has reason to be grateful that it was with the merciful and civilized Sir Thomas Fairfax that the terms had to be negotiated. Even Royalist sources make few complaints of looting or wanton destruction, and none of cruelty. It is characteristic of this large-minded and cultivated soldier that he, a Cambridge man, should have asked the Speaker for the assistance of Laud's old pupil Bulstrode Whitelocke in securing the preservation of Oxford's treasures and that one of his first acts on entering the city was to post a strong guard on the Bodleian.

Among the last Royalist garrisons to have surrendered in the West was that of Barnstaple commanded by Lucy Hutchinson's brother, Sir Allen Apsley. Immediately after the capitulation he came to stay with his brother-in-law, still in office as governor of the Parliamentary town of Nottingham. The Hutchinsons were thus enabled to see at first hand the difference between being on the winning or the losing side. The articles that the victors had promised were not 'punctually perform'd, by which he [Sir Allen Apsley] suffer'd greate expence and intollerable vexation'. Hutchinson, a fair-minded man, exerted himself to get him justice 'and for this was call'd a Cavalier, and sayd to have chang'd his party'. At the end of every war people will be found ready to kick their opponents when they are down; what is unusual is this disinterested concern for fair play. In spite of Hutchinson's support the matter dragged on for years. The most serious claim made against Apsley was that of a woman who sued him for the value of a house of hers 'pull'd downe to fortefie the towne for the King, before he was Governor of the place'. Of course the lady, professing unspotted Parliamentary loyalties, alleged political malice. In fact it appears that she had been a Royalist spy, or at least attempted to claim a reward on these grounds after the Restoration.

It was the prospect of this type of litigation, malicious or otherwise, that made demobilization and a complete return to the ordinary process of law daunting even for the winning side. In any war combatants have to break laws and violate the rights of property. By the oldest of conventions this created no civil liability. *Inter arma silent leges.* But the slightest rift between Parliament as the guardian of the law, and the army, whose power would dissolve once it disbanded, could only too easily be exploited along such lines. And the rifts were there: religion, pay – most of the regiments were months in arrears and knew that once they had dispersed their claims would be forgotten. For the moment the possession of the King brought everyone together against the Scots. What had *they* done to deserve such a political bonus? What city had they captured? What battle had they won? The murmurings and the resentment were such as the King had counted on. And when he had exploited them to divide the Scots from the Parliament, he could use them again to divide the Parliament from its army.

Things, as we know, turned out differently. The Scots, aware of the hard feelings of their allies, prudently retired to their own borders keeping the town of Newcastle as security. Here for several months the King found full scope for the political arts he best understood: obstruction and intrigue. His first absurd hopes of uniting every element in Scotland, the Covenanters, Montrose and the other Royalists who had refused to act with him were quickly dissipated. Argyll and his party hated Montrose much more than they loved the King. His disavowal was the first of their demands. The other, even more impossible, was that Charles should accept what even his Parliament had jibbed at, the rigorous imposition of the Scottish church system on England. The Scots were by no means the only people with whom Charles was negotiating. The Parliament too sent commissioners. And there was a constant flow of secret correspondence with the Queen, the Irish Catholics, agents at the Vatican. The fundamental trouble was that both Parliament and the Scots thought that the King would recognize the palpable fact that he had lost the war as a revelation of God's will. Everyone except a handful of sceptics believed that whatever happened must be accepted as part of the divine plan. Charles himself certainly subscribed to this view. But the difficulty of appealing to history as an umpire in human affairs is that the decision is rarely seen to be final until long after it can have any relevance to what one is to do next. Thus the King, far from accepting the military verdict as a divine ruling on disputed points, took it, as he had taken every defeat, every setback, for God's chastening and punishment for past sins, especially the signing of Strafford's attainder. The same idea had been expressed by Hopton in the closing days of the war when Fairfax had appealed to him to prevent more bloodshed by surrender:

> God hath indeed of late humbled us with many ill successes, which I acknowledge as a very certain evidence of his just judgment against us for our personal crimes, yet give me leave to say, your present prosperity cannot be so certain an evidence of his being altogether pleased with you.

The King knew what God's will was and knew that it was his duty to fulfil it. If this meant plunging the country into another civil war he was ready and anxious to promote it.

From this battering of heads against brick walls some negative conclusions at last began to shape themselves. The Scots and the King could not, with the best will in the world, find a basis for doing business. The French, from whom the Queen expected so much, would in fact do nothing. The Irish situation was now so bedevilled by a criss-crossing of complications that no rational man could expect anything but confusion worse confounded. Montrose had failed to raise the Highlands and had escaped to Norway. Something would

'The King's innocency preserves him.' Beatification is already implicit in this view of the King's predicament after Naseby

Integer vitæ fcelerifque purus
Non eget Mauri jaculis nec arcu,
Nec venenatis gravida fagittis
    Fufce pharetra.
Sive per Syrtes iter æftuofas,
Sive facturus per inhofpitalem
Caucafum, vel quæ loca fabulofus
    Lambit Hidafpis.

have to be done with the King. The Scots did not want to keep him: they did not want to turn him loose. The obvious solution was to hand him over to the Parliament. In January 1647 in exchange for a substantial payment on account for the expense incurred in the war the Scotch army transferred the custody of their exalted prisoner and marched out of Newcastle.

The ending of the first civil war without a political and religious settlement altered the basis of the conflict. From this point it was no longer possible, if it ever was, to contain the struggle within its original terms of reference and to confine the right to take part in it to the political nation of 1640. Humpty Dumpty could not be put together again. Too many people had seen the squire a fugitive, the parson ousted, the farmer's stock driven off, horses commandeered, houses requisitioned, merchandise seized, for the old prescriptive rights of property and degree to slip into place of their own accord. The incidence of military service was small in proportion to the population. By the standards of the two world wars of our century it was tiny. But its effects on a largely static and traditional society are, like those of industrialization, potentially revolutionary. By the mere fact of uprooting men from their familiar and enclosing environments, by forcing them into a collective existence and by demonstrating the unsuspected scale of collective power, a tilth is prepared for ideas that ordinary life would tread underfoot. Soldiering too does not simply teach a man's hands to war and his fingers to fight. It condemns him to long periods of inactivity. The high ideological character of the New Model, the readiness of soldiers and officers to take to the pulpit and the trendiness of its chaplains flowered in the days that were now empty of marching and fighting. The sooner the army could be disbanded the better. There was no time to be lost in cranking up the old constitutional engine of King, Lords and Commons. The longer it lay in bits, the greater the danger of some crackpot Utopian experiment. The Anabaptists of Munster had shown the civilized world what happened when religious enthusiasts got the bit between the teeth. Visions of rape and pillage hardly less dreadful than the fiendishness with which the Pope was credited swam before the eyes of the country gentlemen and lawyers at Westminster.

The growth of English democratic ideas in the seventeenth century dates from this point. To what extent democracy implies social revolution, to what extent the terms are antithetical, is matter for a debate that has gone on intermittently ever since. It has been a dominant theme in much of the most interesting and original work done on this period in the past twenty or thirty years. The sudden blooming of an advanced Republicanism, the discovery, as of some rare ideological wild flower, of an authentic native communism makes a splash of colour. Certainly the very fact that radical opinions whether as to religion, politics or the fundamentals of society were so widely disseminated is crucial to any understanding of what men did and why. This was not achieved only through the sermons and lectures, or even the Army Debates, with which Puritanism will be for ever associated. The pamphlet literature of the two middle decades of the century is vast. Thomason, a Royalist bookseller living in London throughout the period, collected nearly 30,000 which are now preserved in the British Library.

The master of this thriving form was John Lilburne who in his indomitable defiance of any authority that did not satisfy his own moral, religious and historical criteria personifies the transition that the struggle had undergone. Lilburne and his brother Robert served with courage and distinction in the war but it is as the heroic speechmaker from the dock whether before Star Chamber, the King's Council of War, the House of Lords, the House of Commons, or ultimately Cromwell himself that Lilburne acquired a place in contemporary martyrology that no one could rival. His constant imprisonments only stimulated the flow of his publications. At the time of the King's transfer from Scottish to English custody Lilburne was locked in combat with the House of Lords. The origins of this particular dispute lay in the quarrel between Cromwell and Manchester but its importance consisted in the huge publicity that Lilburne secured for his democratic and egalitarian assertions. 'Freeborn John' did more than scholars such as Selden or Prynne to put Magna Carta on the map of popular historiography. How unwelcome and uncalled for such trumpetings sounded in the ears of men who wanted to return to tried and established forms may well be imagined. But to the soldiers these excursions into the past, and especially the recurrent theme of a Norman aristocratic yoke imposed by the conquest on a free unstratified Saxon society, thrillingly confirmed the results of their study of the Bible: 'To bind their Kings in chains and their nobles with links of iron.' That was the stuff to give the troops, or at any rate the stuff that the troops were ready to accept.

The co-operation of the King was imperative if the Parliament were to be able to claim the obedience of Englishmen on the old, safe ground of law and established practice. Charles saw this quite clearly. He seems to have concluded from it that they needed him more than he needed them. He was in any case inflexible on the question of Church government and the liturgy. The usual deadlock ensued during which the King continued to play, or to attempt to play, both ends against the middle. He had been moved south, to Holdenby in Northamptonshire. His conditions of life were agreeable, his treatment courteous. He read widely: Hooker, Spenser and Shakespeare were among his favourite authors at this time. There is no sign that he was anxious or apprehensive. But events were moving to a climax. The Parliament voted to disband the army and prepared to summon the King to London. The army refused obedience and elected its own representative body. Fairfax recently confirmed as commander-in-chief warned the Parliament that he could not answer for the consequences if they held on their present course. They prepared to back down, but it was too late. Cromwell had left London and joined the army. And the army, in the person of a junior officer, Cornet Joyce, at the head of five hundred men had spirited the King away from Holdenby to the headquarters at Newmarket.

Who had given Joyce his orders? When the King asked to see his commission, Joyce made one of the most famous evasive answers in English history, waving his hand in the direction of the soldiers drawn up in front of the house. Whether or not it was Cromwell, it seems overwhelmingly probable that he knew what was in the wind. And he certainly took a leading part in the planning and execution of the policy that derived from this decisive

Charles, Prince of Wales, the future Charles II, at the age of twelve, painted by Dobson shortly after the battle of Edgehill, conventionally represented in the background; the left foreground depicts the diabolical nature of rebellion

act. But this is not to say that he had taken the initiative. Whatever view one takes of Cromwell, short of simplifying him, as many of his contemporaries did, into a hypocrite from first to last, it seems clear that he was a great one for waiting on events. 'No man climbs so high as he who does not know where he is going.' His own words spoken on a later occasion come as close to the revelation of his intellectual processes as we are likely to get. His mind was not analytical but it was, perhaps for that reason, all the more easily made up. His practicality and swiftness of decision were never found wanting. What mattered in the spring and early summer of 1647 was to prevent, if possible, a breach between Parliament and its army and at all costs between the soldiers and their commanders.

The brand names of politics explain little. Men differ too much in their intellectual and moral furniture and in their approach to fit neatly into the sorting boxes constructed for them. Terms such as Left and Right which we use every day will present the future historian with puzzles enough. So much depends on who is speaking, to whom and in what context. From the death of Pym in 1643 to the Restoration in 1660 the labels most regularly employed are Presbyterian and Independent. They were used then, and are used now, to convey many of the same overtones as our Right and Left. The Presbyterians are identified with the Old Guard of Parliamentarianism, Manchester, Holles, Sir William Waller and so on: men of substance and education, very much members of the political nation, conservative and monarchist. In 1647 they are Parliament, while the army is the stronghold of Independency. And Independency stands for every tint and shade of radicalism, religious, political and social, running from a mild and qualified belief in religious toleration to a thorough-going revolutionism. The limitations of such terms of description are obvious. And as in the civil war itself the common ground between people on opposite sides often seems much more substantial than the lines drawn to divide them.

Cromwell in his own time and in every subsequent history has been hailed as the Champion of Independency. To go against the terminology of three hundred years would be perverse but in many important respects Cromwell was deeply and instinctively sympathetic to the Presbyterian position, particularly in its social conservatism. In religion he was unquestionably, heart and soul, an Independent. His dislike of and contempt for forms whether in politics or religion is the recurrent theme of his letters and speeches. And his love for the army he had done so much to create was no mere sentimental affection for the old regiment, profound and powerful though such an attachment can be. Rather it was a sense of mystic union in being the chosen instrument of the divine purpose. There was nothing disloyal to Parliament in such an emotion. It was the Parliament not Cromwell that had been forcing the pace. Faced with an army united under its old commanders, Fairfax and Cromwell, an army moreover that possessed the person of the King, Parliament gave ground. But the city of London which contained strong Royalist sympathies, necessarily submerged, and which was decidedly more Presbyterian than Independent brought direct and popular pressure to bear. There were riots. Parliament wavered and divided, the Speakers of both Houses

The Palace of Whitehall, seen across St James's Park, from a painting by Hendrick Danckerts

headed a party of their members to join the army that had now moved to Hounslow. Early in August Fairfax marched into London, restoring the Speakers and the members who had accompanied them to their places. Militant Presbyterianism had suffered a defeat.

Fairfax's bloodless *coup d'état* had averted a second civil war. But the situation had been so threatening that the King and those who thought like him took heart. The French whose only real interest was to prolong and embitter the divisions that weakened so powerful a neighbour were not slow to encourage him. The reconstitution of the King's original concept of an alliance with the Scots was the basis of this policy. To it could be added the support of the English Presbyterians, including London. The royalist gentry in the country, ready once again to venture all for their King, could be counted on to rise at the appropriate moment. Without a strong dash of romantic optimism it would be difficult to put much faith in such a combination. The Royalists in particular might prove hard to rouse. The war had been long and expensive. The most zealous who had contributed most had little left to give; the more temperate were counting what they had and reckoning what their loyalty had already cost and still might cost them. The terms offered to the defeated were not in general harsh. Two years' annual value of an estate was the suggested norm but there were all kinds of variants. As in the case of recusancy fines the natural instinct of the gentry was not to make things too unpleasant for their neighbours. Many prudent owners of estates had conveyed them to trustees at the outbreak of war to safeguard their families against just such a contingency. It is easy for people who have not voluntarily risked their own lives and the welfare of their children to be censorious from a safe distance. But reluctance to stake everything once again on so disastrous a performer as Charles I is to say the least understandable.

While the King was plotting he was also negotiating with the army leaders. He had been installed at Hampton Court, the palace and park on which he had spent so lavishly as to provoke even Archbishop Laud's remonstrances. The army itself was conducting the great debates that were to shape the tradition of English politics for the next three hundred years. Colonel Rainborough's imperishable phrase, 'I think that the poorest he that is in England hath a life to live as the greatest he', still echoes from Putney Church. To reconcile an ordered liberty and a representative system of government with the existing fabric of society was probably what Cromwell wanted and certainly what Ireton had persuaded him that he did. Such an objective would satisfy the moral and political concern of the soldiers who, as they said themselves, were no mercenary army and would preserve the country from wild experiments in anarchy or communism. All this Ireton successfully achieved in the draft settlement known as the Heads of the Proposals. Regular Parliaments, freedom of debate, the right to petition for redress of grievances, a large measure of religious toleration that undercut both Presbyterian and Prayer Book claims to exclusivity but went a long way to meet the King by specifically providing for the existence of bishops shorn of their coercive power – here if anywhere was a genuine attempt at a compromise that left room for change and development. Charles welcomed it, not as a hopeful sign of a constructive and temper-

ate spirit but as hoped-for evidence of weakness and division. Its generally moderate and conservative tone infuriated the Levellers, as the radical leaders of the soldiers were coming to be called. They were quick to point out how much of the power of the King and the House of Lords would be maintained by such a settlement and to accuse Cromwell of backsliding. *The Old Serpent in a New Form*, the subtitle of one such attack, shows how exposed the position was and what risks Ireton was taking to defend it. Such an offer could not be kept open for long.

It had been made at the beginning of August. By the end of October the Soldiers' Council or Agitators, as they were called, published a manifesto, *An Agreement of the People*, setting out the Leveller programme. In essentials it bears a striking resemblance to the People's Charter of two hundred years later – manhood suffrage, equal electoral districts, triennial Parliaments purged of the hereditary power of the House of Lords. The only mention

Charles I and James, Duke of York, painted by Lely when the King was held prisoner at Hampton Court

NIL ADMIRARI

A Leveller, John Wildman,
by Wenceslaus Hollar

made of the King was in a threatening aside: 'him that intended our bondage and brought a cruel war upon us.' On 11 November Colonel Harrison, the officer whom Cromwell had honoured by sending him to carry the victorious dispatch from Marston Moor, denounced the King in the army council as a man of blood and called for him to be brought to judgment.

On the same day Cromwell wrote to his cousin Colonel Whalley who commanded the soldiers guarding the King at Hampton Court warning him to exercise especial vigilance against a possible attempt at assassination. Whalley showed the letter to the King who promptly escaped that very night in disguise. Well mounted and accompanied by two gentlemen of his bedchamber, John Ashburnham and William Legge, and Sir John Berkeley (a courtier who had served with distinction in Hopton's early campaign), the party arrived safely at Titchfield, the Earl of Southampton's house in the New Forest. The King seems to have been under the impression that Ashburnham, the companion of his earlier expedition incognito from Oxford to Southwell, had laid on a ship. Ashburnham himself denied this. Whether or not he was telling the truth his conduct was certainly odd. Leaving the King at Titchfield he and Legge crossed over to the Isle of Wight to see if Colonel Hammond, the recently appointed Parliamentary governor, would help either by providing a ship or concealing their master till one could be obtained. Hammond's reply was anything but satisfactory: he would give no undertaking that might conflict with the duties of his post and he demanded to know where the King was. Incredibly Ashburnham brought him back with him to Titchfield. When the King heard who was waiting below, he burst out, 'O Jack, thou hast undone me.' Ashburnham broke down and offered to kill Hammond but the King refused. Short of that there was nothing to be done. The King crossed to the island under Hammond's escort and was imprisoned at Carisbrooke Castle.

From the start this story has looked fishy. Why did Whalley show the King, who was known to be frightened of being murdered in captivity, the letter from Cromwell? And how did he come to escape so easily when Whalley had been told to take such care of him? Sir Philip Warwick tells us that only a few days earlier the King, who had long been planning an escape, had formally withdrawn the parole that had enabled him to ride out freely for exercise. The muddle about the ship thickens suspicion. How could there be any doubt on so crucial a question? And why, of all people, pick on Colonel Hammond? The answer that he was nephew of Charles I's favourite preacher, Dr Hammond, who had been one of the King's chaplains at Hampton Court, will hardly do; and the story that the uncle had introduced him to the King as a secret convert to Royalism is too silly to be rebutted. What is much more to the point is that Hammond had married Hampden's daughter and had won Cromwell's particular approval and friendship in the New Model. Moreover Christopher Hill points out in his most valuable study, *God's Englishman*, that Cromwell had paid a recent and otherwise unexplained visit to Hammond who had only been in his post for a very short time. Marvell's Cromwell,

> Twining subtle fears with hope
> He wove a net of such a scope
> As Charles himself might chase
> To Carisbrooke's narrow case,
> That thence the royal actor borne
> The tragic scaffold might adorn

is as convincing an interpretation as any. When the King set out to deceive Cromwell he took on a master at his own game.

Cromwell and Ireton knew all about the King's intrigues with the Scots. They saw, and told him that they saw, that he was trying to play off the army against the Parliament. They knew, as the King did not know, what spirit of revolution was abroad in the army. Within a week of his flight from Hampton Court two regiments had mutinied and at a general rendezvous at Ware had tried to persuade their brothers in arms to join them and seize Cromwell as a traitor. Cromwell rode up to them, his sword drawn. The men faltered. His order to remove the slogans they had stuck in their hats was obeyed. One of the ringleaders was tried on the field and immediately shot. The situation had been saved, but narrowly. The Parliament might, and in fact did, resume negotiations with the King in the Isle of Wight. But Cromwell had gone out on a limb for him once, only to be repaid by discovering that, in his secret correspondence with the Queen, Charles was looking forward to the day that he would see him executed for High Treason. At the end of the year the Engagement between the King and the Scots was concluded. Episcopacy was to be abolished, Presbyterianism established and the King restored by force. The first two points the King could easily shuffle out of once he was back in power. The third gave the signal for the second civil war. In the spring of 1648 it broke out.

Chapter 15
The Second Civil War

The King had been proved right in thinking that if a political settlement were obstructed a further resort to arms would ensue. Sir Jacob Astley's remarks as he leaned against a drum, chatting to his captors at Stow-on-the-Wold, seemed too to have been vindicated by events. Besides the divisions among the victors already referred to, there were the pent-up discontents of the governed. Even the best established Government is only grudgingly obeyed. No one likes paying taxes or conforming to laws that interfere with their pleasure or their profit. When the Government can only claim a dubious legality, when it appears partisan and officious and expensive, when its administration is amateurish, above all when it is weak and uncertain of its direction the temptation to resist it is much increased. This is a long way from accepting the risks attendant on rebellion or revolution but it does provide a certain encouragement to those bolder spirits who are prepared to do so.

The County Committees of Puritan gentry had been an acceptable form of local government in wartime but peace was supposed to bring with it that return to normal so eloquently evoked by Hugh Peter. Their pretensions were often resented. The King's claims, so skilfully insisted on by Clarendon in all the papers he had drafted, that he stood for the known and tried laws were nostalgically remembered, his arbitrary acts forgotten. Moderate and conservative opinion was alarmed by the growth of radicalism in the army, radical opinion by suspicion of a deal at their expense between the officers, the Parliament and the King. The enormous cost of the military and naval establishment far outran the revenue. The soldiers' arrears steadily mounted and there were occasional outbreaks of mutiny or desertion in the navy because of inadequate food and interminable postponements of pay. The gilt of Parliament's victory had worn off.

Army radicalism had made such a noise that too little attention was paid to the no less significant fact of naval conservatism. The ease with which Warwick had secured the fleet for the Parliament and the skill with which he had managed it up to the Self Denying Ordinance had caused its obedience to be taken for granted. Yet Warwick belonged to the Old Guard of Parliamentarians, the party of Pym and Hampden, of Holles and Manchester, whose father-in-law he was. His vice-admiral and successor in the operational command (the naval direction of the war was entrusted to a Parliamentary Committee) was William Batten, a tough, sly, genial old salt. The unforgettably malicious portrait that Pepys has drawn of him in the Diary when they were colleagues at the Navy Board in the next reign should not obscure the fact that Batten was a professional sea-officer of the first quality. In our day he could hardly escape the adjective 'dedicated' but in the seventeenth century self-interest was not thought incompatible with mastery of one's job. The son of a master, he had learned his craft in the hard school of whaling voyages (one at least as a captain) and his experience of the navy and knowledge of the shipwright's art was such that he had been appointed Surveyor of the Navy a few years before the civil war. Left-wing political theorizing would cut little ice with such a man. His masters had begun to suspect as much. In the summer of 1647 a small party of Presbyterian leaders including Sir William Waller were caught off the mouth of the Thames trying to escape to France and brought aboard Batten's flagship in the Downs. They produced the pass issued by the temporary Speaker of the House of Commons – Lenthall, the legally constituted Speaker, had taken refuge with the army – and Batten let them go. For this, and for his unguarded expressions concerning the army's intentions towards the King, he was summoned to Westminster. Batten obeyed but showed his resentment by resigning his commission. The Commons voted that he should be succeeded by Rainborough, not so extraordinary an appointment as it may sound since he had begun the war as a Parliamentary sea captain and had only transferred to the army after his capture by the Royalists. But there were difficulties. First of all Rainborough did not want to abandon his position in the van of army radicalism. And then a few weeks later he incurred the severe displeasure of Cromwell and Fairfax for his part in the abortive mutiny at Ware. The House of Lords at once voted down his appointment. A furious dispute between the two Houses polarized the Left Wing–Right Wing, Independent versus Presbyterian field of force. On 1 January 1648 the Commons openly defied the Lords by ordering Rainborough to repair at once to his command. Batten's wife, who was ill, was turned out of the commander-in-chief's quarters. Royalist agents were not slow to exploit the ruffled feelings of her husband and his many sympathizers in the fleet.

Had the timing of the second civil war been better co-ordinated its outcome might well have been different. But who was to co-ordinate it and how? Hamilton whose leadership made the whole thing possible proved incapable of managing his own army, let alone the disparate and volatile elements that required combination. The war actually broke out with the refusal of the Parliamentary commander of Pembroke Castle to hand over to his relief. He declared for the King and was joined by most of South Wales. That was in the last week of March. At the end of April Sir Marmaduke Langdale and Sir Philip Musgrave who had been in close touch with Hamilton's party in Scotland surprised Berwick and Carlisle respectively. The way was open for the Scots. But Hamilton had been no match for Argyll's skill in political obstruction. As a result it was not till 8 July that the Scots actually crossed the border. By that time a great deal had happened. Most of Kent and much of Essex had risen for the King in the second half of May. The effect had been immeasurably increased by the revolt of the fleet. On 24 May Rainborough reported that two ships detailed to escort a northbound convoy from the Thames might refuse duty. On the 27th the crew of his own ship, headed by her lieutenant, would not let him come aboard and declared for the King. They were soon joined by the whole fleet in the Downs and the sailors landed and secured the forts of

Sieges, battles and bases of the civil wars

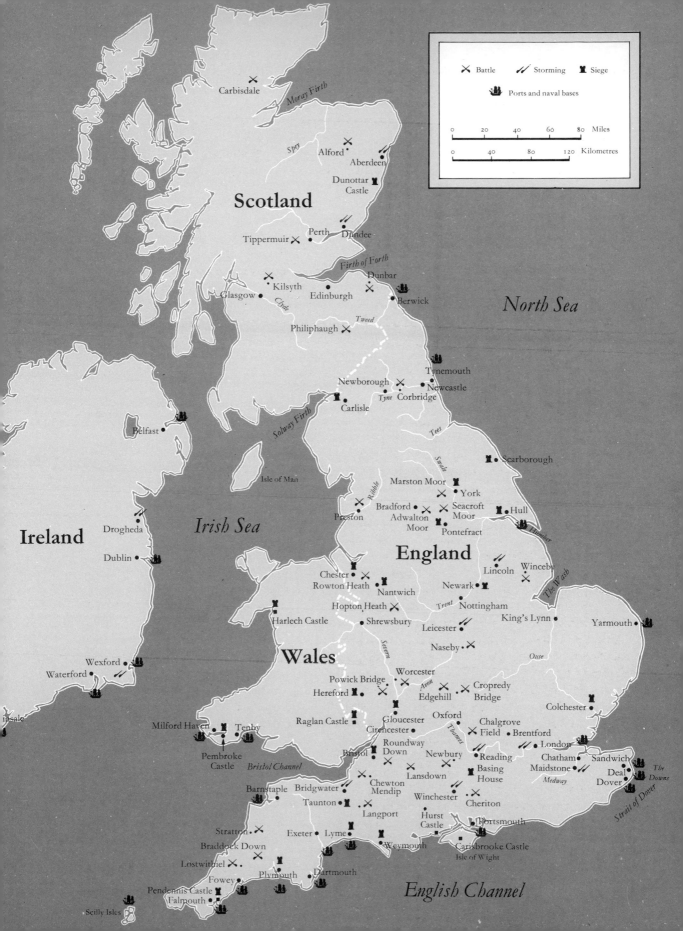

Carbisdale

Moray Firth

Spey

Alford
Aberdeen

Dunottar
Castle

Scotland

Tippermuir
Perth
Dundee

Firth of Forth

Kilsyth
Dunbar

Glasgow
Edinburgh
Berwick

Clyde

North Sea

Philiphaugh

Tweed

Tynemouth

Newborough
Newcastle

Carlisle
Corbridge
Tyne

Solway Firth

Tees

Belfast

Swale

Scarborough

Isle of Man

Marston Moor
York

Ribble

Preston
Bradford
Seacroft
Moor

Ireland

Drogheda

Irish Sea

Adwalton
Moor
Hull

Dublin

England

Pontefract

Humber

Chester
Lincoln
Winceby

Rowton Heath
Newark
The Wash

Nantwich

Hopton Heath
Trent
Nottingham

Harlech Castle
Shrewsbury
Leicester
King's Lynn
Yarmouth

Wexford
Wales
Naseby

Waterford
Ouse

insale

Powick Bridge
Worcester

Milford Haven
Tenby
Hereford
Edgehill
Cropredy
Bridge

Pembroke
Castle
Bristol Channel
Raglan Castle
Colchester

Gloucester
Oxford
Chalgrove
Field
Brentford

Cirencester
Thames
London

Barnstaple
Bridgwater
Roundway
Down
Newbury
Reading
Chatham
Sandwich

Bristol
Lansdown
Basing
House
Maidstone
Deal
Dover

Chewton
Mendip
Medway
*The
Downs*

Taunton
Winchester
Cheriton

Stratton
Langport
Hurst
Castle
Strait of Dover

Exeter
Lyme
Portsmouth

Braddock Down
Weymouth

Lostwithiel
Carisbrooke Castle
Isle of Wight

Fowey
Plymouth
Dartmouth

Pendennis Castle
English Channel

Scilly Isles
Falmouth

✗ Battle ⚔ Storming ⚒ Siege

🚢 Ports and naval bases

| 0 | 20 | 40 | 60 | 80 | Miles |

| 0 | 40 | 80 | 120 | Kilometres |

Deal, Walmer and Sandwich. The emergency was such that Warwick was instantly re-instated as Lord High Admiral. His Old Guard sympathies were well known; his brother, the Earl of Holland, was suspected of Royalism (with only too much reason: he was shortly designated the King's commander-in-chief) but no one impugned his honour or doubted his authority with the sailors. Indeed Rainborough's ship's company had startled their officers by calling for Warwick to resume command after they had declared for the King. Batten too was recalled to service and sent down to Portsmouth to make sure of the squadron there. But Batten's standards were not Warwick's. He was deeply involved in the Royalist plot and tried his best, without success, to subvert the Portsmouth ships to the King. After his return to London he persuaded the captain of the *Constant Warwick*, a frigate of which he was part owner, reputed the fastest vessel of her size, to bring her over to Holland where the revolted fleet had sailed early in July. For Warwick, in spite of the energy and firmness he had shown, had failed to win the seamen back to the Parliament.

The indecision with which the fleet was handled gave Fairfax and Cromwell the chance to stamp out each rising in turn instead of having to fight on five or six fronts at the same time. Had an experienced and resolute commander taken charge in the Downs, there was a wealth of possibilities open to him. He might have sailed to the Isle of Wight and brought the King back into play, dealing with the numerically inferior Portsmouth squadron at the same time. He might have established close contact with the city, where there had been one or two Royalist outbreaks and where feeling against the army was still running high. A fleet at the mouth of the Thames was a powerful argument in London. And everywhere in England, in the West and the North, in the home counties and East Anglia, there were plenty of people waiting to push over an unpopular Government once they saw it swaying on its pedestal. Large and expensive though the New Model was it could not be everywhere at once; and the local forces raised by the counties had been disbanded except for some important garrisons.

Fairfax had been in tighter corners in 1643. He sent Cromwell off to deal with the revolt in Wales, alerted the garrison in Newcastle to watch the east coast route and sent John Lambert, a Yorkshire country gentleman like himself and, after Cromwell, the most capable amateur commander on the Parliamentary side, to keep their native county out of mischief and to provide a mobile force ready to meet the Scots whichever route they chose. He himself marched into Kent to deal with what appeared to be the most serious rising of all. On 1 June he appeared before Rochester to find the town strongly held and the drawbridge over the Medway raised. To outflank a position much too formidable for a frontal assault he swung his army away in a long march through Meopham and Malling, intending to cross the Medway at Maidstone and take Rochester from the east. The Cavaliers anticipated this movement and put strong forces into Maidstone and Aylesford, the other town with a bridge over the river. Again Fairfax swerved away and crossed the river a few miles higher up at Farleigh Bridge. By seven in the evening of 2 June he was in front of Maidstone. His soldiers had been marching with very little pause for three long days of early summer. He attacked at once and after some very stiff street fighting was master of the town by midnight. The road to Rochester was open.

Had the Kentish Royalists had a commander of the same quality as their comrades over the river in Essex Fairfax might not have succeeded so quickly and easily. The numbers favoured the Cavaliers (they were probably nine or ten thousand to Fairfax's seven) and as the fighting at Maidstone showed they were ready to give a good account of themselves. But the command had been vested in old Lord Norwich, George Goring's father, on grounds of rank rather than military talent. He was a spectator of the action at Maidstone; had he brought his forces to participate it might have been a different story. As it was he decided to evacuate Rochester and move on London in the hopes that the city would rise for the King. Unfortunately his supporters thought that they recognized a beaten cause. A large number melted away to their homes while they could still do so with a chance of impunity. Thus Lord Norwich arrived on Blackheath on 3 June, four days after Fairfax had left it, with an army of about three thousand. Now was the time for the Presbyterians in Parliament and in the city to rise. The force Fairfax had been able to leave was very small. There was a Royalist army outside occupying the high ground that commanded not only London but the river and the Dover road. The fleet at the mouth of the Thames was on their side. There were already reports of a Royalist revolt in Essex. Cromwell was still besieging Pembroke Castle with no evidence of early success. At any minute the Scots might cross the border. Not since Rupert took Bristol in 1643 had so favourable a conjunction been offered.

But opportunities require decision. The absurd appointment of Lord Holland to command in chief – Henrietta Maria's last and not least valuable contribution to the ruin of her husband's cause – nullified the hope of effective action and ensured the rapid dissemination of any secret plans that might be formed. Holland was still revolving schemes for sending horses out of London in twos and threes to prepare for a rising that would coincide with Hamilton's invasion. Skippon, the veteran who had drilled the London Trained Bands in the first days of the Long Parliament and had served Essex as his Major-General of Foot, seized the initiative, closing the gates of the city and manning the defences. Norwich, unable to strike a spark of resistance and keenly aware of Fairfax's army coming up behind him, left his troops on Blackheath and crossed the river to investigate the possibilities of joining the reported rising in Essex. He found Chelmsford in the hands of the Royalists and hurried back with the good news. But most of his force had disappeared. Only about five hundred swam their horses across to the Isle of Dogs and joined the Essex Cavaliers. There at least they found capable military leadership in Sir Charles Lucas and Sir George Lisle, and that and more in Lord Capel.

Bold and active as they were, Fairfax's swift pursuit, once he had reduced the last pockets of resistance in Kent, forced the Royalists on to the defensive. They occupied Colchester on 12 June and met Fairfax's army outside the town next day. Outnumbered and beaten back, they yet managed to inflict a sharp defeat on the Ironsides when they pressed into the town intent on taking it

The Earl of Holland

without having to form a siege. In spite of everything Fairfax could do, in spite of the feebleness that let a couple of Parliamentary ships deny them the support that might have reached them up the Colne, this small scratch force held on through thick and thin until the war had been lost. The mere fact of tying down so much of the effective strength of the New Model provided openings that were either neglected or mismanaged. At the beginning of June, after the fall of Maidstone, the most powerful units of the Revolted Fleet sailed from the Downs to see if they could secure Yarmouth. Some base they must have and Chatham was now denied them by Fairfax's victory. But they were too late; the town was firmly held. They sailed back to the Downs and then on 10 June over to the Dutch port of Helvoetsluys. There they welcomed on board as their admiral the King's second son, James, Duke of York, a strikingly handsome boy of fourteen who had escaped from London disguised as a girl a few weeks before. He had been captured at the surrender of Oxford and his escape to the Continent, engineered by a shady Irish colonel particularly favoured by Charles I as a secret agent, had been a great relief to his father's mind. He was staying with his sister, the Princess of Orange, to the annoyance of his mother and elder brother who wanted him to join them at Paris. The removal of the Prince of Wales to Paris from Jersey two years

The siege of Colchester in 1648. Next to Cromwell's victory at Preston, this was the principal military action of the second civil war

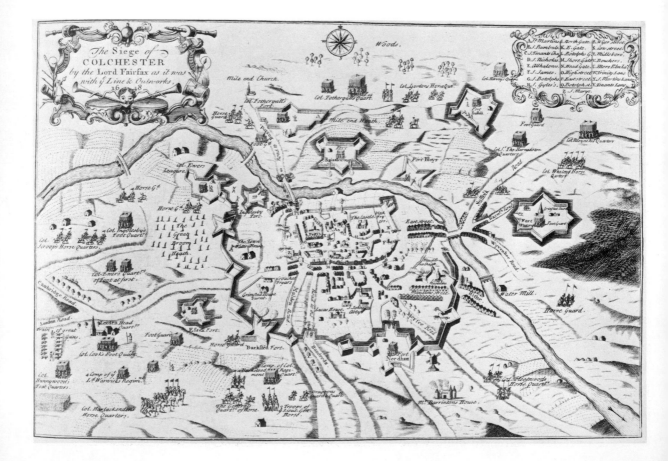

earlier at the express command of Henrietta Maria had been resisted by Clarendon and his friends on the Prince's Council to the point of resignation. It was in that heaven-sent interval that the great minister wrote the first seven books of his masterpiece *The History of the Rebellion and Civil Wars in England*. It was in fact the revolt of the fleet that brought Prince and minister together again. Clarendon had received an urgent summons to attend Charles in Paris. At Rouen he heard that the Prince had passed through on his way to Calais in the hopes of joining the fleet and would send instructions for him to follow. Clarendon's misfortunes in doing so reinforced his distrust of the Continental powers and his detestation of privateering. The smiling governor of Dunkirk who took his money to secure a safe passage was in cahoots with the Ostenders who took his ship and stripped him of everything he possessed.

Meanwhile the Prince had been received with even greater enthusiasm than his brother. Characteristically the Royalists still had time to intrigue and squabble over which brother should in fact command. At fourteen James was surely rather too young: but he had already appointed a Presbyterian peer, Lord Willoughby of Parham, as his vice-admiral and at all costs the Presbyterians and their Scottish patrons must not be offended. Charles managed to

Although Henrietta Maria had visited Prince William of Orange to buy arms during the first civil war, she was bitterly opposed to the Duke of York's staying in Amsterdam while she was in Paris

CHARLES PAR LA GRACE DE DIEV PRINCE DE GALES

Ce Prince Secondant les genereux effortz
Dun Royal pere malgre les destins tres forts
Qui des humains Ça bas choquent la liberté
Par tiltres par courage et par dexterité
Des traistres persistantz fera voir dans le temps
Que des fatalitez mesme il Se rendra exempts
Sus donc renommee Sus clairons esclatans
Par les coins de la terre allez retentissantz
Quil n'y a nulz malheurs qui puissent empescher
Ce prince de regner, et aux siens succeder

LEFT *A French print of Charles, Prince of Wales, during his exile*

RIGHT *A print from an early eighteenth-century edition of Clarendon's History. Of the eighteen supporters surrounding the King, ten preceded or followed him to the scaffold; the other eight died in battle*

persuade the boy admiral to stay behind in exchange for confirming his appointment of Lord Willoughby. He then knighted Batten who had arrived with his splendid frigate and appointed him rear-admiral. It was perhaps as well to have one flag officer whose unrivalled professional experience could

make up for the total ignorance of the other two. But the Cavaliers of every shade, even the moderate and sensible Clarendon, were outraged. Batten was a traitor. He had fired on the Queen when she had landed in Bridlington Bay. Manifestly he was not a gentleman. The seamen did not really think much of him. And so on. Under such curious and uncertain leadership the fleet sailed on 24 June. What was it going to do? Where was it going to go? These interesting questions, it soon appeared, had not been resolved.

In England the Earl of Holland was almost ready to raise the King's standard. More usefully, a party of Yorkshire Royalists had seized Pontefract Castle, the Colchester men were still holding their own and there were unmistakable signs that Hamilton was about to lead his army across the border. Cromwell had still not forced the surrender of Pembroke and, in some ways worst of all, the loyalty of the seamen in the ships remaining to Parliament was highly uncertain. From intelligence reports it seemed that an order to fire on their revolted comrades would provoke a mutiny. Fortunately for the Government the Royalists did not know this. What the real sympathies of the seamen were no one knows and probably no one ever knew. If it were true that the Parliament ships would have refused to fire on their brother sailors under the Prince, how likely is it that such an order given in the Royalist fleet would have been obeyed? Even Batten, a flag officer who had coldly and deliberately changed sides and must be presumed to have reckoned up what was involved, was clearly opposed to any such proceeding. What might, on this scale, be expected from men who had been provoked into their change of allegiance by constant bilking of their wages, increasing dissatisfaction with the victualling and an exasperated conviction that neither Parliament nor the army would do anything for them? In politics and religion the seamen, isolated by their business from the pamphlets, preachings and debates of army radicalism, were no doubt conservative but there is little to suggest that they were Cavaliers.

The uses to which the Prince could put his fleet were therefore circumscribed from the start. In the end he put it to none. He appeared off Yarmouth and even bought some provisions there but made no attempt to secure the town. He sailed to the Downs and landed some Dutch soldiers to reinforce the forts but the landing party were roughly handled and had to be re-embarked. Some merchant ships were captured but were ransomed or even let go free for fear of antagonizing the City whose alliance the Royalists hoped to win. The hungry seamen's hopes of prize money were disappointed. Meanwhile on land the familiar stink of defeat was unmistakable. On 5 July Holland, Warwick's brother, appeared with a few Cavaliers in Kingston and galloped excitedly about Surrey for a day or two before a strong party of troopers caught him at Ewell and chased him back through Surbiton into Kingston. Some lives were lost and the revolt was over before it had begun. Those who had the wit to make for London got clean away but Holland and a small party crossed the river and rode north. The whole escapade came to an end with his surrender in an inn yard at St Neots on 10 July. On the next day Pembroke at last capitulated and Cromwell was free to march north to meet the Scots.

Hamilton's mishandling of his campaign was classic. His troops were raw and needed firm and energetic leadership; such as they got was loose, slow, inert. His English allies, Sir Marmaduke Langdale and Sir Philip Musgrave, had shown speed and enterprise in seizing the two keys to England's northern frontier, Berwick and Carlisle. Not only did he fail to exploit these bold strokes, he allowed Langdale, one of the most experienced and successful of all the Royalist commanders in the civil war, to be recalled from a pre-emptive attack on Lambert's little force before it could be strengthened by local levies. When at last Hamilton did move his army forward from Carlisle Lambert showed great skill in conducting a fighting retreat against forces that outnumbered him by about four to one. So dilatory was the pace of the invasion that the Scots had only reached Stainmore in Westmorland by the time that Cromwell's cavalry had joined Lambert at the end of July. Cromwell himself was marching his infantry north by the central route through Leicester and Nottingham. Besides protecting Yorkshire from the Scottish threat it enabled him to pick up shoes sent from Northampton and stockings from Coventry, both of which were badly needed by his troops. He was at Leicester on 1 August, Nottingham on the 5th and reached Doncaster on the 8th. There he waited three days for the artillery train to reach him from Hull: his own had been sunk in the Severn and, though recovered, was neither so near nor, probably, in such good trim. On the next day, the 12th, he joined Lambert, who had also retreated southeastwards to cover York, at Wetherby. By this time Hamilton, taking the west coast route, had reached Hornby, northeast of Lancaster. He might turn east and cross the Pennines by the road through Settle and Skipton or he might press on south. Cromwell himself decided to take the Skipton road from the opposite end. Either he would meet the Scots head on or he could fall on their flank if they continued south through Lancashire.

Once again it was Langdale moving down the Ribble valley from Settle to guard the flank of the Scotch army who gave Hamilton intelligence of the enemy's movements and urged him to anticipate them. Clarendon recalls that Sir Marmaduke often told him that if he had been sent but a thousand foot – and Hamilton was not short of men – he would have gained the day. But Hamilton and his overbearing second-in-command, the Earl of Callander, had rejected the possibility that Cromwell and his army could be anywhere near them. They had not bothered to provide themselves with intelligence of his movements and they did not want to admit evidence that would convict them of incompetence and compel them to think again, indeed to reverse their every disposition. The Scotch army together with its English allies outnumbered Cromwell's forces by at least two to one. On 17 August it was strung out over great distances: the main body of its foot was just entering Preston from the north while the cavalry had reached Wigan sixteen miles to the south. The weather was filthy, the staff-work rotten. The reckless dissipation of force was largely the result of this. Since no arrangements had been made to feed the troops they had to live off the country and that meant leaving a sizable territory for van, centre and rear to pillage without falling foul of each other. Discipline was bad enough without that. Cromwell had no means of knowing all this so that his decision to attack the Scots from astride their line of communication and retreat was as bold as any in his career. It paid off beyond the highest expectation. An invading force twice the size of his own was defeated and destroyed and its commander-in-chief captured.

The real battle which was far from being a walk-over was with Langdale's force of some 3000, pitted against Cromwell's whole army of nearly 9000, in a narrow lane between Longridge and Preston on the edge of Ribbleton Moor. This was the Thermopylae of the Royalist cause. For four, some accounts say six, hours Langdale's men threw back assault after assault. No field of the civil wars saw stiffer fighting. It was late in the day when the Cromwellians at last dislodged their opponents and broke through to Preston. Hamilton had still kept the great part of his foot north of the Ribble, intending to give battle on Preston Moor. But he was persuaded that the cavalry he had with him were totally inadequate to protect his foot and agreed to put his main body over the river where it could be joined by the cavalry hastily recalled from Wigan. The Ironsides reached the Ribble Bridge before this movement had been completed and fierce fighting ensued. Hamilton's cavalry escort turned tail and bolted for Lancaster, leaving their commander-in-chief and his staff cut off from his army on the wrong side of the river. He tried to cross at a ford but the incessant rain had made the river run deep and strong. At this point he was attacked by a strong party of cavalry from the captured town. Personal courage was one of the many points in which he resembled his cousin the King. He charged them three times and then, having driven them off, put his horse at the river and swam for it followed by his company.

On the next day, 18 August, Cromwell found that the Scots had gone. They had marched south to join their cavalry during the night. The cavalry at the same time had been marching north to rejoin the main body. By a final, dazzling display of incompetence they took different routes and missed each other. In exhaustion and despair they were easy meat for their victorious and disciplined opponents. By the evening Hamilton and a fraction of his forces had retreated on Warrington, hoping to hold the line of the Mersey. By the next day all who were not dead or in flight had surrendered. Hamilton, Callander and a small party of horse made off through Cheshire, hoping to hear of or make contact with Royalist insurgents in Chester or North Wales. But nothing stirred. There was some talk of making for Pontefract Castle but at last the troopers would ride no further and Hamilton himself was taken prisoner at Uttoxeter on the Stafford–Derby border on 25 August.

Three days later Colchester surrendered. For weeks conditions in the town had been appalling. To starve the garrison out, the civil population, men, women and children, had to be starved first. Fairfax, as humane a commander as any, refused to let them through the Parliamentary lines. The second civil war ended with a bitterness and an anger that looked ugly for the losers.

Cromwell headed north to settle affairs in Scotland. This he did easily enough by coming to a composition with Argyll, Hamilton's great rival who had led the opposition to the Engagement, as it was called, with Charles I. Carlisle and Berwick were handed over to the English army whose occupation of the latter is commemorated by a handsome parish church, an uncharacteristic monument to a force that destroyed so much beauty in churches and cathedrals.

Lambert was left behind with a couple of regiments to see that the Scots behaved themselves. Before moving north to mop up Royalist resistance Cromwell had written his dispatch announcing the victory to the Parliament in terms that left no doubt of his disapproving any further attempt at negotiation with the King. But Parliament chose to disregard this clear signal from the victor of the second civil war. In furious reaction to the King's Engagement with the Scots and under pressure from the Army leaders the Commons had passed in January a Vote of No More Addresses to the King. Now, in defiance of those same Army leaders who had just pulled their chestnuts out of the fire for them, they repealed it. Many of the Presbyterian members who had absented themselves, or even, as in the case of Sir William Waller, fled abroad, had taken their seats again. London was still strongly in sympathy. Fairfax was at least half, probably more than half, on their side. Cromwell and Harrison were far away in the North. But Cromwell had won the war and had the power. He would be back.

That Fairfax might now prove less generous to defeated enemies and less anxious to promote a settlement with the King was strongly suggested by his behaviour over the surrender of Colchester. When the garrison at its last gasp sued for peace Fairfax raised his terms. Soldiers and subordinate officers were given no more than security for their lives; senior officers, lords and gentlemen were not even to have that. Probably no one thought that so gentle and chivalrous a man would execute those who had put themselves on his mercy. But he did. On the morning his troops entered the town he called a Council of War to choose the victims. Old Lord Norwich and Lord Capel, natural choices for exemplary vengeance, he reserved for the civil power to deal with. At two in the afternoon Sir Charles Lucas, Sir George Lisle and Sir Bernard Gascoigne, a Florentine soldier of fortune whose name had been anglicized from Bernardo Guasconi, were sentenced to death and told that they would be shot that evening. Gascoigne wrote a letter to the Grand Duke of Tuscany which raised the spectre of diplomatic consequences. He was spared as he was stepping up to the stone on which the bodies of his comrades were still lying. Lisle, a popular officer, met death with a smile. 'Friends,' he said to the firing party, 'I have been nearer you when you have missed me.' Lucas no less brave and an even better soldier was universally disliked. Even Clarendon reports that his presence in Colchester was found harder to bear than the siege itself. But both men pleaded the lawfulness of the King's Commission. Their brother officers, headed by Capel, demanded that if any were to be shot all should be. It was asserted by the Royalists, and with some justice, to be a horrifying departure from the code hitherto respected by both sides.

Yet the righteous wrath of even so moderate and magnanimous a Royalist as Clarendon is somewhat selective. If his tone over the murder (his word) of Lucas and Lisle is compared with that of excited admiration in which he describes the killing of the unarmed Colonel Rainborough a few weeks later it is difficult to sustain a charge of impartiality. Rainborough, to recover from his discomfiture at sea, had been restored to the command of his regiment at the siege of Colchester. A few weeks after its capitulation Cromwell asked for him to be put in command of the siege of Pontefract. Hardly had he arrived at

Doncaster before the Pontefract garrison sent out a commando to capture him and bring him back as hostage for the safety of Sir Marmaduke Langdale who had been taken at an alehouse near Nottingham and was held prisoner in that castle. There were rumours that so eminent and formidable a champion of the King's cause, and a Papist to boot, would be served the same as Lucas and Lisle. The plan nearly came off. Rainborough was hustled out of bed in his inn and led into the yard. When he saw that he was to be carried off he started to struggle and call for help. To avoid being caught his captors killed him and rode hell for leather back to Pontefract. Some of them were executed in their turn when the castle at last surrendered. The mercy generally shown to prisoners by both sides rested on a sensitive equipoise. At the very beginning of the war Lilburne had been among the first prisoners taken by the Royalists. Charles I had only been dissuaded from proceeding against him as a traitor by the threat of reprisals.

For his part Fairfax felt that those Royalists who had once again plunged the country into war had forfeited their right to mercy and might in some cases – Lucas he specifically cited – be held to have broken parole. His soldiers resented the second war even more fiercely. Cromwell and Ireton had already given up all hopes of the King. He had played now right into their hand. If the Parliament tried to stop them winning the game so much the worse for it.

The last embers of the war had been quickly stamped out after Preston and Colchester. The fleet, moving into the Thames after Colchester had fallen, ended as it began in futility. For one alarming day the Royalist Fleet and Warwick's ships rode within sight of each other. Through one hair-raising night the Portsmouth squadron, on its way to join Warwick, and the King's ships blundered into each other. A shot or two was actually fired but no one was hurt. Fortunately both Batten and his old commander-in-chief were each against a general action. Next day Nature came to the rescue: first a storm kept the Royalist ships from closing Warwick's, and then, when that had blown itself out, the Prince's ships found themselves with no water and only one butt of beer. There was nothing for it but to sail back to Holland where they arrived safely on 3 September. Two days later the last of the forts in the Downs surrendered.

The Government had ridden out the threat from the fleet. There remained the King and the Army. If a settlement were to be reached with Charles before Cromwell re-appeared on the scene there was no time to lose. Commissioners were at once sent down to treat with him at Newport in the Isle of Wight. To prevent any further trouble – there had been reports of a Royalist *coup d'état* in the Scillies – Warwick was sent to Helvoetsluys with all the strength that could be spared. He anchored within sight of the Revolted Fleet. A few days later a powerful Dutch squadron under Tromp sailed in and anchored between them. There they all three remained for nearly two months.

The King too thought that he could still play for time. He had, it seems, learned nothing since 1646. He intended no concession, he felt no obligation of good faith. But though his political creed, resting on his profoundest certainties, was unshaken, the confident optimism that he had derived from it was gone. Although better treated by far than he had been at Carisbrooke, allowed the company of his oldest and most valued friends – Richmond, Hertford, Southampton, his favourite divines headed by Bishop Juxon, his old and trusted secretaries and attendants, Sir Edward Walker and Sir Philip Warwick – he left an impression of sadness and resignation on men who had seen him cheerful and unperturbed in ruin and disaster. A quarter of a century later Sir Philip Warwick remembered of this time:

> I never saw him shed tears but once, and he turned presently his head away; for he was then dictating to one somewhat in a window, and he was loth to be discerned; and the Lords and Gentlemen were then in the room, tho' his back was towards them.

A miniature of the King by John Hoskins. The portrait echoes Sir Philip Warwick's description of the King's melancholy

The lords Sir Philip speaks of were not only the men of his own party but the Parliamentary Commissioners, Northumberland, Pembroke, Salisbury, who had been chosen no doubt to give the King what encouragement was possible. Perhaps the presence of old friends and men who if not friends had at least paid him court helped to emphasize the double loneliness of his role as King and as prisoner. Did he now still much believe in the plans of escape and of disavowing every agreement that filled his secret correspondence? Did anyone else much believe in his open professions of goodwill and a readiness to settle all outstanding questions in a spirit of give and take? Cromwell and Ireton certainly did not. On 20 November the officers of the Army laid a Remonstrance before the Commons, demanding that the King be brought to trial and that an end be put to the Treaty. The Presbyterians hesitated. Before they could decide what to do, the Army acted. The King was snatched from the Isle of Wight and brought under strong guard to the cheerless isolation of Hurst Castle, just across the Solent. Apart from a narrow causeway it was surrounded by water. Short of another revolt in the fleet there would be no hope of rescue or escape. On 6 December the Army put a strong guard on the Parliament house, denying access to the Presbyterian members. Pride's Purge, called after the colonel in charge of the operation, set the stage for the climax of the drama, the trial and execution of the King.

Chapter 16
The King's Trial and Execution

Trial and execution were from the start conceived of as integral to each other. There was never any provision for acquittal. It was a disadvantage that a judicial method had been chosen for the attainment of a political end (the elimination of the King) that could be fairly argued in either seventeenth- or twentieth-century terms as a moral necessity. What moral right had any man, King or anyone else, to any other treatment when he was preparing, in the middle of a negotiation, to go back on his word and, if he got the chance, to treat the men he was dealing with as traitors? It was bad faith: it was returning evil for good. In seventeenth-century terms it was also a defiance of the Divine Will as expressed in the result of the civil wars. 'This man against whom the Lord hath witnessed': Cromwell's phrase conveys the player's exasperation at so obstinate a refusal to accept the decision of the referee. And anyone in any age might ask in such a situation: How many more lives are to be lost or ruined because one party to a dispute will not accept a compromise? Why should any be? The King had been admitted to mercy and had abused the grace he had been shown. In such a case there was scriptural authority for exacting the uttermost farthing.

Such in essence was the view common to almost all sections of Army opinion from moderate conservatives like Colonel Hutchinson, Cromwell himself and, apparently, Fairfax to Levellers, Republicans and Sectaries such as Hugh Peter, Ludlow or Harrison. All of these men disagreed with each other, or were shortly to do so, on fundamental political questions. And the execution of the King, though it ushered in a Republic, did so almost incidentally. The men who brought him to the block, Cromwell and Ireton, were not Republicans from choice but from necessity. Fairfax, the dog that did not bark, survived to play an important part in restoring the monarchy in 1660. And some out-and-out radicals, John Lilburne and Sir Henry Vane to cite but two prominent examples, were conspicuous by their absence from the King's trial.

Why were men of this temper unsatisfied by the considerations that their much less revolutionary brethren had at last found compelling? Two answers suggest themselves, the first particular to Radicals and Levellers, the other of a far wider application. Radicals and Levellers were the standard-bearers of democratic theory, a political belief generally abhorred in the seventeenth century. As such they must disapprove the purging of the elected sovereign body, however dubious its democratic title-deeds, by the army. They had not the advantage of the sophisticated rhetoric by which a Left-wing dictatorship can be shown not to be a dictatorship at all but really the purest expression of democracy. Whether or not the King had wronged his subjects was a moral and perhaps a legal question; whether or not he was an impossible man who had to be got rid of before he stirred up any further trouble was a question of expediency. A democrat must in either case require that they be answered democratically, by some body that visibly derived its authority from the people, not by some self-constituted military junta. But dwarfing the idea of democracy, still in its extremest youth, was the prime political notion of English history, the great fundamental about whose interpretation the war had been fought: the concept of law. Here two apparently insuperable objections presented themselves. First, the whole theory of English law rested on the premise that the King was the source of all justice, expressed in the well-known maxim that the King can do no wrong. Second, not only English law but the very idea of law implies that an act can only be justiciable if it offends against a known or declared code. What law, or part of a law, could the King be said to have broken? It was not enough to say, and to get other people to say, that he had acted wrongly. That intensely theological age was constantly reminding itself that no one could live through a day without sin except by God's free grace. But crime and punishment, constitutions and prerogative powers, belonged, and were known to belong, to a much narrower and more certain world.

The force of these objections which the Royalists and the Presbyterians at once asserted in pamphlets and sermons was brought home by the absolute refusal of the front and even the second rank of the legal profession, the heart and soul of Parliamentary resistance to the Stuarts, to have anything to do with the King's trial. Selden, the greatest lawyer of his time and one of the most learned men in Europe, maintained a reverberating silence. Whitelocke, one of the Parliamentary Commissioners of the Great Seal, the joint official head of the legal profession, refused to serve on the committee appointed by the Commons to arrange for the trial. He was joined by Widdrington, his fellow Commissioner, and by the Clerk of the House. Such opposition could hardly have touched Cromwell. Selden and Whitelocke had been among the friends of Clarendon and Falkland. What came much nearer home was the refusal of Oliver St John, now Chief Justice of the Common Pleas, to serve on the Court. St John was one of the inner ring, the Great Contrivers as Clarendon calls them, that cousinhood centred on John Hampden, whose defence counsel he had been in the great Ship Money case. He was not only Cromwell's kinsman but a friend and close political colleague. With Sir Henry Vane he had supplied the Parliamentary ingenuity and adroitness that Cromwell lacked. The fact that St John was joined by the other two Chief Justices probably meant little to Cromwell who counted such matters but dung and dross in comparison to Christ but it underlined the emphatic rejection by the law as a profession of the legality of what was proposed.

In all these proceedings the most baffling figure is that of Fairfax. It is clear that he was anything but the driving force. But it is also clear that he knew what was happening. Though he did not attend the trial or sign the death-warrant he did attend the first meeting of the commissioners appointed to judge the King. Thereafter he dissociated himself from everything that went on, even on the day of the King's execution appearing by one contemporary account to be in genuine ignorance as to his fate. His wife appeared at the trial and made a dramatic demonstration of protest. Yet if, as all this suggests, this brave and chivalrous man disapproved, why did he not do something about it? It was Cromwell who had destroyed the Scotch army and won the war but it was Fairfax who was Lord General and whose standing from his achievements in the earlier war was still, with both soldiers and the general public, hardly inferior to Cromwell's. He was anyhow his superior officer and both men held strict views of military discipline. Everything about Fairfax's subsequent political career, his ostentatious withdrawal into private life, his daughter's marriage to the young Duke of Buckingham, his active part in restoring Charles II in 1660, identifies him with the Presbyterian party. Yet Fairfax was a soldier, the son of a soldier, and had married the daughter of Sir Horace Vere, the pattern and preceptor of those who went to the wars before King and Parliament made England a battlefield. His loyalty to and care for the men he commanded were perhaps his profoundest public sentiments. He had not scrupled to have Lisle and Lucas shot out of hand for their part in causing the death of so many of his men. And when it came to the King might he not, like another great English commander, 'think the King is but a man, as I am: the violet smells to him as it doth to me'?

Of the fifty-nine men who, having sat in judgment on the King, eventually put their names to the warrant for his execution by far the most impressive

A double portrait said to be of Lord President Bradshaw and Hugh Peter. It bears a Latin inscription on the back identifying the two men as divines whose ministrations the King impiously rejected. Its regicide associations are early and strong

and substantial body was that of the army officers, headed by Cromwell, and Ireton. Apart from Lambert, absent on service in the North, it was virtually a roll-call of the regimental commanders of the New Model, supported by several others such as Hutchinson and Ludlow who had not served directly under Cromwell or Fairfax. The attempt to dignify the list with peers, courtiers and independent country magnates disgraced it with the bad hats of each category, men that would never have passed muster with the recruiting officers of the Eastern Association. The last important class to be represented, the lawyers, were not so much crooks as zealots and nonentities. Bradshaw, who presided, was said by Milton to have spent all his early life 'sedulously employed in making himself acquainted with the laws of his country'. This is a baroque way of saying that he had been an attorney's clerk at Congleton in Cheshire and on becoming a barrister had built up a substantial practice in that part of the world. He became mayor of Congleton in 1637 but seems not to have been much heard of in London before the civil war. In politics he was a staunch Republican and soon fell out with Cromwell's dictatorship. Cook, who as solicitor for the Commonwealth prepared the charge and, in the absence of the attorney-general, conducted the prosecution, was even more obscure but much less provincial. He had travelled widely in Europe, had lived for a time in both Rome and Geneva, and had some connection with Ireland. The other barristers who sat as judges were even less eminent.

On 19 December 1648 the King was moved from Hurst Castle under a strong escort. His destination was Windsor where he was to be kept until the curtain was ready to go up on his trial. He spent the first night at Winchester where he was received in state by the mayor and Corporation, and the second and third at Farnham. His last day's ride took him over Bagshot Heath, a wild tract well suited for ambushes and escapes if any were to be attempted. There was, it seems, such a plan. Charles had arranged to dine at the house of a young and spirited peer who was known to keep a stable worthy of his own breeding and temper. Half-way through the meal a message was brought that the King's horse had gone lame. To add verisimilitude Charles had complained that his mount was going badly during the ride over from Farnham. His host at once offered him a replacement, an animal that, like Batten's frigate, enjoyed the reputation of being able to outdistance all pursuit. But the strong, well-mounted escort was under the command of Harrison, not the kind of easy-going officer to take his eye off the job in hand. Before the party remounted he pointedly drew the King's attention to the fitness and quality of the troopers' horses and to the fact that they were riding with their pistols ready spanned. He drove home the hint by keeping them in close order round the prisoner the whole way to Windsor. The last slender chance of escape had gone.

It was dusk and driving rain as he rode in through the Henry VIII gate. There was a man kneeling in the mud apparently waiting for his blessing. When he came close to him he saw that this bedraggled figure quavering, 'My dear Master', was his once masterful and magnificent cousin Hamilton. The King was hustled on, up the slope to the Upper Ward. Cromwell and Ireton had issued strict and specific instructions to the governor on this point only

Sir Edward Massey

the day before: ''Tis good the prisoners, this while, be strictly kept in, and withheld from intercourse or communication with one another.' The Castle at that moment held a number of distinguished prisoners: they were soon to be joined by the Presbyterian leaders arrested after Pride's Purge, among them Sir William Waller and Sir Edward Massey, the King's two redoubtable adversaries of 1643. They and two others afterwards commemorated the fact in a series of portraits with the old, unreconstructed Round Tower demurely miniaturized in the top corner of each picture. The King eagerly enquired after them but was told that they were not there. Emptiness and solitude in the great rooms of his palace were part of the treatment prescribed. On his way to Windsor at Winchester and at Farnham the public had been admitted, at the traditional discreet distance, to watch him dine in state. There was to be no more of that. The whole Castle was to be cleared, during the King's stay, of 'as many . . . loose and idle persons as you can well riddle out and [you are] to stint the number of prisoner's servants to the lowest proportion you well can'. As for the Upper Ward it was to be virtually isolated: even the drawbridge (long since removed) that gave access to it was to be kept raised.

The newspaper reports convey a simple and striking picture of his life at Windsor. On the evening of his arrival, 23 December, after he had made his enquiries, and had been conducted to his apartments, 'The King then went to his chair that was near the fire and leaned his arm on the backside of it, standing in a melancholy posture. A while after he went to supper, and after supper to his lodging chamber.' The portrait sketch is worthy of one who had employed such great painters. 'The King, though the cook disappointed him of mince pies and plum porridge, yet he resolved to keep Christmas; and accordingly put on his best clothes, and himself is chaplain to the gentlemen that attend him, reading and expounding the scripture to them.' His attendants were appointed by his gaolers, not chosen by himself. 'The King is pretty merry and spends much time reading of sermon books and sometimes Shakespeare and Ben Jonson's plays . . .' 'The King goes not out, only walks sometimes upon the terrace and on the galleries . . .' His cheerfulness perhaps was the most taxing part of his performance. Denied the ministrations of his chaplains and the society of anyone he loved or trusted, his books and his dogs were the only refreshment for mind and spirit. Needless to say his choice of reading exacerbated his offences in the eyes of the Saints engaged in preparing his punishment.

The trial of Charles I, as Dame Veronica Wedgwood has shown in the finest study of it that has been written, was an astonishing combination of skilfulness and bungling, of craft and naïveté. Beside the one great unifying theme, 'stone dead hath no fellow', echoing the attainder of Strafford that preyed so much on the King's mind in his last months and of which he was to repent on the scaffold itself, every other purpose was divided. The trial was to be a show trial, a great act of propaganda such as is only too familiar in our century; yet at the same time it was to be hurried, hustled, almost hushed up. The sovereign people was to assert itself in the face of the world, yet admission was to be by ticket only. It was to exalt the law and to abase arbitrary power, yet the court was to look like a Council of Officers with hardly a lawyer in sight. It was to carry out a bold deep-laid political plan, yet the most obvious contingencies had been neglected. The story is too subtle and too thrilling to condense. It is it-self an epitome of the issues over which the civil war was fought and to which it had itself given birth. Its theatricality offered the role of a lifetime to a man whose apprehension of reality was at its deepest in the arts and on the stage.

> That thence the royal actor borne
> The tragic scaffold might adorn

Marvell's famous couplet calls up the masques in which the King had not disdained to perform to the final scene outside the Banqueting House, itself the work of the greatest masque designer of the age. Whatever moral, legal or political criticisms the King's trial may be open to, aesthetically and dramatic-ally it is one of history's masterpieces.

On 19 January 1649 the King was moved, at the shortest notice, to St James's. Next day he was carried across the Park in a sedan chair, its blinds drawn down, hedged in for further security, by a close escort of infantry, to the palace of Whitehall. He was conducted through its long-deserted rooms to the river stairs, where a barge was waiting, its curtains drawn. A short row brought him to the garden of Sir Robert Cotton's house fronting the river, conveniently adjacent to Westminster Hall where the trial was to open that very afternoon. This, his lodging till the trial ended, fell below the standards of propriety that the officers had so far maintained. The King was not allowed privacy even to relieve nature or to say his prayers. The troops on duty smoked and talked in his room, paying him no respect. On the other hand his lot was lightened by the presence of Juxon. The King's request that he might be allowed his services as chaplain was granted on the condition that Juxon shared his master's imprisonment and did not come and go.

During the course of his trial, Charles I was painted by Edward Bower (see frontispiece)

On the great stage that had been set for him the King transcended his present miseries and past mistakes. Alone, with no resources, no advisers, no friends, denied even the elementary justice of being allowed to see the charge brought against him or to speak in his own defence, the King turned the tables on the men who had him at their mercy and won the clearest victory of the whole war on the fiercely disputed battlefield of constitutional law. Sitting there in the hall in a huge loose-box thick with attendants not of his choosing, facing his judges in a grandstand under the great window crowned with the blazon of St George, not his own Royal Arms, his back to the body of the hall in which soldiers clanked and stamped and hawked (it was very cold), his lateral vision dominated by more soldiery with a few boxes and galleries of spectators behind them, his impotence, his isolation, his atomism were made palpable. In that vast space, among all the stir and shift of humanity, there was nothing and no one that promised a shred of comfort or compassion. To maintain dignity and self-possession in so dismal a situation cannot have been easy. To rout his opponents, as the King did, was a triumph. He showed with extraordinary skill the complete illegality of the proceedings and the inconsistency of the arguments by which they were defended, twice driving both President and Prosecutor back against the ropes so that in their double capacity as referee they were forced to bring the round to a premature conclusion. He established as brilliantly as Selden could have done that the court for all its imposing flummery rested on nothing but naked force. He was able, most convincingly, to appear as the champion of law, Parliament and people:

But it is not my case alone, it is the freedom and the liberty of the people of England; and do you pretend what you will, I stand more for their liberties. For if power without law may make laws, may alter the fundamental laws of the Kingdom, I do not know what subject he is in England, that can be sure of his life, or anything that he calls his own.

Evidence was brought that the King had permitted or encouraged the ill-treatment of prisoners and the plundering of innocent people, that he had, during his captivity, intrigued and plotted for a resumption of the war. The second was certainly true and very likely the first; but these points were not remotely relevant to the central issue, that of arbitrary power, about which the war had been fought and by which, it now appeared, the King was to be executed. In any case charges of this kind could easily and endlessly be preferred against commanders on both sides. The King's unexpected dialectical superiority began to shake a few nerves. One of his judges, an insignificant placeman who had speculated in land confiscated from the Church, broke down and began to howl. The Court had to adjourn for Cromwell to deal with him. But it became ever more obvious that delay could only be dangerous. On 27 January the King was sentenced to be beheaded. On the 29th the Death-Warrant, which had almost certainly been made out and signed by a number of judges during the actual course of the trial, was signed by the remainder of the fifty-nine regicides and transmitted to the King's gaolers. The King was to die the next day.

In the afternoon Charles was allowed to see his children, the Princess Elizabeth, aged thirteen, and Henry, Duke of Gloucester, a boy of eight. All the rest of his family were on the Continent and these two were living under the care of the Earl of Northumberland who had looked after them throughout the civil war. Indeed they had only come to know their father during the time that he had been held prisoner at Hampton Court. The King's domestic affections were strong, the parting poignant. With all the tenderness of which he was capable he impressed on them the importance of not letting themselves be used by his enemies to divert or divide the succession to the Crown. The children heartened him by the passionate loyalty of their promises. So gentle and sensitive a father could not but be aware of the intolerable strain such a meeting must impose on a child. He gave them what was left of his jewels, blessed them and sent them off. The evening he spent in prayer and meditation assisted by Juxon. Later he passed some hours in private devotion. Even on his last night a man of punctual regularity he retired at his usual hour and slept soundly till the early morning.

Henry, Duke of Gloucester, Charles's third son, and Princess Elizabeth spent the war in the custody of the Earl of Northumberland, where their elder brother James, Duke of York, joined them after the surrender of Oxford, until he escaped to the Continent (see illustration on p. 4)

As soon as he was dressed – he put on two shirts against the bitter cold in case he should be seen to shiver on the scaffold – he gave directions for the disposal of his personal possessions, his Bible and other devotional works, his gold watch, among his elder children and oldest friends. He took particular care over the neatness of his appearance, saying that it was his second wedding day. That this was more than a figure of speech to a man of strong and deep personal religion, a man whose experience of symbolic truth was perhaps more immediate than his response to the material world, we can hardly doubt. Charles I and Cromwell had in common with each other and with many vehement spirits of their generation a power of transfusing the imagery of religious language into consciousness that our age cannot share. When the King was ready Juxon joined him in preparing to receive the sacrament and then gave him Communion. A knock at the door announced the presence of a posse of Puritan divines ready even at so extreme a moment to convince the King of his errors in theology. They were sent away. Between nine and ten another knock warned the King that the time had come for his last walk across the Park to Whitehall.

By a final touch of incompetent cruelty he was then kept in suspense. What had happened was that Cromwell and Ireton had forgotten that by law Charles, Prince of Wales, must be proclaimed King as Charles II as soon as his father's death was known. The Lord Mayor of London, whose sympathies were strongly Royalist would do so with enthusiasm and so would many others in authority. There had been no move, so far, to depose the King or to abolish the monarchy. 'We will cut off his head with the Crown on it', Cromwell had crushingly replied to one of the Council of Officers who had objected to the illegality and irrationality of trying the King for treason. But the objection was valid. There was no point, or not much, in executing Charles I if the throne were to pass straight to Charles II. But what was to take the place of the established system? Were the officers, as Charles had feared, going to nobble the young Duke of Gloucester, disinherit his elder brothers and proclaim a Regency, with Cromwell in the role of Protector Somerset or Duke Humphrey? Was Cromwell himself to found a new royal house? Was there to be a Republic and if so what form would it take? These questions were too large and too difficult to be disposed of in a morning. But what could be, and was, done was to hurry a Bill through three readings in the Commons declaring the proclamation of a new king illegal. That done, they could set in motion once again the machinery that had trapped the King in so agonizing a situation.

About two o'clock there was a knock on the door of the room in which he was waiting with Juxon. It had been Charles's intention not to eat or drink between taking the sacrament and entering the new life that it had bought for him. But Juxon expostulated with him, urging the length of time he had fasted, the sharpness of the weather and the consequent risk of fainting from weakness when he stepped out on to the scaffold. The King gave way and ate a little bread and drank a glass of wine. For the last time he walked through the cold corridors of his great palace to the Banqueting House, now dark and lifeless, that more than any other building in his capital is still instinct with his taste and personality. One of the windows had been unblocked to give access to the scaffold. A friend of Sir Philip Warwick's watching from close by 'saw him come out of the Banqueting-house on the scaffold with the same unconcernednes and motion, that he usually had, when he entered into it on a Masque-night'. The huge crowd was heavily policed by soldiers, of whom a strong guard was drawn up round the scaffold itself making it all but impossible for the general public to come close enough to hear whatever the King might say. Undeterred Charles took a small piece of paper from his pocket, confident that someone would report his speech. He denied any responsibility for the war but accepted in an oblique but unmistakable allusion his guilt over Strafford's death. 'An unjust sentence that I suffered to take effect is punished now by an unjust sentence on me.' He made his own profession of faith as a Christian, emphasizing his unchangeable loyalty to the Church of England. As befitted that profession he forgave and prayed God to forgive all the world 'and even those in particular that have been the chief causers of my death'. As to law and the rights of the subject he occupied once again the inexpugnable position that Clarendon had seized for the Royalist party in the great manifestos of 1641–2 and that Charles himself had manned so memorably at his trial:

A contemporary Dutch print of the King's execution. He is shown handing his George – the insignia of the Order of the Garter usually worn round the neck – to Juxon before kneeling to the block (here represented as higher than it probably was)

Truly I desire their [the people's] liberty and freedom as much as anybody whomsoever; but I must tell you their liberty and freedom consists in having of government, those laws by which their life and their goods may be most their own. It is not for having a share in government, Sir, [who was the King addressing? Colonel Tomlinson, the senior officer present on the scaffold or the notional Speaker of some cosmic House of Commons?] that is nothing pertaining to them. A subject and a sovereign are clear different things . . .

The speech concluded with a beauty of cadence and a dignity of language that must touch any heart unhardened by a previous certainty of political opinion. Not for nothing had the King spent so much of his last months reading Shakespeare and the New Testament in the version authorized by his

An allegory of the King's execution. The besotted people assist at the ruin of their institutions, the Church, the Crown and the Common Law, at the diabolical inspiration of Cromwell, whose own motives are entirely mercenary

father. The King knelt in prayer, laid his head on the block (it was inconveniently low) and stretched out his hands in the pre-arranged signal to the executioner. The axe came down hard and true. When the severed head was held up, a fearful groan rose from the crowd, expressive of horror more than grief or pity. An unmentionable act had been committed, a point of no return passed. Like the chorus in a Greek play the Londoners bore witness to its moral and historical significance. The famous lines in Marvell's *Horatian Ode* were to immortalize its pathos.

As the soldiers dispersed the crowd, where had their officers taken the country? At home sympathy with the King, admiration for the courage and consistency he had shown in his last weeks, horror at his killing, almost blotted out all other considerations. Almost but not quite. The clever, cocksure schoolboy Samuel Pepys, then aged fifteen, watched the proceedings with the highest satisfaction and told his schoolfellows that were he to preach on the subject he would take as his text, 'The memory of the wicked shall rot'. Paine's famous rebuke to Burke that 'he pitied the plumage but forgot the dying bird' might be applied with far more justice to the threnodists of Charles I.

Louis XVI and Marie-Antoinette had not written the parts they had to play as Charles I and Henrietta Maria had. The King's performance compels admiration but it does not dispose of the question of authorship. Pym in 1640 and Cromwell in 1647 had been forced to recognize that there was no doing business with the King. Whatever may be thought of Cromwell's methods, that problem not of his choosing or creating was now solved.

Perhaps it was not so much solved as resolved into a host of consequent problems, practical and theoretical. Abroad reaction stretched through every shade of hostility short of outright war. The Dutch had sent ambassadors to try to prevent the execution. The Tsar of Russia expelled all English merchants from his dominions. But the country with the most substantial grounds of complaint was Scotland. Charles was her King just as much as he was England's. And whatever the House of Commons might or might not legally do to prevent the proclamation of his son as King of England, there could be no question of the legality of Charles II's claim to the kingdom of Scotland. He was in fact so proclaimed as soon as the news of his father's death reached Edinburgh. And then there was Ireland, whenever that fragmented, scorched and scarred country should regain some political existence. How, exactly, were the Commons of England to claim sovereignty there? Putting the juridical questions on one side for the moment, what were the facts of power? Scotland was nominally and for the time being controlled by Argyll who had opposed Hamilton and the Engagers defeated in war a few months ago. But whether he could hold on without changing to the Stuart side looked more than doubtful. Ireland was under no central control. The Catholic confederacy, the Ulster Protestants, the Parliamentary forces, the official Royalists under Ormonde, the tribal chieftains who changed sides with every shift of the local balance were all just strong enough to maintain confusion but too weak to assert authority. Ormonde believed that he could win the whole country and the Royalists still held the southern ports of Waterford, Wexford and Kinsale. For these the remains of the Revolted Fleet under Prince Rupert were known to be making. Warwick had had to raise his blockade of Helvoetsluys to avoid being frozen in late in November. The Scillies, the Channel Islands and the Isle of Man were still in Royalist hands. Finally Montrose was in Brussels recruiting for a new attempt on Scotland, a plan that Rupert had encouraged and hoped to assist with his fleet.

If these were all matters of some urgency, they were all at a distance and could be dealt with one by one. In the wake of the King's execution Cromwell had cause to echo the scriptural truth that 'a man's foes shall be they of his own household'. The divisions in the old Parliamentarian front that had held together through the first civil war had been made irreparable in the second. Of the Army that was now effectively in power the Right Wing of the officers, men such as Fairfax or Mountagu, the first Cromwell's superior officer, the second his protégé, were dismayed by the King's execution and anxious to retire from political life. Of the Left Wing, headed after Rainborough's death, by officers such as Overton, Lilburne and Cromwell's own ex-trooper Sexby, the real strength lay among the men and their preachers. They had had little or no hand in the King's death and they were already deeply suspicious of

Cromwell and Ireton. Of the Republicans who were not Levellers and not connected with army Radicalism, men such as Harry Marten and Sir Arthur Hesilrige, even Cromwell's erstwhile close political ally Sir Henry Vane, were too articulate and independent-minded to follow any Government in dumb obedience. Consent, or the more negative formulation of that concept that Cromwell was to re-iterate – 'Acceptation' – was to elude him. It is hardly surprising. What is surprising is how high a degree of toleration he managed to combine with strong government.

To assert that strength first against the Presbyterians or crypto-Royalists and then against any challenge from the Left was the immediate task. Down went the House of Lords reduced by this time to an insignificant handful. Down went the monarchy. The coffins of both were nailed down by an Act declaring England 'to be a Commonwealth and Free State' and defining 'the supreme authority of this nation' as 'the representatives of the people in Parliament'. On the surface this might appear to accept the principal points of the Leveller programme. In reality it did no such thing. The Levellers, like any body of reformers who are not impeded by the intractable responsibilities of governing, were in constant motion. By the time that Cromwell and Ireton had reached their point of departure they were over the hill into the Chartist territory of the nineteenth century, calling for annual Parliaments, equal electoral districts, salaries for MPs and so on. An important part of the movement had begun to question, even to deny, the rights of property on which the social order rested.

> Take but degree away, untune that string,
> And, hark! what discord follows; each thing meets
> In mere oppugnancy.

Cromwell no doubt disapproved Charles I's reading Shakespeare but he would have identified himself to the core of his being with the social philosophy expressed in Ulysses' great speech. His opponents in the Leveller movement, Lilburne chief amongst them, were quick to recognize that and to denounce him as a secret upholder of the very things whose outward forms he was destroying.

In March, the same month that the office of King and House of Lords had been abolished, the Leveller leaders were arrested and brought before the Council of State. After Lilburne had spoken with his usual fearlessness he was asked to withdraw into an adjoining room while the Council discussed what he had said. He heard Cromwell thump the table in emphasis: 'I tell you, sir, you have no other way to deal with these men but to break them, or they will break you.' Lilburne and his friends were sent to the Tower. The dangerous mood of the army showed itself in ever more serious incidents. At last in May a regiment marching westwards to embark for Ireland mutinied at Salisbury and turned north to join a rising at Banbury that had been fomented by an ex-corporal with a long record of indiscipline and agitation. Cromwell and Fairfax marching from London with lightning speed – in one day they covered nearly fifty miles – caught the mutineers asleep and not dreaming of pursuit at Burford in the small hours of 15 May. Only a few resisted and of these three

The King is thrown overboard; lightning strikes St Stephen's; discord and anarchy break out among the citizens, behind whom can be seen the military: a vivid allegory of 1649

were subsequently executed in the churchyard. The Banbury rising had already been suppressed, its leader refusing quarter. 'These men' had been broken.

In this uncertain period it was all the more important to deter the Royalists from any foolish adventure. The King's execution had been followed in March by that of three of the leaders of the second civil war, Hamilton, Holland and Capel. Hamilton's sentence had in the circumstances a certain fitness. Holland's, though as much deserved as any, made it impossible to continue employing his brother Warwick as Lord High Admiral. The execution of Capel, widely liked and respected on both sides, was a much more direct warning that the Government would not tolerate any further questioning of the verdict of history. For the rest of his life Cromwell, though ready to employ ex-Royalists in the highest commands abroad or in the sister kingdoms, continued to execute a few irreconcilables from time to time, choosing his victims with a certain indifference to their importance or to the gravity of their offence. Sir Henry Slingsby was one of the last to be so made an example in June 1658. Even the crusty old Republican Edmund Ludlow observed 'in the opinion of many men he had very hard measure'.

With Royalists and Levellers crushed it was high time to deal with Ireland and Scotland. Charles II in exile though negotiating with the Scots was planning to go to Ireland and to co-ordinate with Rupert's naval squadron and Montrose's intended revolt in the Western Highlands a fresh challenge to the Commonwealth. Ireland therefore was the first priority. Cromwell landed in August and by the end of the year his victories had made it clear what the result would be. Of the hideous brutalities both in hot and cold blood that he committed there can be neither doubt nor defence. It can be asserted with only too much truth that he was neither the first nor the last to figure in that recurrent nightmare. But Ormonde had shown that these odious traditions fuelled by bigotry and propaganda could be transcended. In the spring of 1650 Irish resistance though by no means at an end could be left to Ireton as Lord Deputy. The southern ports and those of the Irish Channel were in Commonwealth hands. Rupert and the Fleet had escaped to Lisbon. Charles II was on the point of sailing for Scotland. Cromwell was recalled to London.

Chapter 17
Charles II and Cromwell

Of the Royalists leaders who survived from the first Act few had parts in the last, now about to open. Rupert and a few bold spirits some of whom were, like himself, to hold high command in the Restoration navy, had sailed off into the blue. Only seven ships could still find hands enough to work them. Lisbon was their first refuge. But the Commonwealth navy soon smoked them out and chased them about the western Mediterranean until it had caught or sunk all but two or three. Escaping from the Mediterranean the Prince made an adventurous voyage down the West African coast and then across the Atlantic to the West Indies, returning to St Nazaire with several prizes and some valuable loot in March 1653. This remarkable performance had no effect whatever on the war.

The new King's little court was sharply divided over the proposed treaty with the Covenanters. Henrietta Maria and the Earl of Bristol were, as ever, enthusiasts. The King's oldest and best counsellors, Clarendon, Hopton, Cottington and Nicholas, the heart and mind of English Royalism, were strongly opposed, as, of course, was the great Scottish fighting leader whom the Covenanters abominated, Montrose. Charles II like his father did not feel obliged to return the straightforward loyalty of his tried and faithful friends. He expressed his entire confidence in and support for Montrose. But behind his back there were nods and winks to the plenipotentaries of the Covenanters, and, after he had sailed for the Orkneys on his last adventure in December 1649, a formal agreement that would involve his laying down his arms in exchange for a safe conduct out of the country. A guerrilla leader stands or falls by the undivided support of the people among whom he is operating. The fissure here opened soon proved fatal. For lack of intelligence his raw little army was surprised and destroyed at the battle of Carbisdale in Sutherland on 27 April 1650. Montrose himself made his way westward through the mountains to the country of the Macleods of Assynt. His host arrested him and handed him over to his enemies who had already reached an understanding with Charles II. Montrose met his end with the courage, the style, the sense of occasion that had marked every phase of his life. His major-general, Sir John Urry, who had on changing sides for the first time been the immediate cause of the death of John Hampden, was executed a few days later.

To the Kirk party Charles II was no object of loyalty, as he had been to Montrose, but simply a means towards their chimerical scheme of imposing a rigid Presbyterian discipline on their lax and libertarian neighbours. It was the betrayal of the Church of England implicit in the King's acceptance of Scotch demands that scandalized Clarendon and those who thought as he did. On

Charles, 2nd Earl of Dun-
fermline, one of the noblemen
who accompanied Charles II to
Scotland. At the Restoration he
became a Privy Counsellor and
later Lord Privy Seal

2 June, only a day or two after he had heard of Montrose's execution, Charles sailed from Holland. He had not then accepted all that his detested taskmasters demanded of him and he had defied them to the extent of bringing with him his own chaplains and some of his English courtiers. But the voyage so precipitately undertaken proved longer than he had expected. The winds were contrary or fell light. The interminable delays, the relentless pressure of the Scotch Commissioners with whom he was cooped up wore down the King's resolve. What did it matter? If he won, he would be back on his father's throne in England and could laugh in their faces. If he lost, all bets would be off. The one prospect he could not contemplate, a reign confined to Scotland hedged in by serried ranks of dour provincial killjoys, was fortunately impossible. By the time his ship reached Speymouth on 23 June Charles had given way on almost every point. At hardly any turn in the civil war can two allies have detested and despised each other as cordially as the King and his hosts. No opportunity was lost of humiliating him. The friends he brought with him were either sent away or allowed access to him only under supervision. His own movements were severely restricted. He was forced to listen to the turgid self-righteous pulpiteering of an unbridled clergy who did not hesitate to disparage either his parents or himself. Probably the boredom was harder to bear than the insolence. In any case he stored up a hatred for Scotland and the Scots that lasted the rest of his life. It was on England that his eyes were fixed, his hopes concentrated.

There was, however, little chance of a Royalist rising as long as the Council of State looked as formidable and as decisive a Government as it did in the summer of 1650. Cromwell had returned from the virtual conquest of Ireland to find that a London jury had acquitted Lilburne of a charge brought under the new Act by which the Government made it treason to challenge its legitimacy. This Lilburne had in fact done in the roundest terms, retaliating the charge of treason on Cromwell himself in the title of a pamphlet. The Londoners resentful of military rule had huffed and puffed but the house had not been blown down. The Army had not stirred. And the growing threat of another Scotch invasion strengthened the Commonwealth. However unpopular it might be it was better than having the Scots back again. It was thus with confidence and energy that the Council prepared to meet the challenge. An army would be sent north at once to fight the war on Scottish soil.

Fairfax was designated commander but scrupled at a preventive blow against an ally of the first war. In spite of Cromwell's urging, he resigned his commission and retired to Nun Appleton, outside York, where Andrew Marvell shortly joined the household as tutor to his daughter.

> For he did, with his utmost skill
> Ambition weed, but conscience till.

Did conscience shrink from the proposed action against the Scots or was the execution of Charles I the real but unavowed objection? Whatever Fairfax's reason, Cromwell was the only conceivable alternative. Ireton was still heavily engaged in Ireland. The place that he would no doubt have taken was supplied by Charles Fleetwood, a much less masterful character, who was to succeed

Ireton two years later as Bridget Cromwell's husband. Two other officers selected for command were John Lambert and George Monck, the ex-Royalist. The personalities of the Protectorate and Restoration have almost replaced the men who were prominent in 1642 and 1643.

Leaving London toward the end of June Cromwell gathered his forces as he marched north, concentrating at Berwick in the middle of July. On the 22nd he crossed the border and reached Dunbar without opposition. His army, consisting of some 5000 horse and nearly 11,000 foot, was closely supported from the sea. David Leslie, the experienced professional soldier who confronted him, had been careful to destroy or remove everything that could ease the problem of supply. As so often in a northern summer the weather was cold and wet. Leslie's tactics took full advantage of this. Although the army he commanded was much larger, probably about 6000 horse and 16,000 foot, it was far inferior in quality. Most of the troops were raw and indisciplined; their officers were subject to the ideological purgings of the Kirk. One of the disadvantages of playing the match on the home ground was the ubiquitous presence of these assertive dominies. On the other hand it did mean that the troops could be lodged and fed, while their opponents, soaked and hungry, were shivering on exposed hillsides.

Cromwell's aim conversely was to bring on a battle. Moving up the coast to Musselburgh he found the enemy occupying a strong position, his left resting on the port of Leith, his right on Edinburgh itself. This was at the end of July. For most of August Cromwell circled round Edinburgh to the south and west like a boxer looking for an opening. But Leslie never let down his guard and never let himself be cornered. In the middle of the month, unable to bring his supply ships into Musselburgh against the prevailing westerly wind that drove the rain clouds scudding overhead, Cromwell retreated to Dunbar. The harbour was easier to work into and the troops were given a square meal and a few days' rations. Back outside Edinburgh Cromwell made a determined effort to break through to the Forth and cut off access from the north and west. That would force Leslie to fight as there was not much food in the city. But again Leslie manoeuvred impeccably, blocking Cromwell's every move. By the end of the month the English army was seriously weakened by disease and hunger. Cromwell again retired to Dunbar, this time without hopes of doing more than extricate his army from a dangerous situation. But this time Leslie followed him and, by-passing the town, seized the strong position of Doon Hill to the south, commanding both Dunbar itself and the Berwick Road. Cromwell was trapped with his back to the sea.

The battle of Dunbar fought on 3 September 1650 was an even more striking victory than Preston, in that it was won against a commander who had consistently out-generalled Cromwell in the campaign and had himself chosen the field of battle. Cromwell's military talent is here seen at its strongest in his choice of subordinate commanders – both Lambert and Monck performed prodigies of bold and brilliant fighting leadership – and in the magnificent quality of the troops he had trained and led. Dunbar was a soldiers' battle in that only soldiers of the first quality could have fought so superbly when everything was against them. They were outnumbered; the enemy was astride their communications and enjoyed an overwhelming superiority of position; they knew their own situation to be desperate; a less disciplined and self-confident body of men might have lost confidence in their officers. Yet splendidly as the soldiers fought it was the quickness of eye followed up by instant irresistible unexpected attack shown first and most conspicuously by Lambert and seconded so stoutly by Monck that carried the day. But, like Nelson at the battle of St Vincent, Lambert could only defy conventions and preconceived plans because he knew that his commander-in-chief would exploit the opening he had seized and would support him through thick and thin.

The key to the battle was the excessive concentration of the Scotch foot in the centre. If they could be attacked on the flank they would be unable to deploy and their numbers would impede the necessary defensive movement. Everything turned on breaking the Scotch cavalry on the right of the line covering the Berwick Road. The attack which Lambert was to lead was to go in while it was still dark and was to be supported by the full weight of the English army. These movements are more easily executed on paper than on a night made darker by driving rain over unfamiliar country where at all costs the enemy must not be prematurely alarmed. This meant that Lambert came on the enemy before he had support on anything like equal terms. He instantly charged and though the Scots cavalry stood their ground and even counter-charged, the fire and spirit of the New Model horse had more than half won the battle in the first few minutes. In an hour the whole Scotch army was in head-long retreat, Cromwell, as so often, exulting over the slaughter: 'Our men had the execution of them for eight miles.' Three thousand Scots died on the field or in the pursuit. Ten thousand of the foot were taken prisoner. Leslie lost all his artillery and stores but got away with about four thousand men.

The decisive effect of the defeat at Dunbar was that, as Cromwell succinctly put it in a letter to Sir Arthur Hesilrige, then governor of Newcastle, 'it's probable the Kirk has done their do.' The stranglehold of the Presbyterian fanatics on the political life of the country had been loosened. The imposition of the Scottish ecclesiastical system on the population of England and Ireland was no longer a credible aim. This immediately widened the permissible basis of Royalist support in Scotland, most notably amongst the experienced army officers, often younger sons of nobles or gentry who had learned their trade in the armies of Gustavus or the Dutch Republic. Such ungodly and carnal persons had been the chief objects of the purgings in the lately defeated army. But if breadth had been gained, intensity had been lost. Charles now stood on his own legs as the lawful King, and as such was crowned at Scone on New Year's Day 1651. But in Scotland national consciousness had long found the focus of its loyalty in the Kirk rather than the royal dynasty. And indeed there was not much that was identifiably Scotch about Charles II.

Meanwhile there was a victorious English army on Scottish soil. Cromwell at once moved on Edinburgh, occupying the city without resistance and laying siege to the castle. In October he entered Glasgow. On Christmas Eve, not that the festival was kept under the new regime, Edinburgh Castle surrendered. Cromwell was master of all the richest part of Scotland south of the Forth and

RIGHT *A detail from The Execution of Charles I by Weesop*

OVERLEAF *Stumpwork from the seventeenth century depicts Charles II and Charles I as a martyr (this scene derives from the frontispiece of Eikon Basilike or The Pourtraicture of his Sacred Majesty in his Solitude and Sufferings – see p. 216)*

the Clyde. Leslie's army strongly posted at Stirling was secure as long as it did not venture out of the hills. The bitterness of the winter made campaigning impossible but when the warmer weather came Cromwell was still faced with the task of dislodging this dogged enemy from his fastness. For months he met with no success. At last at the end of July he made a throw to end the game. Securing the passage of the Forth by his command of the sea he put the great part of his army on the north shore and marched boldly up to Perth, taking the town on 2 August. He had thus taken Leslie's position in the rear and had cut him off from the supplies and reinforcements he was expecting from the north and east. But he had also, and much more importantly, opened the road to England.

What was Leslie to do? His shrewd realism left him undazzled by the visions of cheering crowds and easy victories that swam before the eyes of his young sovereign. He knew that his army was weak. He knew how unpopular a Scots invasion would be and how little mercy his men might expect if, as was probable, the whole enterprise ended in disaster. On the other hand the country could not support a war for another year even if he did elude the threat now posed by Cromwell's presence to the north. The bet on invading England was at long odds but a win would transform the situation. Scrambling out of Cromwell's reach into the Highlands would solve nothing. To the King the choice presented itself in very different terms. He had good cause to believe that the country gentlemen of England, appalled by his father's execution, alarmed at the alternatives of military rule or Left-wing republicanism, would gladly see him ensconced on his father's throne. And in all his travels was there ever a country that he left with a greater enthusiasm to be gone than Scotland in 1651?

The King and his army crossed the border on 6 August, making for Penrith which they reached two days later. Massey, the successful defender of Gloucester for the Parliament in 1643, had been appointed lieutenant general and sent on ahead to rally support. He had been one of the Presbyterian prisoners enquired after so eagerly by Charles I on that dark December afternoon at Windsor and had made his escape just before the King was brought to trial. It was hoped that so gallant a veteran of the Parliamentary cause would reach the widest range of political opinion capable of conversion to active Royalism. To say that the result was disappointing would be an understatement. Except for the passionate Royalists, the men of substance in the northwestern counties had had enough of wars and risings. They had in particular had enough of Scotch armies traipsing through their country and looked with no friendly eye on the cause that brought them there.

The wider Royalist rising that was supposed to break out in sympathy from the Wash to Land's End proved equally delusive. Too many people had known too much. The Council of State had caught some very talkative prisoners and had rounded up and even executed some of the most energetic promoters of the scheme. In consequence Charles abandoned his original plan of a direct march on London and determined to find a base in the West, so long the bastion of his father's cause. Shrewsbury declined the honour so that it was Worcester, the Loyal City that had already suffered a great deal for its attachment to the

Staunton Harold Church (see pp. 208–9); *view of the east end from across the lake*

This contemporary print of the battle of Dunbar, 3 September 1650, brings out very clearly the superiority of the Scottish position and the full use of the Commonwealth navy in close support of the army. Note the stand of pikes surrounded by musketeers, the characteristic fighting formation of the civil wars

Hiberniæ PROTECTORI præpotentissimo F.F. Fælicitatem, victorias, Triumphos
Elitiæ viris Primipilaribus, hanc calcographicam Prælij Dunbarrensis Iconim DDL
Sold by Pet. Stent

House of Stuart, at which the King eventually halted on 22 August. He had met no opposition apart from a skirmish at Warrington on the 16th when Lambert and Harrison contemplated contesting the passage of the Mersey but decided at the last moment to withdraw and await a more favourable occasion.

Cromwell had heard that the Scotch army was heading south on the very day he captured Perth. Leaving Monck and four or five thousand troops to clear up the remaining centres of resistance, notably Dundee and Aberdeen, he started south at once with the rest of the army. He reached Leith on 6 August, the day that Charles II crossed into England. From there he detached Lambert with about three thousand men to shadow the Royalists but avoid action. Harrison was ordered to collect a strong force of cavalry and mounted infantry and to strike off down to the West Midlands at top speed. He was to join Lambert as soon as their forces were in touch but even then they were to avoid a pitched battle. Cromwell himself, as in 1648, would come down well to the east of the invaders so that he could cover the old Royalist counties of the northeast in case Charles were to try his luck there. Lambert and Harrison, as we have seen, had joined forces before the Royalists approached the Mersey on the 16th. Cromwell with the artillery and the bulk of the foot followed down the North Road as far as Ferrybridge and then swung southwest through Rotherham, Chesterfield and Burton-on-Trent, joining the other two at Warwick on the 24th. On 27 August he reach Evesham. The Scotch army, feverishly throwing up defence-works round Worcester whose walls had been pulled down as a punishment for its Royalist past, sent out a detachment to hold and partially destroy the bridge at Upton-on-Severn. Massey, whose resolution and efficiency had made the Royalists smart at Gloucester in 1643, was in charge of this operation, but it was mishandled. Cromwell's men caught the guard napping, carried out temporary repairs to the bridge and got enough troops across to secure it before a counter-attack was mounted. Everything was running against the Royalists. Gloucester had refused support to its old defender. Reinforcements poured in to Cromwell's already ample army. On the day that he took up his position outside Worcester he probably disposed of about 30,000 men against Charles's 12,000.

The battle was fought on 3 September, the anniversary of Dunbar Charles and his Council of War surveyed the scene from the tower of the cathedral. To the south and east they could see the main body drawn up on the rising ground that covered the road to London. To the southwest Fleetwood was attacking the Scotch infantry that held the north bank of the river Teme. This force was further threatened in the rear by a strong detachment under Cromwell's personal command which had thrown a bridge of boats across the Severn about a mile below the city. The Scots fought until overwhelming numbers and shortage of ammunition forced them back to the city. At this point the King decided on a bold stroke. He saw that the main army had lost a good deal of its strength by pouring men across the Severn. He therefore opened the Sudbury Gate that gave on the London Road and himself led a charge that drove the Cromwellians back and even overran some of their artillery. If this had been the Ironsides charging some half-starved disconsolate body of peasants officered by amateurs, a great victory against huge odds might have

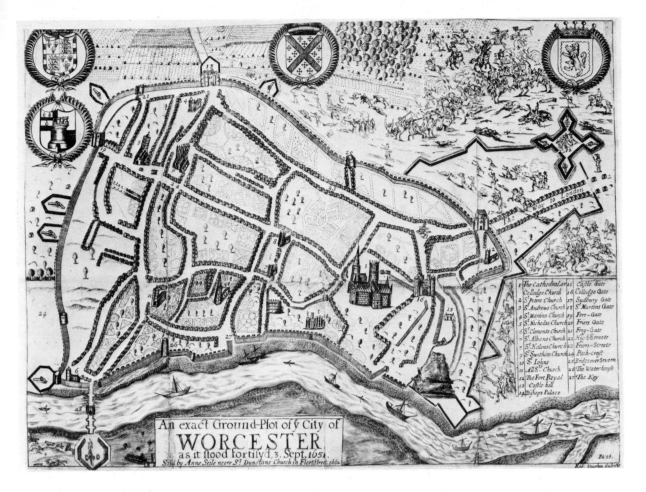

Ground plan of Worcester and its fortifications at the time of the battle

crowned the day. Some Englishmen like Clarendon sourly observed that if only David Leslie had thrown in the Scotch cavalry, hitherto uncommitted, the thing might yet have been done. But Cromwell quickly saw what was happening and calling off the pursuit of the beaten defenders of the Teme brought his regiments back across the Severn. The Royalists had anyhow been checked; they now gave ground and the battle was lost. The civil wars were over.

Charles II had given a remarkably good account of himself in the fighting. He was now called on for coolness and courage of a different sort. Capture would be the final humiliation; might, indeed, be final in the most elementary sense. The Commonwealth Government was humane. It had been on the point of sending Charles I's two young children, Princess Elizabeth and the Duke of Gloucester, to join their family abroad when the approach of war with Scotland brought a check. But if Capel and the others had suffered, if the men found guilty of conspiring to overthrow the Government had been sent to the scaffold, would it be easy to admit Charles to mercy on the grounds of his youth or to argue that he was simply an accessory manipulated by others?

The face that the Government set against those who tried to rekindle the wars was stern, and justly so. The whole Scotch escapade from first to last had cost untold misery and had turned out just as Clarendon and the soberer Royalists had said it would. As Charles rode northwards with the nobles who had managed to escape, Lauderdale, Wilmot, Buckingham and Derby, he can have been in little doubt that he must expect the worst.

Eluding pursuit sorted well with Charles's genius. Deception and deviousness came easily to him. His quick intelligence and powers of observation, his sociability, his charm were additional advantages. But even with all this it was certainly a stroke of good fortune that brought him to a Catholic household at the start of his adventures. Years of concealing priests, evading recusancy laws and outwitting the malice of authority had forced such people to acquire the skills and instincts of clandestine activity. During the first few days the pursuit was at its hottest and closest. The tight-knit little recusant community on the borders of Shropshire and Staffordshire took no unnecessary risks, tested each step, never moved too soon, and never relaxed vigilance. It was nearly a week before the King was returned to the familiar world of Church of England country gentlemen who conveyed him from Worcestershire to Somerset in the hopes of finding a ship at Bristol, then south to the Channel coast in Dorset and finally to Sussex and the coal-brig *Surprise*. The story is one of the most fascinating in English history and adds a welcome touch of colour to the closing scene of the war.

No further Royalist rising of any significance was to take place until after Cromwell's death. The ceaseless activities of the Royalist Underground were to lead to some pathetic follies like the rebellion of Penruddock and Grove in Wiltshire and Dorset in the spring of 1655. Scotland was reduced by Monck without trouble except for the sack of Dundee two days before the battle of Worcester. The Isle of Man surrendered at the end of October, a fortnight after its lord, the Earl of Derby, had been executed for levying war against the

The Speaker investing Cromwell with the insignia of his Protectorate, 1653

Commonwealth: it was then that he was charged with killing the first victim of the civil war in his raid on Manchester in July 1642. Jersey and the Royalist Castle Cornet on Guernsey surrendered to Blake in December. He had already dealt with the Scillies in May. He was now free to move against Rupert who might in the absence of any other base be expected to take his fleet across the Atlantic where some of the West Indian islands and the colonies of Maryland and Virginia still adhered to the Stuart cause. A squadron under Sir George Ayscue brought them to a better frame of mind in January and February 1652. Rupert did eventually turn up there at the end of May, just after Ayscue had sailed for home but by that time hand-to-mouth piracy was all that his force was equal to. The end of May saw also the surrender of the last remote Scottish fortress, Dunottar Castle, that had held out for the King. The death-throes of Irish Confederate resistance to the New Model were then all but over, though two small and unimportant places held out till April 1653. The relevance of that bitter and fearful struggle is, however, tangential to the civil war.

The war, it soon became clear, had ended in stalemate. The Parliament had won an outright military victory but the period of *ad hoc* political experiment that followed Cromwell's expulsion of the Long Parliament in April 1653 could hardly be said to bear much relation to the aims and principles avowed in 1642. That it gave England and, more surprisingly, Scotland, forcibly incorporated into the Union, several years of good government and that it transformed the standing of the country in Europe would hardly be contested. Cromwell's genius as a ruler was liberated by the civil war but not to any great extent shaped or conditioned by it.

The opposition offered by the existence of Charles II's court in exile and by its secret correspondence with Royalists in England seems to have had little effect on what Cromwell did or did not do, on what constitutional expedient was or was not adopted. Cromwell's intelligence service under John Thurloe was generally considered the best in Europe. It penetrated from the beginning

In this attack on Common wealth Rule, Magna Carta is linked with the traditional Royalist insignia of Church and King. Unpopular exactions and infringements of liberty are given their full weight

A Dutch view of events under the Protectorate: Cromwell breaks open a barrel of gold using the Speaker's mace. Scobell, the Clerk of the House, Oliver St John and Speaker Lenthall assist, while the ghost of Dr Dorislaus – Parliament's ambassador to Holland murdered by Royalists to avenge Charles I's execution – holds the candle. In the background, a view of Parliament House

the High Command of the Royalist Underground known as the Sealed Knot. One of its members Sir Richard Willis, the ex-governor of Newark who was displaced by Charles I in 1645, agreed to betray every conspiracy on the understanding that no one about whom he gave information should be put to death. The civil war had been fought often enough: there was no point in a replay. Until Cromwell had vanished from the scene and the army that upheld him had either been disbanded or induced to favour a restoration of the monarchy there was nothing for the Royalists to do but keep quiet.

The enormous financial requirements of a Government that kept up a military and naval establishment so far beyond the ordinary revenue naturally exposed them to penal taxation in the proper sense of the term. If they behaved themselves, they were allowed to compound for their estates at a rate that did not really hurt. If they plotted and conspired or even refused to take the Engagement 'to be true and faithful to the Commonwealth of England, as it is now established, without a King or House of Lords', the screw was tightened. Most of them gave no trouble. But the supporters of Church and King too had their Hampdens. At Staunton Harold in Leicestershire the young Royalist squire defied the Puritan regime by building next door to his house a church that expressed the purest Anglicanism in all the beauty of holiness for which Archbishop Laud had striven, sometimes by such inappropriate means. There was an altar, then strictly forbidden. Its frontal, still surviving, was probably worked by members of the dispersed community at Little Gidding. There were paintings, not, it is true, directly representing persons and thus liable to be characterized as idolatrous, but none the less suggestive of spiritual truths better left to exposition from the pulpit. There they still are in an interior that, as no other, consciously represents a type of English piety for which

Laud and Charles I tried to live and for which they were ready to die. The young man who did these things was sent to the Tower and died there. The inscription over the west door of his church may serve for an epigraph on Royalism in eclipse:

In the yeare 1653
when all thinges Sacred were throughout ye nation
Either demolisht or profaned
Sir Robert Shirley, Barronet,
Founded this church;
whose singular praise it is
to have done the best things in ye worst times,
and
hoped them in the most callamitous.
The righteous shall be had in everlasting remembrance.

Chapter 18

Exits and Entrances

The age of Cromwell has more in common with the age of Charles II than either have with the England of the early 1640s. The dissimilarities of character and temperament between the Protector and the restored King disguised underlying affinities. Both men, for very different reasons, promoted toleration in religion. The limits to Cromwell's achievement in this field were set by his own ardent certainties, those of Charles by external pressures on a lightly held scepticism. But the result in both cases was that England was the less intolerant for their presence on the scene. Both men, again for very different reasons, presided over a policy of aggressive commercial imperialism based on the assertion of sea power. Cromwell indeed did a great deal more than preside: he was the prime mover. But Charles II in his amused lackadaisical way lent the policy considerable if unsystematic support. Under both intellectual life stretched and flowered as it has in few ages. The Royal Society, granted its charter by Charles II, originated during Cromwell's time in a group of Oxford men, one of whom, John Wilkins, the Warden of Wadham, married the Protector's sister. Both men were served and advised by many of the same people. In military and naval affairs Monck and Mountagu and Lawson are the most eminent of a long and distinguished list; in diplomacy, Lockhart and Downing and Maynard. Cromwell's regime was notably efficient and free from corruption, Charles II's the reverse. Yet both are obviously similar in methods and technique, partly, no doubt, because the same people were operating the machine and partly because the tone and flavour of the age that had changed in the course of the civil wars did not change in any substantial way when the King came back. That there were changes on the surface hardly needs to be said. The theatres opened again. The bishops came back to their palaces and to the House of Lords, the deans and chapters returned to their much-damaged cathedrals, the Prayer Book came back to the parish church. Christmas was kept again and cakes and ale were accorded a relation to virtue that Sir Toby Belch would have approved. But to a man of the nineteenth or twentieth century there is a recognizable kinship with his own time about the Cromwellian and Restoration periods that is absent from the age of Charles I. Their government, their society, look modern, his antique.

The difference can be detected very clearly in the attitude of Lord Chancellor Clarendon when the King's restoration had brought him to effective power. Early in the reign his old friend Ormonde had suggested to him that the burden of detail he had to bear as Chancellor should be delegated to a subordinate and that he should assume the office of Prime Minister. Clarendon was horrified. Detail was what offices of state were about. It stopped their holders from getting ideas above their station. The volume of work kept them out of mischief. It did them good and would do the King good too. Finally the term 'First Minister' and the position it suggested (but did not define) was a nasty invention of the French and should be turned back at Dover.

An even more instructive instance can be found in Clarendon's reaction to the King's proposal on the death of Lord Treasurer Southampton, who had long been past the discharge of his duties, to put the office into commission. Clarendon answered:

'The business would be much better done by a single officer, if he could think of a fit one; for commissioners never had, never would do, that business well.' The duke of York said, 'that he believed it would be best done by commission; it had been so managed during all the ill times' (for from the beginning of the troubles there had been no treasurer:) 'and he had observed (and the king found the benefit of it) that though Sir William Compton [Master of the Ordnance: an official much admired by that severe and expert critic Samuel Pepys] was an extraordinary person, and better qualified than most men for that charge, yet since his decease, that his majesty had put the office of the ordnance under the government of commissioners, it was in much better order, and the King was better served there than he had ever been; and he believed it would be so likewise in the office of the treasury, if fit persons were chosen for it, who might have nothing else to do'. And the king seemed to be of the same mind.

The chancellor replied, 'that he was very sorry, that they were both so much delighted with the function of commissioners, which were more suitable to the modelling of a commonwealth, than for support of the monarchy: that during the late troubles, whilst the parliament exercised the government, they reduced it as fast as they could to the form of a commonwealth: and then no question the putting of the treasury into the hands of commissioners was much more suitable to the rest of the model, than it could be under a single person.'

Clarendon further thought that such people would be under a grave disadvantage, 'having no revenue of their own, but being to raise one according to their inventions and proportionable to their own occasions . . .' As to the instance quoted by his son-in-law, the Duke of York:

The ordnance was conversant only with smiths and carpenters, and other artificers and handicraftsmen . . . whereas the treasury had much to do with the nobility and chief gentry of the kingdom; must often have recourse to the king himself for his particular directions, to the privy-council for their assistance and advice, to the judges for their resolutions in matters of difficulty; and if the ministers of it were not of that quality and degree that they might have free recourse to all those, and find respect from them, his majesty's service would notoriously suffer . . . and that how mean an opinion soever some men had of the faculties of the late excellent officer . . . the vast sums of money which he had borrowed in these late years had been in a great measure procured upon the general confidence all men had in the honour and justice of the treasurer; and that the credit of commissioners would never be able to supply such necessities.

Clarendon's view expressed with his usual eloquence and lucidity is essentially medieval. The Treasurer is a great officer of state and must, therefore, be a grandee in his own right. When he raises money for the Crown he does so

The Great Seal of the
Protectorate

not on the security of the public revenue but on his own credit. The concept of a treasury as a ministry of Government finance run by officials chosen for professional ability and experience is perfectly comprehensible to him and perfectly abhorrent. Yet it is this essentially modern conception, borrowed from the Commonwealth and Protectorate ('the ill times'), that the Stuart brothers, not generally accused of dangerously progressive notions, are championing. It is not that Clarendon is just a buffleheaded old fogy. Pepys, the brightest star in the heavens of Restoration bureaucracy, was 'mad in love with my Lord Chancellor, for he doth comprehend and speak as well, and with the greatest easiness and authority, that ever I saw man in my life'. The times had changed, not just the catchwords. Clarendon was not too old to learn new tricks. There were some that on principle he did not wish to learn.

Through all the storm and smoke of the civil war it is his mind, his personality that rises above the scene and remains, when the battlefield has fallen silent, to explain its significance. Cromwell and Milton are greater figures in our history and our literature, but Cromwell has stamped a whole era with the impress, warts and all, of a political genius essentially somnambulist ('No man climbs so high as he who does not know where he is going') and Milton begins where the civil war ends. It is Clarendon who experiences and even while experiencing tries to understand the war and to record it. It is he who evolved and consistently adhered to a political programme that was ultimately vindicated by events. Yet for all his intellectual rigour, the outrage, the shock, the pathos have not vanished from his pages into unfelt generalities. Of the Royalist leaders who survived the diaspora of the Interregnum he and Ormonde were the two who still effectively and recognizably stood for the constitutional legalism that Charles I had proclaimed so memorably from the scaffold. The old Earl of Southampton and Sir Edward Nicholas were other seniors of the group, but Clarendon was, as he had always been, the most vigorous and the most articulate exponent of its creed.

Of the men who had led the Royalists in battle Astley and Hopton were long dead. The Earl of Newcastle returned to enjoy his enormous estates and to publish another treatise on horsemanship. Sir Marmaduke Langdale, beggared by his proportionately greater sacrifices, had first taken service with the Venetians against the Turks and had then retired, for reasons of economy rather than piety, to live in a monastic house in Germany. Before sailing for England Charles made him a peer but his poverty was such that he was unable to afford his coronation robes and did not attend. Rupert who had quarrelled with the King after his return from the West Indies in 1653 was rewarded with pensions and offices and high command at sea in both the Dutch Wars. But the dislike and suspicion that he had always too easily excited isolated him still further. Pepys tells us that the King looked on him as a madman. One eminent survivor was slow to return and quick to go away again. Henrietta Maria found that England no longer suited her.

Of the Parliamentary generals Fairfax and Waller had worked for the Restoration, and others had either long made their peace or were allowed to do so. Lambert and Harrison were notable exceptions. Harrison as a regicide and an unrepentant one was executed with the revolting barbarity prescribed for High Treason. Lambert had not signed the King's death-warrant but he had twice led an unsuccessful *coup d'état* in the turbulent eighteen months between Cromwell's death and Charles II's return and had repulsed repeated overtures from the Royalists. Imprisonment for life was his punishment. A great gardener he was allowed to pursue his taste in a pleasant house and grounds in Guernsey until his daughter rashly married the son of the governor. The authorities felt so close a relation to be dangerous and moved him to St Nicholas Island in Plymouth harbour.

The humanity that had been generally shown by the Parliamentarians was wisely reciprocated. Of the forty-one surviving regicides, nine suffered the full penalty. Three escaped to America, and a dozen to the Continent, of whom three were handed over through the treachery of Downing, their old comrade now ambassador in Holland. Two of the King's gaolers, his prosecutor and the preacher who had exulted over him in his misfortune, Hugh Peter, also went to the scaffold. So too did the Republican Sir Henry Vane who had so conspicuously disassociated himself from the King's trial. 'Too dangerous to lett live', Charles II's reported justification of this political killing avows a departure from justice and from his own pledges of mercy.

The civil war thus left much less of a *damnosa hereditas* than any comparable political convulsion. The fierce vendettas of Restoration politics were rooted in the characters of the men who conducted them and in the standards of their own society, not in the grudges and wrongs bequeathed by the preceding generation. The conduct of the war had reflected the tragic sense of personal moral responsibility so finely expressed by Waller in the letter from which the title of this book is taken. These men were faced with questions that they felt it dishonourable to evade but they did not feel obliged to uncharitableness towards those who answered them in a different sense. And what questions they were. The civil war may not have produced a settlement in politics or religion that many of the men who spent their blood in it would have found satisfying. But the whole conflict showed a level of political maturity and of humanity towards opponents in which any age or any country might take pride.

It is the misfortune of the contestants that they have offered posterity, through the very universality and intelligence of the issues that engaged them, a temptation to re-enlist them, as they themselves so often re-enlisted the defeated soldiery, under flags other than their own. The Whig aristocracy, the men of the American Revolution, the paladins of Victorian liberalism, have with a greater or lesser degree of plausibility asserted if not identity with, at least a direct and indefeasible right of inheritance in the cause of Pym and Hampden, of Warwick and Fairfax. The martyrdom of Charles I was long part of Tory faith. A form of service to commemorate the event was introduced into the Prayer Book of 1662 but under the Hanoverians its use grew rare and it was finally withdrawn in 1859. A bold effort was made by the Left Wing of the Anglo-Catholic party in the first half of the twentieth century to claim Laud and Strafford as forerunners of Socialism against the Capitalists disguised behind Puritan vizards who haunted, and to some extent still haunt, the fashionable historiography of the period. But the most substantial claims advanced and the most lively debates provoked proceed from those to whom the word 'Revolution' is both a battle-cry and a term of art. Victorian and Edwardian gentry were fond of dressing up as Roundheads and Cavaliers. The anxiety to rig up an English float in the Marxist pageant of history may be an expression of the same taste. Certainly there are to be found in the period immediately following the end of the civil wars instances of primitive Communism, notably Winstanley and the Diggers; and some, but by no means all, Levellers could fairly be said to advocate a violent dispossession of some citizens and a remodelling of the social order. Whether this constitutes a revolutionary situation (and what may be the proper definition of that term) are questions with which this book is not concerned. The Levellers and the Diggers, like the Protectorate, are products and consequences of the civil war, not causes, and not present to the minds and hearts of those who experienced that catastrophe.

That we and the generations that separate us from it have benefited, that the bells have rung a finer peal from being recast and rehung, may well be true. But for the generation that lived through the wars, destruction, dislocation, uprooting and loss were obvious. That they turned immediate disaster

The cult of the Royal Martyr

Looking to Iesus so our Soveraigne Stood
Praying for those who Thirsted for his Blood:
But high in Bliß with his Celestial Crowne
Now with an Eye of Pity hee Looks Downe.
While some Attaqu his other life, his Fame,
Ludlow reviv'd to blott the Royal Name
On Sacred Majesty Profanely treads,
Madd to sett up ye Beast with many Heads:

New Regicides bad as the Old dare call
The Martyr's blood on their own heads to Fall;
And black as those who Frocks & Vizors Wore,
These barefac'd Hangmen trample on his Gore:
Can it bee Silent can it cease to cry?
Such Feinds forbid it in repose to Lye:
Tis well the blood of God speaks better Things
Then that of Abell or a Murder'd Kings

W. Faithorne fec

E. Cooper ex.

The frontispiece of Eikon Basilike, the great best-seller of Royalist hagiography

to ultimate advantage is a measure of the quality, so much praised by Clarendon, of the age that was ending. If its religious bigotry has much to answer for, its real piety redeemed much more. The sense of eternity (not simply crude notions of eternal rewards and punishments) imposed on men who disagreed about Church and state a perspective and an individual responsibility. Except, and it is a terrible exception, in the case of the Irish, opponents were considered as human beings, and immortal souls. Participants on both sides thought of themselves as involved in a general collapse, as actors in a tragedy. Actors, not authors. The parts assigned them had been written, most of them believed, by God. A revolutionary is a man who believes that he is to some degree at least writing his own role. As Marx put it in the *Theses on Feuerbach*, 'The philosophers have only *interpreted* the world in various ways: the point, however, is to change it.' That idea, or something like it, might be discerned in obscure corners of the army radicalism and the millenarianism of the late 1640s. There is little trace of it in the Great Civil War.

To·Marvell, who served with Milton in Cromwell's secretariat, as to Clarendon, the civil war was to be recollected as a sad and terrible breach in a nation blessed above all others in the happy and peaceful relations of its citizens:

> When gardens only had their towers,
> And all the garrisons were flowers,
> When roses only arms might bear,
> And men did rosy garlands wear.

Illustration Acknowledgments

The following abbreviations are used:
Ashmoleam: the Ashmoleam Museum, Oxford; Sutherland Collection
NPG: Reproduced by courtesy of the Trustees, The National Portrait Gallery, London

Asterisks* denote colour plates on facing page

HALF TITLE Oliver Cromwell by Samuel Cooper, unfinished miniature, c. 1650. Courtesy of His Grace the Duke of Buccleuch and Queensberry, VRD. Photo: Derrick Witty

FRONTISPIECE Charles I at His Trial by Edward Bower, 1648. Copyright reserved

4 Three Children of Charles I. attr. to John Hoskins, miniature. Fitzwilliam Museum, Cambridge

7 Henry Ireton by Samuel Cooper, miniature, 1649. Fitzwilliam Museum, Cambridge

8 Henrietta Maria by John Hoskins, miniature, c. 1632. Copyright reserved. Photo: A. C. Cooper

11 LEFT Henrietta Maria, artist unknown, NPG
RIGHT Charles I by Daniel Mytens. NPG

13 The Earl of Clarendon. Ashmoleam

14 LEFT John Hutchinson by Robert Walker. Courtesy of The Earl Fitzwilliam. Photo: NPG
RIGHT Lucy Hutchinson by Robert Walker. Courtesy of The Earl Fitzwilliam. Photo: John Bethell

16 Henry, Prince of Wales, by Isaac Oliver, miniature. Copyright reserved. Photo: A. C. Cooper

19 Title page. The Divine Right and Originall of the Civill Magistrate from God by Edward Gee. Ashmoleam

20 1 James VI and I by Nicholas Hilliard; Anne of Denmark by Nicholas Hilliard; Frederick of Bohemia by Nicholas Hilliard; Princess Elizabeth by Isaac Oliver; Charles I as Prince Charles by Nicholas Hilliard; miniatures. Victoria and Albert Museum, London

22 LEFT King Charles in Masque Dress by Inigo Jones, 1640. Devonshire Collection, Chatsworth. Reproduced by Permission of the Trustees of the Chatsworth Settlement

RIGHT The Queen, or a Masquer, in Amazon Costume by Inigo Jones. Devonshire Collection, Chatsworth. Reproduced by Permission of the Trustees of the Chatsworth Settlement

25 Title page, The Holy State by Thomas Fuller. Ashmoleam

28 Alexander Henderson, artist unknown. Scottish National Portrait Gallery

29 Detail from engraving. 'The Trance and Vision of William Laud.' Ashmoleam

30 1 Part of Berwick fortifications. Crown Copyright, reproduced with permission of the Controller of Her Majesty's Stationery Office

31 'The English and Scotts Armies as first ready to fight, lovingly embrace each other and part kinde freinds.' Ashmoleam

*33 A View of Greenwich by Adriaen van Stalbemt and Jan van Belcamp. Copyright reserved

*33 Henry, Prince of Wales, in the Huntingfield, artist unknown. Copyright reserved

34 5 'London before the burning of St Pauls', folio 21 of Vol. I of Samuel Pepys's 'My Collection of Prints and Drawings . . . Relating to the Citys of London and Westminster . . :', 1700. The Master and Fellows, Magdalene College, Cambridge

36 TOP Engraving by Hollar of Arundel House, London. Ashmoleam
BOTTOM Sir Theodore Turquet de Mayerne by Peter Paul Rubens. The Trustees of the British Museum, London

39 Lucius Cary, 2nd Viscount Falkland, attr. to Van Dyck. Devonshire Collection, Chatsworth. Reproduced by Permission of the Trustees of the Chatsworth Settlement

40 Bulstrode Whitelocke, artist unknown. NPG

44-5 Dutch and Spanish sea battle in the Downs. Ashmoleam

46-7 York. Ashmoleam

*48 TOP The Family of Arthur, Lord Capel, by Cornelius Johnson, c. 1639. NPG
*BOTTOM Algernon Percy, 10th Earl of Northumberland, by Van Dyck. Courtesy of His Grace The Duke of Northumberland, Photo: Photo Centre, Alwick

*49 TOP see credit to half-title illustration
*MIDDLE see credit to p. 7
*BOTTOM Oliver Cromwell by Samuel Cooper. The Fitzwilliam Museum, Cambridge

50 Execution of Strafford. Ashmoleam

53 Whitehall. Ashmoleam

57 Sir John Hotham, Governor of Kingston-upon-Hull. Ashmoleam

58 Summoning Hull. Ashmoleam

62 Setting up the King's standard at Nottingham, 22 August 1642. Ashmoleam

64 Lady Frances Devereux by Van Dyck. Courtesy of His Grace The Duke of Northumberland. Photo: Country Life

65 William Goffe. Ashmoleam

66-7 Henry Ireton, attr. to Robert Walker. NPG

67 Detail of Horace, Lord Vere of Tilbury, attr. to M. J. van Mieveveldt, 1629. NPG

68 Prince Rupert, Count Palatine, attr. to Gerard Honthorst. NPG

71 The Earl of Essex's hearse. Ashmoleam

73 Detail of the battle of Edgehill from Mercurius Rusticus. Ashmoleam

75 William Walker. Ashmoleam

77 TOP Sir Edmund Verney's ring. Courtesy of Sir Ralph Verney, KBE, Photo: John Bethell
BOTTOM Grocers Hall, London. Ashmoleam

81 Sir Bevil Grenville. Ashmoleam

85 Frances Howard, Countess of Somerset, attr. to William Larkin. NPG

84 Sir William Waller. Ashmoleam

86 'Maistre Pin, L'Archicagot politique Parliamentaire.' *Ashmolean*

87 Burning holy pictures; hanging of Challenor and Tomkins, May 1643. *Ashmolean*

*88 Robert Rich, Earl of Warwick, by Van Dyck. *The Metropolitan Museum of Art, New York; The Jules S. Bache Collection, 1949*

*88–9 The Salusbury Family, artist unknown, c. 1640. *Courtesy of Edmund Brudenell, Esq. Photo: John Bethell*

*89 Peter Pett and *The Sovereign of the Seas* (detail), artist unknown. *The National Maritime Museum, London*

90 Robert Devereux, Earl of Essex. *Ashmolean*

95 'The Trance and Vision of William Laud.' *Ashmolean*

96 'The souldiers in their passage to York turn unto reformers, pull down Popish pictures, break down rayles, turn altars into tables.' *Ashmolean*

97 Archbishop Williams. *Ashmolean*

98–9 Prince Rupert with Colonel William Murray and Colonel John Russell by William Dobson, c. 1644. *Private collection*

100 *Mercurius Rusticus. Ashmolean*

101 Dr Bruno Ryves, author of *Mercurius Rusticus. Ashmolean*

103 Gardens at Wilton House. *Ashmolean*

107 Henry Marten by Sir Peter Lely. *Courtesy of the Rt Hon. Hugh Fraser*

108 TOP Siege helmet. *The Grosvenor Museum, Chester*
BOTTOM Lobster-tail helmet. *The Grosvenor Museum, Chester*

109 Bust of Sir Thomas Fairfax, artist unknown; lead, 26 in. high. *The City Art Gallery, York*

111 Parliamentary commanders. *Ashmolean*

112 Plymouth. *Ashmolean*

113 Sea battle, 1652. *Ashmolean*

116–17 Horses bowing to the Earl of Newcastle. *Ashmolean*

123 'Englands Arke Secured.' *Ashmolean*

124 The Earl of Manchester by Sir Peter Lely, 1661–5. *NPG*

125 'Hugh Peters, ye first and ye last.' *Ashmolean*

126 1st Marquis of Montrose, after Honthorst, c. 1634 *Scottish National Portrait Gallery*

127 'Popish Recusants disarmed, for the greate security of the kingdom.' *Ashmolean*

130 Oliver Cromwell by Robert Walker, c. 1649. *NPG*

134–5 ff.42–3, *Anglia Rediviva* by Joshua Sprigge, 1647. *Photo: John Freeman Ltd, London*

139 Raglan Castle, Gwent. *Photo: John Bethell*

140 Detail of memorial tablet to Sir William Penn, St Mary Redcliffe Church, Bristol. *Courtesy of Mardon Son & Hall Ltd, Bristol*

*144 George Gilbert Digby, KG, 2nd Earl of Bristol, by Justus van Egmont, 1653. *Collection A. R. Dufty, Esq., on loan to the Armouries, H.M. Tower of London*

*145 Painted window at Farndon Church, Chester. *By kind permission of the Revd Marcus Hasted. Photo: John Bethell*

146 Prince Rupert of the Rhine by William Dobson, unfinished, c. 1646. *Courtesy of Lord Dartmouth*

147 Charlotte Stanley, Countess of Derby, probably by Gilbert Jackson, c. 1635. *Victoria and Albert Museum, London*

148–9 'The Siege of Bazinge House.' *Ashmolean*

150 Inigo Jones by William Dobson. *Crown copyright, reproduced with permission of the Controller of Her Majesty's Stationery Office*

152 LEFT William Laud (detail), artist unknown. *NPG*
RIGHT James, Duke of York, playing tennis. *Ashmolean*

153 'Winter', from *The Seasons*, a set of four etching by Wenceslaus Hollar, 1643. *Copyright reserved*

154–5 Siege of Newark. *Ashmolean*

158 'Integer vitae . . .' *Ashmolean*

*160 Charles II as Prince of Wales by William Dobson. *Scottish National Portrait Gallery, Photo: Tom Scott*

*161 The Palace of Whitehall by Hendrick Danckerts. *Berkeley Castle*

163 Charles I with James, Duke of York, by Sir Peter Lely c. 1647. *Courtesy of His Grace The Duke of Northumberland. Photo: Country Life*

164 'Nil Admirari.' *Ashmolean*

171 Henry, Earl of Holland. *Ashmolean*

172 Siege of Colchester. *Ashmolean*

173 Henrietta Maria visiting Prince William of Nassau, September 1644. *Ashmolean*

174 Charles, Prince of Wales. *Ashmolean*

175 Royalist *dramatis personae* from Clarendon's *History of the Great Rebellion. Ashmolean*

181 Charles I by John Hoskins, miniature, c. 1647. *Copyright reserved*

184 Lord President Bradshaw and Hugh Peter, attr. to Lely. *By permission of The Lord Tollemache. Photo: Courtauld Institute*

186 Sir Edward Massey, artist unknown. *NPG*

190–1 Execution of Charles I. *Ashmolean*

192 'The Royall Oake of Brittayne.' *Ashmolean*

195 Allegory of 1649. *Ashmolean*

198 Charles, 2nd Earl of Dunfermline, by Van Dyck. *Scottish National Portrait Gallery*

*200 Execution of Charles I (detail) by Weesop, 1649. *On loan to the Scottish National Portrait Gallery. Courtesy of the Earl of Rosebery. Photo: Tom Scott*

*200–1 Stumpwork, third quarter of seventeenth century. *Victoria and Albert Museum, London*

*201 Staunton Harold Church. *The National Trust. Photo: John Bethell*

202–3 Battle of Dunbar. *Ashmolean*

205 Town and battle of Worcester, 1651. *Ashmolean*

206 The Speaker investing Cromwell with the insignia of his Protectorate. *Ashmolean*

207 'The Commonwealth ruling with a standing Army.' *Ashmolean*

208 Dutch print of the English Parliament under Cromwell. *Ashmolean*

212 The Great Seal of Oliver Cromwell. *City Museum and Art Gallery, Worcester*

215 'Corruptibilem pro incorruptibile.' *Ashmolean*

216 *Eikon Basilike*, frontispiece, engraving by William Marshall. *Ashmolean*

Index